INVENTING
AUTHENTICITY

FOOD AND FOODWAYS

SERIES EDITORS:
JENNIFER JENSEN WALLACH
AND MICHAEL WISE

INVENTING AUTHENTICITY

*How Cookbook Writers
Redefine Southern Identity*

Carrie Helms Tippen

THE UNIVERSITY OF ARKANSAS PRESS

FAYETTEVILLE | 2018

ISBN: 978–1–68226–065–4
ISBN cloth: 978–1–68226–064–7
eISBN: 978–1–61075–640–2

22 21 20 19 18   5 4 3 2 1

Designer: April Leidig

∞ The paper used in this publication meets the minimum requirements
of the American National Standard for Permanence of Paper for Printed
Library Materials z39.48–1984

Library of Congress Cataloging-in-Publication Data:
  Names: Tippen, Carrie Helms, author.
  Title: Inventing authenticity : how cookbook writers redefine Southern
  identity / Carrie Helms Tippen.
Description: Fayetteville : The University of Arkansas Press, 2018. | Series:
  Food and foodways | Includes bibliographical references and index. |
Identifiers: LCCN 2017052577 (print) | LCCN 2017053205 (ebook) |
  ISBN 9781610756402 (electronic) | ISBN 9781682260647 (cloth : alk.
  paper) | ISBN 9781682260654 (pbk. : alk. paper) | ISBN 9781610756402
  (eISBN)
Subjects: LCSH: Food writing—Southern States—History. | Cookbooks—
  Social aspects—Southern states. | Food writers—Southern States. |
  Cooking, American—Southern style—Social aspects. | Southern States—
  Social life and customs.
Classification: LCC TX644 (ebook) | LCC TX644 .T57 2018 (print) |
  DDC 641.30975—dc23

LC record available at https://urldefense.proofpoint.com/v2/url?u=https-3
A__lccn.loc.gov_2017052577&d=DwIFAg&c=7ypwAowFJ8v-mw8AB
-SdSueVQgSDL4HiiSaLKo1W8HA&r=4fo1OqKuv_3krqlYYqNQWNK
NaWxXN20G1PCOL-2ERgE&m=fCPk67ueF84JvVY85jR32dmplwM1nE
EKszrLc7TrHLk&s=kPvooD_p1GEHgxek-I94UEbpD6hqkoK_pLYoC
8bz50g&e=

CONTENTS

SERIES EDITOR'S PREFACE

The University of Arkansas Press series on Food and Foodways explores historical and contemporary issues in global food studies. We are committed to representing a diverse set of voices that tell lesser-known food stories and to provoking new avenues of interdisciplinary research. Our strengths are works in the humanities and social sciences that use food as a critical lens to examine broader cultural, environmental, and ethical issues.

Feeding ourselves has long entangled human beings within complicated moral puzzles of social injustice and environmental destruction. When we eat, we consume not only the food on the plate but also the lives and labors of innumerable plants, animals, and people. This process distributes its costs unevenly across race, class, gender, and other social categories. The production and distribution of food often obscures these material and cultural connections, impeding honest assessments of our impacts on the world around us. By taking these relationships seriously, Food and Foodways provides a new series of critical studies that analyze the cultural and environmental relationships that have sustained human societies.

In *Inventing Authenticity: How Cookbook Writers Redefine Southern Identity*, Carrie Helms Tippen takes cookbooks seriously both as historical documents and as literary texts. She examines the rhetorical strategies that authors of Southern cookbooks use to authenticate their visions of Southern food and Southern culture, highlighting the complications inherent in any attempt to wrest a positive version of regional foodways away from the weight of a complicated history. Tippen does not shy away from difficult topics like cultural appropriation and the tendency among some to conflate whiteness and Southern-ness, or from thorny questions about authorship and intellectual property in the food world. She guides her readers through these issues deftly as she combines academic analysis with her own reminiscence. In this layered and reflexive study, Tippen not only analyzes texts written by Southern food writers, but she also joins them, simultaneously creating and critiquing her own narrative of Southern authenticity. In doing so, she reveals the promises and perils of navigating this rich but troubled cultural terrain. Tippen's interdisciplinary approach is representative of the best work in food studies, which forsakes fidelity to genre or discipline in order to push readers into reaching profound but sometimes difficult conclusions about what food choices reveal about the values and aspirations of the people who created them.

Jennifer Jensen Wallach and Michael Wise

PREFACE

I come from a family of writing women. The women in my family are committed diarists. They have written memoirs and school plays. They have written poems, songs, local newspaper columns, Sunday School lessons, newsletters for national conventions of music educators, digital databases of American folk songs. I come from saving women, inheriting and bequeathing women. They saved journals and songs and scrapbooks. They saved necklaces and brooches. They saved newspaper clippings, photographs, quilts, dresses, family records, and, yes, recipes. I came to know the women in my family most intimately through their recipe boxes when I began to learn how to cook. I was twenty-six, living far from home, and what I wanted most in the world was a genuine buttermilk biscuit.

I had resisted learning to cook, always. As a child, when it was time to cook or clean or do anything so mundane as set the table, I was somehow never where my mother could find me. Then, as a young adult and fledgling feminist, I had an idea that my mother's cooking was a mechanism of her oppression, that the time she spent preparing meals for men and children would have been better spent in her "real" work. When I got married and received cookbooks for wedding gifts, I resented them and the implication that cooking was a condition of wifehood. The beautiful silver serving trays may as well have been manacles; *The Joy of Cooking*, my ball and chain. I'd have nothing to do with them.

But on a snowy day in West Virginia, on what felt like (but probably wasn't) the tenth snowy day in a row, I wanted a real Thanksgiving meal with Grandma Taylor's angel biscuits. My grandfather, Buck Welty, had died in July, and in early November, my beloved grandmother, Nella Jo Welty, had passed away, too. That Thanksgiving, in the snow, far from home, in a world without either of my grandparents, I was hungry. If I wanted that Thanksgiving meal, I was going to have to do it myself.

I called my mother, Joburta Welty Helms, and as she read recipes for broccoli and rice casserole and pecan pie over the phone, I took them down in a spiral-bound notebook. I knew that she was reading the recipes from three-by-five notecards that had an avocado and harvest-gold colored spray of flowers in the top right corner. I knew the cards were kept in a wooden box with a cluster of grapes painted on the lid. I knew that the card for angel biscuits was misspelled —"Angle Biscuits." Maybe I never cooked a meal, but I had baked a few cookies, and I knew those cards. I knew that most of the cards were written in my mother's own handwriting but that they came from my great-grandmother, Mary Bearden Taylor, of whom I have no memory.

I knew that Grandma Taylor had taught my mother to cook when she was a young bride in 1972. I remembered my father telling how Grandma came to stay with them, and for a week, my mother made scratch biscuits and gravy every morning and a dessert every night until she got them right. I knew that my other grandmothers and great-grandmothers were in that box, too. So were my babysitters, my Sunday school teachers, my mother's college friends, the women who taught me to read. These were flashes of childhood memories and stories that I remembered as if they were my own memories. They brought me home when I most wanted to be there.

I cooked Thanksgiving dinner. My husband and I ate it. I did not feel that power had shifted in our marriage because I had cooked. I did not feel manacled. I felt satisfied, connected, delighted, and full. Suddenly, I felt a great responsibility. I had lived a life with a casual relationship to this inheritance. I had lived alongside it, listening to it, watching it, eating it, and never really knowing it, and now a generation had passed from the earth and I was the weak link. I had to learn it now, to find its archives, to question its practitioners, to record and codify and teach. Or else watch two grand civilizations — the West Texas Helmses and Weltys — disappear back into the cotton fields, oil fields, pastures, and canyons from whence they came.

In the months that followed, I mined the cookbooks and recipe boxes of everyone I knew. I started a habit of carrying my recipe book with me, and when conversation lagged at a dinner, I'd clear the plates and then ask to see The Goods. I wrote and I cooked and I ate. I started a blog, and I wrote in it every other day for a few months, exploring in writing what it meant to be a woman who cooked and a woman who saved recipes. Even after my husband and I moved back to Texas, even after I returned to graduate school, I kept cooking and eating and saving, digging and archiving. I soon discovered that the questions I had thought about in my blog were the same questions other people were asking in the formal, academic study of foodways.

When word got out that my recipe collecting had turned into serious study, people started showing me The Real Goods. When my paternal grandmother, Dorothy Helms Grady, passed away, the family had gathered at my Aunt

Barbara's house. I had just finished copying down my aunt's recipe for marble pound cake when a longtime family friend who played the piano at the church where I grew up brought me a cookbook that had been wrapped carefully in brown paper. It had belonged to her grandmother in the 1930s. It was commercially published, not a manuscript, though it had some handwritten notes tucked inside. She knew that it was old, and that her grandmother had mostly used it for making Christmas candy. She went out of her way to bring it me — to let me unwrap it and investigate — because she thought that I should see it. I think she hoped that I could tell her what it was, what it meant. That as a scholar and someone who would know, I could tell her that her cookbook was important.

This book is how I tell her that her cookbook was important.

ACKNOWLEDGMENTS

As this project will repeatedly emphasize, texts of all kinds have invisible collaborators, though only my name appears on the cover. I thank those collaborators without whom this work would not be possible. First thanks to editors of this series, Jennifer Jensen Wallach and Michael Wise, for taking on this project with so much enthusiasm and shepherding it so efficiently into print, and to the reviewers whose thoughtful feedback shaped the final product in vitally important ways. To my dissertation committee, who expertly and patiently reviewed and supported the dissertation from which this present work derives: Sarah Ruffing Robbins, Charlotte Hogg, Rebecca Sharpless, and Elizabeth Engelhardt. More thanks to my doctoral program mentors: Bonnie Blackwell, Australia Tarver, Mona Narain, Alex Lemon, and the late David Vanderwerken. To my incredible colleagues and on-the-job mentors who helped move this project from dissertation to book: Anissa Wardi, Lynne Bruckner, Jessie Ramey, and Jennie Sweet-Cushman. To my dearest friends and tireless hype-persons, Tyler Branson, James Chase Sanchez, Heidi Hakimi-Hood, and Amanda Barnett: thank you.

Special thanks go to my husband, Jay Tippen, a partner in the truest sense. To my parents, Eddy and Joburta Helms, who are always impressed but never surprised when I reach some goal, and to my parents-in-law, Philip and Pamela Tippen, who taught me to eat so that I could learn to cook. To my grandmothers, Dorothy Helms Grady and Nella Jo Welty, who are not mere grandmother figures but true flesh and blood, who bequeathed to me their kitchen knowledge in stacks of papers and thousands of meals, who left me their legacies in days spent, stories told, and memories made.

INVENTING
AUTHENTICITY

RECIPE ORIGIN NARRATIVES

Arguing Authenticity in New Southern Cuisine

Welcome to the black, white, Asian, male, female, sweet, spicy,
boiled, boozy, farm-fresh, foraged, locally sourced, globally
inflected future of Southern food and drink.
—Sarah Camp Arnold, *Gravy*[1]

Food and speech share space in the human mouth.
—Candice Goucher, *Congotay! Congotay!*
A Global History of Caribbean Food[2]

IF THIS WERE A COOKBOOK, I'd open this introduction with a memory. I'd tell you about my childhood on a cotton farm in West Texas, about my family's huge vegetable garden and the summers I spent with my mother and my sisters picking, preserving, and eating those vegetables. I would tell you how I loved cucumbers sliced in vinegar at every meal in the summer and cherry tomatoes still hot and dusty, eaten in the garden itself. I wouldn't tell you that I hated everything but the eating. Instead, I would tell you that historically (I won't be too specific about this) the South has always been a proud cotton-growing, vegetable-canning region.

I'd tell you that my father's people, the Helms or Helmses, came from England to Virginia before the Revolution, then were granted land in Kentucky after 1812. Helm's Landing, the ancestral home, is a flat little space on the Cumberland River with a wooden dock. I've been there. The Helms made that *s* permanent somewhere along the line as they moved into Arkansas and Texas.

I'd tell you that my mother's people, the Weltys, are obviously, though distantly, related to that great Southern lady of letters, Eudora Welty. I can't prove it, but you won't ask me to. And with just these few anecdotes, I'd tie myself to a Southern geography, a Southern history, a Southern literature, a Southern identity.

Depending on the kind of cookbook I'm writing, I might be expected to give you some sense of my unique cuisine, what original moves I'm making and how I came up with the idea to make them. Or I might explain why my cuisine is traditional, faithful to long-lasting customs. I might even have a subsection of the introduction called "My Manifesto"[3] or "How I Cook,"[4] and I'd tell you all the things I believe about food and cooking, what it's for and why it's important. And near the end, I'd give you ideas about how to use this book. I'd tacitly give you my permission to be creative with my recipes, to treat them as friendly suggestions. I'd invite you to imagine coming into my kitchen and being my friend.

The scholarly monograph introduction is no less conventional than the cookbook introduction. In the next few pages, I'm going to need to tell you who I am, how I got here, why you should trust me. I'm going to need to connect my life and my work to recognizable fields of study. I'll need to tell you what I've read and who taught me. I'll need to convince you that I've read enough of the right things, that the source of my knowledge is appropriate. And then I'll need to convince you that the arguments in this book are both completely original and the logical heir of long-standing schools of thought. I'll need to tell you exactly what it is that I believe about cookbooks and the study of cookbooks. I'll need to convince you to keep reading, to assign my work to your students, to cite my pithy sentences in your seminar papers, to take the recipes and methods I've developed and apply them to your next project in the study of cookbooks. I'd invite you to come into my office and be my colleague, a fellow traveler in the fascinating study of literary cookbooks.

Who I Am and What I Cook: An Introduction

You already know that I'm a Texan. My CV will tell you that I'm a professor of English and creative writing. I came to the study of cookbooks as literature almost entirely by accident. When I was thinking about enrolling in a doctoral program, food had recently become an important part of my real life. I was just beginning to learn how to cook, and I was teaching a course called "The South in Literature and Film." Our class focused on the construction of a distinct Southern identity and the many ways that writers and artists contributed to and profited from that distinction. It was a small class, and I was excited about showing off my new skills, so I decided to cook for them when we watched films together. I would cook Southern food. In my brain, that was the food of my childhood: black-eyed peas and cornbread, fried chicken and fried okra, pound cake and peach cobbler. I took down recipes from my mother's recipe box, and I looked up recipes online from Paula Deen and Alton Brown and *Southern Living,* sources I trusted to tell me how to be Southern. It wasn't until the third meal that I began to ask the same questions about food that the class had been asking about novels and film: Who says this is the "real" South? What made me so sure that my West Texas farm food was "Southern?" I wanted to give students an authentic Southern experience, but what does *authentic* even mean? And where is the South?

The cookbooks of Southern cuisine had a lot to say about this. They seemed to know exactly what made an authentic Southern recipe. The writers in *Southern Living* did not have any doubts about where the real South was or what its people were like. The more I read, the more I began to see patterns and conventions across the genre. I saw that there was a toolbox of strategies for defining authenticity and that the strategies themselves were worth studying. A whole field of scholarship opened up when I learned that smart people already knew what I seemed to have just found out. Susan Leonardi wrote in 1989 that there was something to study in recipe texts: a textual record of a complex and gendered system of exchange. The actions and motives surrounding recipe texts — whether they happened in the grocery store, in cookbooks, or in novels — were the subject of study.[5] Anne Bower's 1997 collection *Recipes for Reading* showed me what that study would look like. How do you read a cookbook like a novel? Where is the story when there aren't any long prose passages?[6] I found the story of exchange in the recipe headnotes. I set out to discover what I could about this conventional paragraph of introduction that precedes recipe ingredients and instructions.

Fusion Cuisines: An Interdisciplinary Review

This volume is a bit difficult to classify because it speaks to six academic fields at once: literature, rhetoric, history/historiography, American and Southern studies, women and gender studies, and food studies. My home is literature, and the central argument of this book is that cookbooks are suitable for literary study because they are made up of stories that attempt to reflect and reshape reality. This view of story as formative of reality is linked to the study of rhetoric, and my focus on arguments of authenticity that depend on an exchange between speakers and audiences speaks to rhetorical analysis. I am also interested in history and the writing of history in cookbooks, especially in Southern cookbooks where history is sometimes hard to talk about in frank terms. This study seeks to understand how stories about the past are used as a rhetorical tool for making an argument — and to understand what other tools are available when history fails to be convincing.

Of course, the focus on regional foodways appeals to Southern studies and food studies, but I also think about how popular cookbook practices intersect with scholarly methods of regional studies — what these fields learn from one another and where they fail to communicate. The interdisciplinarity of my methods and the focus on "ordinary" or popular texts will perhaps be more familiar to American studies than to literary studies. So, too, women's and gender studies and food studies take up neglected domestic texts like cookbooks. Leonardi argues that recipes and cookbooks, whether written by men or women, are part of a feminine discourse of exchange within networks of women, with women as the imagined audience of cookbooks.[7] Food studies is inextricably linked to the study of women and gender as food practices across many cultures tend to fall on women and marginalized laborers. In introductions to scholarly works of food studies, it is conventional to note that the late arrival of food studies to academic standing is attributed to a devaluing of women and their labor. As you will see, this study examines many texts authored by men because *gender* does not only mean *women*; this study attempts to examine what strategies are available to men and women writers as they negotiate the rhetorical situation of the cookbook, and how the expectations of a sex-gender system based on binary constructions affect how the gendered speaker appeals to a gendered audience.

Food talk and food writing may take many forms, from menu boards and advertisements to television cooking shows and government-issued diet recommendations, including seed catalogs, primers and memoirs, little magazines and zines, and born-digital texts like food blogs and websites, as well as fiction, poetry, and documentary film. Among the many genres of food writing, cookbooks have a long history of scholarly analysis, perhaps because they have a long history as texts themselves. Cookbooks have been in homes and in hands for centuries, and they have been the subject of study in history and anthropology for decades. Food studies scholars recognize the value of cookbooks as cultural objects in addition to their value as historical objects. Put another way, cookbooks not only contain the evidence of a culture's daily practices, but they also play a functional role in the formation and performance of cultural identity. Arjun Appadurai argues that codifying "authentic" cuisine in cookbooks is "an effort on the part of some variety of specialist to standardize the regime of the kitchen, to transmit culinary lore, and to publicize traditions guiding the journey of food from marketplace to kitchen to table."[8] In this way, Appadurai concludes that cookbooks are tools in the institutionalizing of hegemonic power; they are "revealing artifacts of culture in the making."[9] That process of "culture in the making," which takes place in narrative recipe headnotes, is the subject of this study.

The culture in question is the contemporary South, a region whose identity is still in the making—or perhaps, more accurately, always in the remaking. Though popular representations would suggest that Southerners have an intensified relationship to food as a part of their identity, the South is certainly not alone in its deployment of food talk as a method of setting boundaries around its public identity. Donna Gabbacia, examining the struggles of immigrant populations in negotiating ethnic and national identity, argues that patronage for ethnic cookbooks, festivals, and small ethnic restaurants are a kind of "culinary conservatism," a response to an anxiety that ethnic culinary traditions can be lost to the forces of assimilation and homogenization.[10] Certainly, the US South shares this anxiety over a potential loss of distinction through homogenization. In 1974, John Egerton predicted the death by assimilation of a unique Southern identity in *The Americanization of Dixie: The Southernization of America*: "For good or ill, the South is just about over as a separate and distinct place."[11] Fifteen years later, in *Southern Food*, Egerton's position is modified only slightly: "The South, for better or worse, has all but lost its identity as a separate place." However, Egerton quickly turns to food as one of the last distinct markers of Southern-ness: "But its food survives—diminished, perhaps, in availability and quantity, but intact in its essence and authenticity—and at its best, it may be as good as it ever was."[12] The texts examined in this project all speak for this remnant of Southern foodways, claiming the culture maintains its distinction and relevance.

The centrality of food to the definition of Southern identity has opened up food studies as a vibrant agenda for scholars of the US South from a variety of fields, appealing equally to popular and professional audiences. Joe Gray Taylor's *Eating, Drinking, and Visiting in the South* (1982) and Egerton's *Southern Food: At Home, on the Road, and in History* (1987) are targeted at general audiences rather than scholarly ones, but both continue to be touchstones for scholars of Southern food because of their encyclopedic coverage of Southern food traditions and their rich bibliographies of historical Southern cookbooks.[13] Karen Hess's scholarly editions of *Martha Washington's Booke of Cookery* (1981), *The Virginia Housewife* (1984), and *What Mrs. Fisher Knows About Old Southern Cooking* (1995) set a precedent in the South for doing scholarship on historical cookbooks, and, perhaps more importantly, made historical cookbooks available in print from academic presses for scholarly use.[14] These texts together establish a defining feature of food studies in the US South: a permeable boundary between interdisciplinary scholarship and popular publication.

More recently, Elizabeth Engelhardt's *A Mess of Greens: Southern Gender & Southern Food* (2011) demonstrated a methodology for examining middlebrow literature and archival materials in the context of Southern food, contextualizing fictional texts in the lived experiences of working-class women.[15] Influential texts about African American food culture in the South and beyond, including Doris Witt's *Black Hunger: Food and the Politics of U.S. Identity* (1999), Andrew Warnes's *Hunger Overcome?* (2004), Psyche Williams-Forson's *Building Houses out of Chicken Legs: Black Women, Food & Power* (2006), Rebecca Sharpless's *Cooking in Other Women's Kitchens: Domestic Workers in the South, 1865–1960* (2010), and Jessica Harris's *High on the Hog: A Culinary Journey from Africa to America* (2011) all examine African American foodways through a variety of lenses — domestic history, literary analysis, material culture, art history — to argue that African American food culture shapes and is shaped by racial politics and hegemony in the South and in the United States more broadly.[16] In each of the preceding texts, the authors specifically identify race, class, and gender — that mirepoix of cultural studies — as important factors in the creation and interpretation of food writing.

New work in Southern Food studies is coming steadily from a variety of interdisciplinary academic fields, from cultural histories like Marcie Cohen Ferris's *The Edible South: The Power of Food and the Making of an American Region* in 2014 to rhetorical analyses like Ashli Quesinberry Stokes and Wendy Atkins-Sayre's *Consuming Identity: The Role of Food in Redefining the South* in 2016.[17] A number of recent studies focus on the intersections of race and foodways, especially in the civil rights era, demonstrating how the greatest contests for racial equity were, and still are, fought out over food. Frederick Douglass Opie's *Southern Food and Civil Rights: Feeding the Revolution* (2017) offers a history of "the organizations and individuals, home cooks and professional chefs, who — with the food they donated, cooked, grew, and distributed — helped various activists continue to march and advance their goals for progressive change and self-determination." Opie's history includes recipes gathered from cookbooks and black newspapers of the time, along with many historic photos.[18] Similarly, Angela Jill Cooley's *To Live and Dine in Dixie* (2015) focuses especially on the segregation and desegregation of public eating spaces like restaurants, saloons, and cafes.[19] John T. Edge's 2017 history *The Potlikker Papers* emphasizes the important role of food in the civil rights struggle as both a symptom of inequality and a tool to resist and reform it. Edge describes how African Americans in the South used food and cooking to sustain the movement financially and physically, and describes the restaurants and barbecue joints where white Southerners reinforced entrenched white supremacy and, at times, plotted and committed violence. Edge also focuses on the malnutrition, hunger, and food scarcity that resulted from generational structural inequalities, and the projects aimed at relieving (sometimes perpetuating) food insecurity.[20]

This current study relies heavily on precedents set by a 2013 collection of essays, *The Larder: Food Studies Methods from the American South.* The essays in this collection come from historians, anthropologists, ethnographers, social science researchers, and interdisciplinary practitioners in American studies, Southern studies, and women's and gender studies.[21] The ongoing work of the Southern Foodways Alliance, under the direction of John T. Edge, continues to bring the work of oral historians, documentary filmmakers, archivists, chefs, activists, and eaters together for popular and academic audiences. Conversations about Southern food and authenticity on social media, on blogs, and in magazines feature the voices of powerful figures like Michael Twitty and Sean Brock, who blur the lines between celebrity chefs and public intellectuals. Whether the conversation takes place in the classroom, in the cookbook, or on Twitter, there remains a broad interest in the meaning of Southern food past, present, and future.

Furthermore, Southern food studies (and food studies in general) has a longstanding relationship with literary studies. Recently, Tara Powell and David Davis's edited collection of essays on food in Southern literature called *Writing in the Kitchen* (2014) explores the role of food as symbolic and significant in historicizing and interpreting fiction.[22] Though this present volume examines cookbooks themselves as literary documents, my teaching and other writing is focused on ways that understanding food as a cultural object and a rhetorical practice can enrich the experience of reading novels, poems, and plays.[23] However, Jennifer Cognard-Black and Melissa Goldthwaite point out the limits to which food studies has been welcomed into departments of English and the literature classroom. Cognard-Black and Goldthwaite write about teaching a course called "Books That Cook" that includes canonical literary genres like poetry, fiction, nonfiction prose, and film, as well as hybrid texts like the cookbook-memoir, "food fiction," or "recipe novels."[24] They recognize in the "raised eyebrows" of colleagues the unspoken accusation that the introduction of middlebrow food writing into the canon of literature may strain an already stretched reputation for literary studies: "You English folk will teach anything and call it literature."[25] At the 2015 MLA convention, a panel convened on "Horizons of Literary Food Studies: Genres, Material, and Methods" demonstrated areas of growth in literary food studies. However, the panelists themselves also demonstrated the limits of food studies in English to date: four out of five members of the panel held joint appointments in English and interdisciplinary programs.[26] The field of literature is still in the process of adopting food studies into its department structures, but the interdisciplinary conversation described above suggests an argument for reading recipes as literary and cultural productions as well as rhetorically constructed arguments for identity.

The suggestion that cookbooks be approved for literary study is also supported by the cognitive practices of cookbook readers. Barbara Kirshenblatt-Gimblett argues in "Playing to the Senses: Food as a Performance Medium" that experienced cookbook readers approach these texts as books to be read and perhaps never used: "Cookbooks, now more than ever, are a way of eating by reading recipes and looking at photographs. Those books may never see the kitchen. Indeed, experienced readers can sight-read a recipe the way a musician sight-reads a score. They can 'play' the recipe in their mind's eye."[27] The famed author Margaret Atwood opens the introduction to her 1987 literary cookbook *The CanLit Foodbook* declaring, "I'm one of those people who read cookbooks the way other people read travel writing: I may not ever make the recipe, but it's fun to read about it, and to speculate on what kind of people would." Atwood goes on to make the less flattering genre comparison between cookbooks and soft porn: "There's a certain sybaritic voyeurism involved, an indulgence by proxy."[28] In these comparisons between recipes and musical scores, travel writing, and porn, the common factor is an imagined participation that effects a very similar result compared to active participation in reality. Just as a reader of science fiction can imagine a trip to Mars without ever having to unpack a spacesuit, a reader of cookbooks can imagine the details of preparing and consuming a recipe without having to leave the chair. The vivid and descriptive language of recipes supports this view of recipe reading as imaginative exercise.[29]

Contemporary cookbooks appeal to the imaginative reader by offering more text for the reader to consume, creating a subcategory of cookbooks that can be described as literary. Atwood, for example, describes the compilation of poetry, prose, and recipes in *The CanLit Foodbook* as both "a civilized literary symposium on the subject of food," featuring the work of Canadian literary authors, and, with self-deprecating humor, "a collection of recipes preceded by some amusing verbal shenanigans."[30] Many of the contemporary cookbooks examined here have literary aspirations; their long prose interludes, full-color photographs, detailed ingredient lists, and adjective-filled instructions cater to an audience that has more interest in imagining the cooking process than replicating it. Still other cookbooks behave more like souvenirs or advertisements for restaurants, representing a chef's cuisine in print and picture for the purpose of engaging the senses in imagination or remembrance. In this way, today's cookbooks have more in common with literary texts than with their utilitarian forebears from the early domestic science movement.

What I Mean When I Say . . . : Defining Terms

I've made my case that my book is an heir to the long-standing traditions of recognizable fields. This is the part of the cookbook where I would do the complicated dance of declaring that even though I have received those traditions, I am making a wholly original contribution to interdisciplinary scholarship. The first chapter of Kevin Gillespie's 2012 cookbook *Fire in My Belly: Real Cooking* is called "What I Mean When I Say . . ." In it, Gillespie breaks down "Kevinspeak," his particular vocabulary in the kitchen.[31] Perhaps this is a good model for what I need to do now.

The stories in this book come from recipe headnotes. Contemporary cookbooks tend to have an introduction to the book as a whole, introductions to chapters, and shorter introductions to each recipe. These headnotes may be a few sentences describing the ingredients or procedures of the recipe or making a suggestion about the appropriate occasion or method of serving. They may also run several paragraphs long, giving details about the writer's personal memories or the historical and traditional function of the dish in a particular culture. Though these headnotes vary in length and content, they are ubiquitous and conventional in twenty-first-century cookbooks. The basic form of cooking instruction varies little across the genre; each recipe is presented with a title, headnote, ingredient list, numbered instructions, and serving suggestions, usually opposite of a photograph.

The headnote is one generic feature of the cookbook where readers find stories; the "recipe origin narrative" that is the focus of this study is one conventional type of headnote. I define the recipe origin narrative as a story about where food traditions come from and who invented them. This may be a historical narrative about the distant past, the very first instance of this dish's appearance and the subsequent canonizing of that dish in the culture at large. The origin narrative might also document the source of the recipe text, citing the individual who is responsible for innovating this particular version of the dish. Another form of the origin narrative describes the *writer's* origins and how their personal identity and experience authorize them to present this recipe to the audience.

I draw my interest in origins from Michel Foucault. In "Nietzsche, Genealogy, and History," Foucault questions the project of using narrative to establish any single genesis for any of the conditions of existence. The search for a first ancestor in genealogy must always end in disappointment, with one more unknowable ancestor lost in prehistory. According to Foucault, the suggestion that any concept moves in logical, linear, upward progress ignores the dynamic relationship between language and meaning.[32] Instead of looking for purity in the moment of origin and clarity in the lines of inheritance, genealogical analysis questions the possibility of purity and insists on the messiness of beginnings. So rather than a pursuit of origins, genealogy as a method "opposes itself to the search for 'origins,'"[33] and can critique the historical narratives of concepts without ever "confus[ing] itself with a quest for their 'origins.'"[34] Through the method of genealogy, first proposed as a philosophical paradigm by Nietzsche and then adopted by Foucault, one can critique naturalized concepts that appear to be "without history."[35] Genealogy, the method, asks: What is at stake in this narrative, and who are the stakeholders? The end goal is to trouble the narrative, to subject it to rigorous analysis with the hopes of shaking off the ivy and overgrowth that made it appear natural, and exposing the scaffolding and construction underneath. What appears as a substance, a material fact, is exposed as an act, a repeated and entrenched performance. The narrative — and those who have stock in the narrative, surely — are troubled.

Recipe headnotes that tell stories about the roots of food traditions are origin narratives, and I argue that these narratives are important sites for examining regional identity as they reflect and reform the narratives of the culture they claim to represent. Some of the origin narratives in cookbooks are genealogies in this sense. They throw doubt on the project of finding a single origin point. They reveal the complex forces and interconnected accidents at the moment of origin, thereby suggesting that a single origin is impossible. In that way, they are points of resistance to power. In the case of the recipe, the origin narrative is a means by which the writer struggles "against forms of exploitation that separate individuals from what they produce."[36]

Identifying people and people groups as creators of culinary knowledge can potentially offer those ordinary cooks a stake in shaping the identity of the region and its people, making an implicit argument about who may have insider status in a particular identity group. Each cookbook has its own rhetorical agenda when it comes to telling origin narratives; some do so to establish the author's own ethos as iconoclast while others do so to direct attention to unacknowledged or underappreciated figures. The stories of the founding of Southern cooking traditions can be used to validate certain individuals and groups as true Southerners. However, those narratives can just as easily take cultural power away from founders by revising or rejecting the received origin narrative. The *stories* are the subject of this investigation because *stories* are the tools that authors use to define and readers use to enact legible regional identities.

Authenticity and *identity* are intricately linked in this study through story. Origin narratives are stories that claim a recipe belongs in a cuisine, arguing that the borders of that cuisine can be drawn with certainty, and that the moment of origin (and the characters, settings, and circumstances present at the moment of origin) is convincing evidence of belonging to that cuisine. An authentic cuisine exists and is knowable. A distinct cuisine must belong to a distinct culture with defined parameters for group membership. Implicit in an argument about a recipe's authenticity is an argument about the writer's or innovator's identity and belonging.

Authenticity is an especially difficult term to pin down in foodways scholarship. Scholars disagree on what factors determine authenticity or whether authenticity is a useful term in making food choices. In *Exotic Appetites* (2003), Lisa Heldke interrogates the implications of "the [food] adventurer's intense desire for authentic experiences of authentic cultures."[37] Heldke argues that food adventurers garner cultural capital by trying out foods from cultures to which they are outsiders. However, the value of that capital is determined by the perceived authenticity of the food and its source. The emphasis on authenticity is misguided, according to Heldke, because it suggests that middle-class Euro-Americans have the knowledge and power to determine the authenticity of traditions from cultures not their own, and this form of appropriation mirrors the practices of colonization. Heldke identifies some definitions of authenticity that seem to be in use in popular culture. One is that the authentic is "the true cuisine, unmediated by any outside influences."[38] This definition reduces the authentic to an essential quality that Heldke argues does not match reality. Ingredients and recipes move, and cuisines adapt to natural and political changes. Heldke concludes, "To seek after some pure, unchanging, authentic essence in a cuisine is to look for something that does not exist. But the very search for it contributes to the essentializing of the Other that makes the search for authenticity part of the 'conquering spirit of modernity.'"[39] Though Heldke doubts that authenticity is useful — and even suggests that the search for authenticity is culturally violent — she does not deny that authenticity dominates the discourse of food in the United States. Therefore, it is vital to critique the employment of that term and concept in popular culture and food discourse.

Josee Johnston and Shyon Baumann take up Heldke's call in *Foodies: Democracy and Distinction in the Gourmet Foodscape* (2010). Johnston and Baumann argue that foodies (the same group of consumers that Heldke calls "food adventurers") rely on the category of authenticity to "evaluate and legitimate food choices," emphasizing that authenticity is an unstable, socially constructed category.[40] The authors identify five qualities used in the discourse of authenticity that operate in a "symbolic economy" to determine the value of foodways: "People understand food as being authentic when it has geographic specificity, is 'simple,' has a personal connection, can be linked to a historical tradition, or has 'ethnic' connections."[41] All five factors depend entirely on origins. Geographic specificity asks, "Where did this recipe originate?" Historical tradition asks, "When and how did this recipe originate?" Personal and ethnic connections ask, "Who originated this recipe?" "Simplicity," as Johnston and Baumann's scare quotes suggest, has multiple meanings, but it refers to the qualities of "honesty and effortlessness . . . a trait that hearkens back to the association between authenticity and individual sincerity, or being 'true to oneself.'"[42] It also connotes "small-scale and non-industrial production techniques" and "the purity of 'simple' high quality ingredients."[43] This category of "simplicity," too, depends on origins, asking if the recipe emerges from the right kind of source: a natural confluence of cultural and geographic factors, a sincere artist without ulterior motives, an honest writer sharing a part of his or her heart, a local and ethical supplier. I return to Johnston and Baumann's five factors of authenticity throughout the book like my favorite seasonings. Authenticity, as it is discussed in this study, depends on origins deeply connected to identity and place.

In Southern food studies, authenticity is a particular point of contention. Andrew Warnes argues in his essay for *The Larder* (2013) that the study of Southern food is polarized between those who want to excavate and preserve an authentic Southern food and those who want to undermine the authenticity of foodways by describing how traditions are invented. Warnes describes the field of Southern food studies in conflict, with nostalgia and authenticity on the one hand and cynicism and invention on the other; one focused on celebrating the pleasure of food, and the other on uncovering the pain.[44] This project is meant to answer Warnes's call for a scholarship that does not see authenticity and invention as mutually exclusive approaches. Instead, I hope to continue the conversation Warnes began about the complicated relationship between the primacy of pleasure in food experiences and the potential for cultural violence of food narratives.

To that end, I argue that authenticity is invented. Despite the scholarly conflict on the meaning of authenticity — or whether such a thing exists in any measurable form — the discourse of authenticity in food culture and food writing persists. *Authenticity* is an informally agreed upon set of signs, symbols, certificates, badges, and strategies that speak to an audience invested in evaluating authenticity and collecting authentic experiences. This project takes on the issue of authenticity from a rhetorical position, examining narratives from cookbooks that make arguments about authenticity, identifying and naming the linguistic, narrative machinery that constructs and supports these arguments in origin narratives.

New Southern food, in particular, has much invested in arguments of authenticity, in part because the authenticity of these recipes is contested. The "newness" of New Southern cuisine is a threat to authenticity as it separates current food culture from traditional practices. The texts of New Southern Cuisine are preoccupied with an authentic Southern identity and history because they often address the reader and cook as a Southerner displaced or adopted, one whose authentic Southern identity is suspect or in need of fortification. Cookbook authors like Nathalie Dupree encourage readers to use cooking to reconnect with an authentic Southern identity by way of performing an authentic Southern past. Dupree writes in *New Southern Cooking* (1990) that she knows her readers may be "young Southerners (and Northerners, too)" who might not be familiar with cooking techniques or traditional Southern dishes because of a missing link in the chain of inherited culinary knowledge: "I made a point of stopping to explain techniques that many might not understand because they didn't learn cooking at Mama's knee as people did in past generations (Mama may have been too busy, or she may not have even come from the South)."[45] Dupree promises to "make you a Southerner for a time" through the performance of these recipes, which will connect the cook to the history of the South and the memories of their collective, and potentially adoptive, Southern family.[46]

I have purposefully chosen the verb *perform* to describe cooking a recipe. Diana Taylor's *The Archive and the Repertoire: Performing Cultural Memory in the Americas* (2003) describes performance as "vital acts of transfer, transmitting social knowledge, memory, and a sense of identity" through "twice-behaved behavior."[47] Recipes are scripts of a performance, whether they are read and performed in the imagination or physically performed in the kitchen. They are always at least "twice-behaved" between the cook who writes them and the cook who reads them. But recipes linked to an authentic group identity are behaved potentially in the thousands, over generations and across geographical space. As Nathalie Dupree's promise to "make you a Southerner for a time" suggests, the repeated performance of the recipe is an act of transfer, as Taylor defines it, moving "social knowledge, memory, and a sense of identity" in a continuous narrative from an original innovator to the present performer, preserving the authenticity of the performance as valid cultural capital. Authenticity is an important factor in making a successful act of transfer. There is a need to validate the knowledge, memory, and identity as the right knowledge, memory, and identity to serve the reader.

Therefore, the stories of Southern cooking found in recipe headnotes are a rich site for investigating the role that recipe reading, cooking, and storytelling play in the formation of individual and group identities. The fact that the headnote is conventional is not a liability of this study but further evidence that the innovations, variations, and deviations within that convention are meaningful as a part of a larger conversation with the form of the genre, the expectations of the audience, and the purposes of the author.

And that brings me to the last word that needs a definition: *author*. One potential complicating factor of the analysis of narrative strategies in this book is that while the chef- and restaurant-centric cookbook is most often written with a single authoritative voice from a first-person pronoun point of view, ghostwriting and coauthoring are common practices that can become nearly invisible. Where some cookbooks like Faye Porter's *At My Grandmother's Knee* (2011) borrow from the practices of community cookbooks to be explicitly collaborative and composite in terms of authorship, chef-centric cookbooks typically appear to have a single author whose ethos is established and confirmed throughout the text.[48] Some cookbooks are quite honest about the collaborative writing process. Sara Foster of Foster's Market in Chapel Hill, North Carolina, shares cowriter credits in each of her cookbooks: Emily Wallace (*Foster's Market Favorites: 25th Anniversary Collection*, 2015), Tema Larter (*Sara Foster's Southern Kitchen*, 2011), Carolyn Carreno (*Sara Foster's Casual Cooking: More Fresh Simple Recipes from Foster's Market*, 2007; *Fresh Every Day: More Great Recipes from Foster's Market*, 2005), and Sarah Belk King (*The Foster's Market Cookbook: Favorite Recipes for Morning, Noon, and Night*, 2002).[49] The names of Foster's cowriters are credited in various ways. Sarah Belk King's name is on the cover in very small white print (while the name of the author of the foreword, Martha Stewart, is only just slightly smaller than Foster's own name). Emily Wallace and Tema Larter's names do not appear on the outside covers.

Wallace is clearly credited on the title page, but Larter is named only in the acknowledgments and the Library of Congress publication information. In the acknowledgments, Foster writes thanks to "Tema Larter, my co-author, who developed a distinctive voice throughout the pages of this book. Her knowledge and love of Southern food brought my memories and experiences to life."[50] While Foster's name appears on every cover in the title, as the author, or sometimes both, she signals clearly to readers that the work in front of them is collaborative. The book represents Foster's personal "memories and experiences" and recipes, but those are "brought ... to life" through a "distinctive voice" that is acknowledged as the narrative creation of another writer.

While Foster makes her coauthors easily visible, Pat Conroy goes a bit further, clarifying in his introduction the specific roles assigned to himself and to his coauthor and long-time friend Suzanne Willamson Pollack: "Suzanne is the great workhorse and beauty behind the recipes in this book. I provide hot air and sense of story," Conroy writes.[51] Foster's and Conroy's cookbooks demonstrate opposite definitions of what it means to author a cookbook and what is being sold between the covers. Foster is first author of *Sara Foster's Southern Kitchen* because the recipes are her original contributions; the recipes are the authored product. Conroy is first author of *The Pat Conroy Cookbook* even though, by his own admission, the recipes are Pollack's contribution; the stories are the authored product. In both cases, the author is the product. The persona one pays to see is Foster as chef or Conroy as writer. Even when the collaboration is made visible, there is no single rule for how to differentiate between a cookbook's author and the writer of a headnote.

To complicate matters further, the common practice of ghostwriting is designed to be far less visible than coauthoring. The absence of a credited coauthor does not signify the absence of collaboration. As cookbook ghostwriter Julia Moskin wrote in a *New York Times* Dining and Wine column in 2012, ghostwriting today is both more common and more visible than in the past. "Years ago," Moskin writes, "there was a quaint trust among cookbook buyers that chefs personally wrote their books and tested their recipes, and a corresponding belief among chefs that to admit otherwise would mean giving someone else credit for the tiniest part of their work — unacceptable, in those macho and territorial times." However, Moskin also admits that "today, in a content-driven media environment, the role of the writer is given far more respect, and many chefs do not pretend that they do their own writing." She quotes TV chef–personality Bobby Flay who admits, "I consider myself an 'author,' in quotes, but not a writer. ... I have skills in the kitchen, but the writers keep the project on track, meet the deadlines, make the editor happy." The ghostwriter, according to Moskin, is tasked with invisibly packaging the chef persona into a marketable product, "bundling the voice, knowledge and vision of a chef between the covers of a book."[52]

In this formulation, the chef-author functions as a chef-auteur, a creative force and vision that is the raison d'être for the book, even if he or she has not typed a word. This term *auteur* comes from film studies and describes the way that a film's director — as the final decision maker and holder of a holistic aesthetic vision — is the more deserving of the credit as "author" of a film than any of the collaborators who are responsible for individual parts of the film (screenwriters, actors, designers, technicians, etc.). This word is especially relevant to the study of cookbooks because, as Marilyn Fabe argues in *Closely Watched Films* (2014), the auteur theory emerged as an argument for the artistic and literary merit of film as a genre:

> Despite film's status as primarily a commercial entertainment medium, it could potentially be an art form as powerful in its means of expression as literature or poetry. In order to propose filmmaking as an art, however, *there had to be an artist*, a central consciousness whose vision is inscribed in the work. . . . For the French New Wave theorists, the author of the film (the auteur) was the director. (emphasis added)[53]

Like the artistic film that depends on an artist, the literary cookbook depends on an author to fit into the conventional understanding of how meaningful texts get made. Though this convention is itself a construction with a history, not inevitable (see more about this in chapter 2 in the discussion of intellectual property law), literary and rhetorical analysis requires a speaker and an audience to make claims and interpretations, even if both of those entities are imagined.

I recognize that the practices of ghostwriting and coauthoring may make it more complicated to assign motives or intentions in a narrative to the chef-author when it is not always clear what role the chef-author has actually played in composing the narrative. When I make claims about what Sean Brock or Virginia Willis or Edward Lee are doing or suggesting or arguing in a particular narrative, it is with the understanding that the hand that crafted the meaningful sentence may indeed belong to a visible or invisible collaborator. However, I argue that these shared composition practices nonetheless emphasize the central argument of this chapter: the chef's person and persona are carefully crafted products whether they are crafted by the chef-writer or a ghostwriter speaking as chef-author. A narrative written by a professional ghostwriter on behalf of a chef may be even more self-consciously aware of how it contributes to a rhetorical purpose than if the chef was writing alone. When I speak of chef-authors in this book, it is with the understanding that I refer to the imagined speaker of the narrative, the personal pronoun that represents the chef-auteur at the center of the text.

How I Cook: A Methodology

To accomplish this analysis of narrative strategies and draw conclusions about cookbooks as a genre and headnote writing as a practice, I rely on some methods of "distant" or "surface" reading. Surface reading, as described by Stephen Best and Sharon Marcus, is a reaction against "symptomatic" or "close" reading that "took meaning to be hidden, repressed, deep, and in need of detection and disclosure by an interpreter."[54] In this way of reading, the surface of a text is a trick, a façade, not to be trusted, and the work of textual analysis assumed that a text never meant what it said. But Best and Marcus point out that "not all situations require the subtle ingenuity associated with symptomatic reading,"[55] and that "certain kinds of forgotten literature do not need to be decoded to be understood."[56] Symptomatic reading and its requirement for professional readers is perhaps another reason for the slow adoption of food writing and other middlebrow texts into literary analysis: these texts appear to have no mysteries in need of solving. Their meanings are manifest in their surfaces, and they do not require professional readers to tell regular readers how to make sense of them. However, surface reading as a practice seeks to undo the surface/depth binary to suggest that "underneath the surface there is only more surface."[57] Surface reading does not suggest a shallow reading, but does define the focus of study as "what is evident, perceptible, apprehensible in texts; what is neither hidden nor hiding. . . . A surface is what insists on being looked at rather than what we must train ourselves to see through."[58] Though I would continue to vehemently argue that cooking instructions are rich texts with unexplored depths, I would not suggest that the richness comes from disguised meanings under artistic or symbolic uses of language. Rather, the richness of cookbooks comes from understanding the way cookbook writers establish relationships with audiences, attempting to move those audiences into action in the physical world. Cooking instructions tend to straightforwardly mean what they say and declare their intentions directly. But unlike many other kinds of literary texts, these stories move from the ideological to the material, affecting both the ways audiences think and the ways they move their bodies, encouraging audiences to incorporate the text from the surface of the page to the depths of their stomachs. The material surfaces of cooking instructions — complete with dog-eared, batter-splatted, hand-annotated pages — offer plenty of meaning themselves.

Another aspect of surface reading also implies the exploration of patterns across many texts. Best and Marcus describe this kind of critic as having two functions: "anatomist" and "taxonomist." The anatomist "break[s] down texts or discourses into their components," while the taxonomist "arrang[es] and categoriz[es] texts into larger groups."[59] In this project, I play both roles. By examining many alimentary texts from one region and a short period of time, I am able to draw conclusions about the component parts common between them and the conventions of genre. I read across the genre to diagram its body systems; the recipe headnote is one such system that behaves in predictable ways. As taxonomist, I group texts around the variations in those systems and give them names. The aim is not to reveal that cookbooks are so complex as to deserve critical attention, but to question that complexity is a prerequisite for critical attention at all.

This project is also an exercise in close reading. I do, indeed, look at small portions of texts for figurative uses of language. And I do, indeed, examine absences and silences in the surface of texts as meaningful deflections and misdirections. I do conclude that some texts mean more than what they are saying. The combination of these reading techniques — distant and close — appears to me to be the most productive way of reading recipe texts. It recognizes that cooking instructions are valuable because of their surfaces and distant patterns, and that recipe writers are rhetors and authors because of their skillful language use. The combination of surface and close reading methods are required to fully explore the significance of cooking instructions because, as Leonardi has argued, cooking instructions are an "embedded discourse."[60] They communicate in a system of complex social relationships, historical times and places, and rhetorical and narrative strategies. Both methods are required to evaluate the significance of cooking instructions as meaningful texts and cultural objects.

Through methods of distant reading as "anatomist," I looked for patterns and generic conventions across the body of Southern cookbooks published in the last two decades. Besides recipes, all the texts also had in common the practice of composing headnotes. Within the headnotes emerged patterns of content, including the origin narrative: the narrative of how this recipe came to be in this book. Within that category of origin narrative emerged subcategories or types of origin stories that differed in content. Some described the historical origin of the dish or the food tradition. Others described the provenance of the specific set of instructions from contributor to writer. Still others described the origins of the recipe writer, the personal memories and moments of inspiration for particular innovations. As "taxonomist," I grouped these narrative types into named subcategories that became the chapters of this book: historical narratives, citation narratives, and personal narratives.

In chapter one, I examine origin narratives that use historical origins as evidence of authenticity. In this subcategory, historical narratives, I explore the implication of the origin narrative as historiography and as genealogy. The textual analysis in this chapter begins with an attempt to account for the appearance of Brunswick stew in the canon of Southern recipes. A distant reading revealed that the recipe for Brunswick stew was predictably accompanied by a discussion of the disputed historical origin of the dish. I track the changes in the historical narrative for this dish as cookbook writers engage in an intertextual conversation about the origins of Brunswick stew and about the value of the project of narrating historical origins at all. As cookbook writers narrate the conflict or narrate a single origin story, they use specific changes in language from their source documents to alter the character of the innovator — and by extension, the value of the innovator's culinary knowledge and the productive power of his or her status as innovator to shape culture — in reaction to the political needs of the present or the rhetorical needs of the writing situation.

Chapter two explores a second category of origin narratives that use provenance as evidence of authenticity. These citation narratives describe the movement of a recipe from an innovator to the cookbook writer. In this chapter, I discuss the role of copyright and intellectual property law in the development of citation practices in recipe origin narratives. By excluding recipes from protection, the law considers recipes as documents without authors and without histories, separated from the individuals who created them. The narrative citation resists the law and its definition of literary value by writing a history for the recipe and establishing the authorship rights of a named contributor and knowledge creator. However, even as a recipe narrator resists the negative power of the law (power that oppresses or restricts), that same narrator exercises a form of positive power that produces the category of knowledge creator. As the texts for analysis in that chapter demonstrate, narrators use the citation narrative as means to a variety of ends, some of which produce power for the contributor while others produce power for the cookbook writer (recipe citer) or for the cookbook reader.

Like citation narratives, the personal narratives in the third chapter are also narrowly focused on "small pasts." Chef-authored cookbooks of New Southern Cuisine have a simultaneous need to provide readers with original haute cuisine recipes and to connect to a long-standing tradition of distinct regional identities. This connection is often made through the chef's personal ethos and credentials: the chef is certified to innovate without losing authenticity because of authentic origins. The personal narrative is often employed to authenticate chef-authors who are not born and bred in the South or who identify themselves as racially or ethnically outside of the black/white racial binary that dominates the imagined South. This kind of headnote attempts to justify the chef's "right" to appropriate, innovate, or otherwise claim authentic Southern cuisine. These headnotes utilize ancestry and genealogy, personal memory, and professional experiences as measures of authenticity superior to history or geography. Instead of engaging with the systemic injustices in the public history of Southern food and agriculture, personal narratives focus on the individual.

I argue that all forms of the origin narrative described above are designed to affirm the perceived authenticity of recipes as valid methods for performing an authentic cultural identity in public. For the writers of Southern cooking instructions, the concept of authenticity is an argument central to the text, requiring writers to employ strategic arguments to convince readers that their recipes are authentic Southern cuisine and good to eat. Moreover, they must verify their own authenticity as chefs who can provide reliable recipes and, as "real Southerners," who can provide reliable guidance in the performance of Southern identity. The writers of cookbooks are focused on convincing readers that their recipes are not just good to eat but good to perform. The preoccupation with the construct of authenticity is one manifestation of the South's efforts to preserve a distinct regional identity in the face of homogenization. The origin narrative (in its several forms) is one specific rhetorical strategy that writers use to argue for authenticity.

Contemporary cookbooks are an especially apt site for an investigation of the rhetoric of authenticity and Southern identity. According to data collected by Lily Kelting, the last two decades have seen a marked increase in the use of the words *South* and *Southern* as intentional regional branding in cookbook titles, increasing from 2 percent of cookbooks published in the United States in 1990–2000 to 7.5 percent in 2010–2015.[61] The market share of cookbooks representing Southern cuisine and identity appears to be on the rise. As more cookbooks claiming a Southern identity appear on bookstore shelves and kitchen counters (or perhaps coffee tables and bedside nightstands), right now seems to be a good moment to examine how these cookbooks variously define the South as a geographic region, a distinct culture, and a unique cuisine. This volume focuses intentionally on this period of growth in the Southern cookbook market from John Egerton's *Southern Food* (1987) and Nathalie Dupree's *New Southern Cooking* (1990) to the moment's most critically acclaimed texts like

Ronni Lundy's *Victuals* (2016) and Asha Gomez's *My Two Souths: Blending the Flavors of India into a Southern Kitchen* (2016).[62]

I had set for myself only two requirements for choosing texts at the start of this project. The book should be published between 1990 and the present, and it should be clearly marked as representing the South or Southern cuisine. As the project grew, it became apparent that I needed a more sophisticated strategy for identifying texts for case studies. What I most wanted to examine in this study was arguments of authenticity, and so to choose primary texts for analysis meant first establishing what kind of rhetorical situation I wanted to explore. The rhetorical situation, in its most simplified terms, is a relational context between the speaker and the audience, the "exigence" or purpose for speaking, and other "constraints" that call forth and shape the utterance.[63] These factors determine how the rhetor creates discourse to achieve a goal or persuade an audience. A savvy rhetor will purposefully present their identity and ethos in writing to suit the purpose and appeal to the audience's beliefs and biases. Similarly, the rhetor will strategically choose arguments that accomplish their goals, and may even purposefully address their arguments to a specific imagined or real audience most likely to be moved by those arguments. Any change in the context of discourse may result in a completely different product. For example, a recipe writer whose primary purpose is to entertain an audience of home cooks will construct a very different argumentative narrative from a chef whose purpose is to inform (and impress) fellow food professionals. In order to identify rhetorical patterns across cookbooks, it was important to build a sample responding to similar rhetorical situations. All of the cookbooks in this sample have similar kinds of speakers, similar target audiences, and the same primary exigence: to define a distinct Southern cuisine. Like answers to the same open-ended question, it is the similarity of the rhetorical situation that highlights the unique strategies of each author as they respond to the same exigence, attempting to achieve very similar outcomes under widely diverging constraints.

First, I chose to limit the scope to cookbooks with a central speaker (or small group of speakers) who could be identified by name, as opposed to collective or corporate authors. Because I was interested in a kind of personal authenticity with a focus on the complexities of authorship and identity, a personal author was needed. For this reason, I excluded collaboratively authored community cookbooks and cookbooks that identified editors (rather than individual authors) in favor of books with strong, central authorial personalities. Thus, the study leans toward celebrity chefs and television personalities, but it also includes career food writers, historians, and scholars.

Also for this reason, I did not include in this study cookbooks branded by *Southern Living* or printed by its publishing arm, Oxmoor House, unless they named a specific author. Cookbooks like *The Southern Cookie Book* (2016) and *The Southern Baker Book* (2015) both credit "The Editors of *Southern Living*" on their covers.[64] These collaborative or edited collections seemed to be of a different rhetorical situation from the chef-authored cookbooks that make up most of this study. However, Oxmoor and *Southern Living* have also released cookbooks with named authors who have significant reputations as food writers: Sheri Castle (*The Southern Living Community Cookbook*, 2014), Morgan Murphy (*Bourbon and Bacon*, 2014), Matt Moore (*A Southern Gentleman's Kitchen*, 2015), and Tasia Malakasis (*Southern Made Fresh*, 2015).[65] A few of these apparently single-authored texts do make good examples, or counterexamples, in this study. Still, while a single person is identified as author on the cover, some remain corporate in nature; in Castle's *Community Cookbook*, recipes are collected from popular and historical community cookbooks with editorial commentary from Castle. Similarly, while Kelly Alexander is author of *No Taste Like Home: A Celebration of Regional Southern Cooking and Hometown Flavor* (2013), the recipes are "inspired and contributed by *Southern Living* readers, chefs, and locals-done-good in each region" of the South.[66] These cookbooks remain explicitly collaborative in authorship, which means they respond to a very different rhetorical situation when compared to (at least apparently) single-chef-authored works like Hugh Acheson's *A New Turn in the South* (2011).[67]

Secondly, to fit into the study, at least one rhetorical purpose of the cookbook should be to represent, define, revise, claim, or reclaim some version of Southern cooking or cuisine. Of course, most single-authored cookbooks had other implied purposes: developing a chef-author's unique brand, driving traffic to the chef-author's restaurants, advancing an argument about what foods are delicious or what methods of farming are ethical. I relied on the authors' explicit statements of purpose, often found in their introductions and manifestos, and the implied purposes communicated by strategic and rhetorical language in the titles and narratives. A title on the cover announcing "New Southern Cuisine" was one way of identifying this purpose, but relying on Southern titling alone to identify candidates excluded useful texts. For example, the title of Sean Brock's *Heritage* (2015) merely implies that the heritage in question is Southern, but the book clearly and repeatedly makes claims to represent Southern cuisine from the first page of the introduction.[68] By contrast, Ashley Christensen's cookbook, titled after her Raleigh, North Carolina, restaurant *Poole's* (2016), is clearly Southern in origin, but the content of the cookbook is strongly linked to the American tradition of diners like Poole's. The first words of the book are these: "Welcome. Diners are an American tradition."[69] While a few recipes like pimento cheese and deviled eggs are presented as specifically Southern traditions, and Christensen is pedigreed in the introduction as "a kid who grew up in the sticks of North Carolina," the book makes very few claims to a distinctly Southern identity or cuisine.[70] The book's rhetorical purpose is to represent the modern diner as a national phenomenon, so it did not suit the needs of this study. I focused on texts that announced an intention to represent the South or Southern cuisine.

By focusing on this explicit statement of a primary exigence to represent Southern identity, I may have set up criteria that would necessarily limit writers of color and give preference to white male chefs. As James C. Cobb explains in *Away Down South*, black Southerners have often been excluded from Southern identity. A focus on Old South plantation nostalgia and segregation as the definition of Southern identity "effectively excluded the South's black residents in much the same way that both black and white southerners had been 'othered' out of the construction of American identity."[71] Ashley B. Thompson and Melissa M. Sloan point out in "Race as Region, Region as Race," that everyday conversation about the South tends to conflate Southerners with white Southerners, as in "'southerners are racist,' or 'southerners owned slaves.'"[72] Patricia G. Davis writes about this exclusion very personally in the introduction to *Laying Claim: African American Cultural Memory and Southern Identity:* "Whether the content of and implication of dominant ideas about southernness took the form of the celebrated elegance and splendor of the Old South aristocracy or of the proudly defiant, so-called redneck culture epitomized by *The Dukes of Hazzard,* they invoked cultural memories and, by extension, a sense of belonging, to which I could never lay claim."[73] However, each of these authors also describes black Southerners taking action to claim membership in Southern identity, against some resistance. Cobb argues that black Southerners "served notice of their determination to offer an alternative version of southern identity" after emancipation and "began to assert their identities as southerners and to embrace the South as their homeland" through the civil rights struggle.[74] Similarly, Thompson and Sloan cite black Southerners' actions against "symbols of the Confederate past" in the public sphere as evidence that "at least some black southerners are reclaiming their identity as southerners."[75] Still, as Davis demonstrates throughout *Laying Claim*, black and white Southerners do not necessarily share a common view of Southern history and identity.[76] Obviously, black residents of the South have played a key role in creating Southern culture, particularly in foodways; however, their relationship to the label of *Southerner* continues to be contentious, and their power to claim a fair share of credit for Southern identity often meets with resistance.

The conflation of Southerners with white Southerners affects even how cookbooks are classified in libraries. Library of Congress subject headings separate African American cookbooks from Southern cookbooks even though they can be similar in content, explains Gretchen Hoffman in "What's the Difference between Soul Food and Southern Cooking? The Classification of Cookbooks in American Libraries." As Hoffman argues, this separation is in line with other categorical distinctions in the Library of Congress system that make dominant identities invisible as the norm while highlighting difference. For example, Hoffman notes, the library subject headings create classifications for "nurses" and "male nurses" but not "women nurses," suggesting that "nurses are women, and male nurses are the exception to the norm."[77] Similarly, the subject heading of "African American cooking" is in a completely different pattern from any other form of geographically bound ethnic cuisines (i.e., "Cooking, Italian" or "Cooking, American — Southern style").[78] Therefore, a search for cookbooks classified as "Southern style," like the one I conducted for this project, would likely exclude cookbooks with African American authors unless, as Hoffman points out, "a cookbook stated explicitly it contained 'southern' recipes."[79] In fact, no Library of Congress number exists that will classify a cookbook as both Southern and African American; cataloguers must choose which of those headings will define the book, often arbitrarily and inconsistently. Hoffman suggests that soul food cookbooks may represent this juncture of Southern and African American, but they are rarely classified as Southern by librarians. Just as subject headings like "male nurses" and "women executives" make a privileged norm invisible, this system of classification "excludes soul food cooking from Southern cooking and privileges white Southern cooking" while also making African American cookbooks generally difficult to find in library holdings.[80]

Though I agree with Hoffman that the system for categorizing cookbooks by African American authors unjustly marginalizes minority writers and cuisines, for the purposes of this study, I did not include cookbooks representing soul food in this sample unless the authors explicitly linked "soul" and "Southern." As many writers have pointed out, soul food and Southern food are not synonymous. Adrian Miller explicitly connects soul food with national cuisine in *Soul Food: The Surprising Story of an American Cuisine, One Plate at a Time* (2013). When choosing which "plates" to examine in the book, Miller chose to exclude some "iconic soul food items" that represented "African American–inspired regional cuisines" like "fried pork chops, grits, okra, rice, sweet tea" and others.

"I had to make these hard choices," Miller writes, "in order to discern whether or not soul food is a national cuisine. Therefore, I've put together what I think African Americans . . . are most likely to have for lunch or dinner, living in any part of the world and not just the South."[81] Similarly, Frederick Douglass Opie's definition of soul food in *Hog and Hominy: Soul Food From Africa to America* (2010) describes a global African cuisine, one branch of which developed in the South as a result of Atlantic slave trade.[82] To limit soul food to a reaction against dominant white culture in only the South, according to Opie, is to exclude "the equally African-influenced cuisines that began to proliferate in multiethnic communities of color" in urban centers all over the United States.[83] Though the ingredients and signature dishes of soul food overlap with those thought of as Southern food, the label "soul food" tends to take in far more territory geographically and culturally.

According to Miller, soul food emerged as a means for people of color to identify with a national community of African Americans or the global community of the African diaspora. "Soul food" is a label that connotes that kind of membership in an expansive category of identity that transcends geography. Miller makes clear that throughout history, black and white Southerners ate very similarly, arguing that "the illusion that blacks and whites ate differently reinforced [white Southerners'] sense of racial superiority."[84] However, as Miller explains, Southern-born African Americans who moved to Northern urban centers continued to cook and eat many of the foods they had grown up with in the South, especially foods connected to church and emancipation celebrations.[85] Though whites used these foods to "create vicious caricatures" and reinforce a caste system of "low" and "weird" foods associated with "other" cultures, African Americans in the 1950s and 1960s embraced these differences.[86] As John Lewis commented in 1964, "I think people are searching for a sense of identity and they are finding it," in part, in a particular way of eating associated with the black church.[87] According to Miller:

> Soul food was now a rallying cry for black solidarity. A cuisine 400 years in the making, melding African, European, and Native American influences, was now wholly black-owned. No matter where one lived, any black person could bond with another over this type of food. . . . It took food to a place where whites couldn't go — the black experience.[88]

Again, Miller points out the artifice and arbitrariness of the choice to equate what had come to be known as soul food with blackness, a choice that both ignored the similarities to the diets of white people and "glossed over the rich and varied culinary traditions within the black community."[89] Miller is up-front about the critiques of soul food from inside and outside the African American community, but there is little disagreement that the label "soul food" connotes a race-based identity and not a place-based one. When representations of Southern identity fail to include the experiences of black Southerners (as Cobb and Davis have argued), black writers may choose instead to align their personas as authors with national and diasporic identities. Therefore, cookbooks by African American writers living in the South may strategically claim to represent soul food instead of Southern food as an act of resistance, a purposeful declaration of identity and alliances that supersede narrow geographic boundaries.

Therefore, in respect to the rhetorical choice of the author, I have chosen not to include soul food cookbooks in this sample. If the author has purposefully chosen not to link their work primarily to Southern identity, I did not impose the link upon the work by conflating the two cuisines and categories of identity. Thus, I have included Bryant Terry's *Afro-Vegan: Farm-Fresh African, Caribbean, and Southern Flavors Remixed* (2014), but I have excluded Terry's *Vegan Soul Kitchen: Fresh, Healthy, and Creative African American Cuisine* (2009).[90] In the same way, Alice Randall and Caroline Randall Williams's *Soul Food Love: Healthy Recipes Inspired by 100 Years of Cooking in a Black Family* 2015) would not fit into this study. The speakers of the introduction align their family both with black Americans and Southern families, and they make clear that the story of their family is not isolated geographically: "The kitchens we will recollect were located, at various times, in three different Southern states — Georgia, Alabama, and Tennessee; in the Midwestern metropolises of Detroit and Chicago; and in the imperial black city of the East Coast: Harlem."[91] Randall and Williams are not interested in representing a particular geographic or cultural tradition; instead, their primary exigence is to make a record of a black family and provide recipes for other black American families. As the authors state in their introduction, "If you're a black American, our roots are likely to cross yours. We cover a lot territory."[92] This is not a book positioning itself as Southern; therefore, it does not match the rhetorical situation I've chosen to examine in this study.

Though I would want this present work to resist reifying the distinction between Southerners (where whiteness is invisible) and black Southerners, or to repeat the false dichotomy of historically separate diets, I also want to respect an African American author's choice to purposefully construct personal authorial identity. Including soul food cookbooks would certainly increase the diversity of my sample; however, to conflate soul food and Southern food is to undo the act of resistance that soul food necessarily is — a purposeful separation, a self-selection of an identity not tied to place. There are many cookbooks by African American authors in this sample that do claim a Southern identity. Perhaps the best-known African American chef to claim Southern identity is Edna Lewis. Lewis's first cookbook, *Taste of Country Cooking*, was first released in 1976, outside the chronological scope of this project, but it is Lewis and her farm-to-table, seasonal approach to cooking that set a precedent for many of the Southern chef cookbooks of the last decade. Lewis died in 2006, and her epitaph identifies her as "Dr. Edna Lewis . . . Grande Dame of Southern Cooking." Francis Lam explains in his 2015 article "Edna Lewis and the Black Roots of American Cooking" that Lewis intentionally connected herself to Southern food to highlight black Southerners as founders of a sophisticated cuisine. In fact, Lam writes, "Lewis publicly distanced herself from soul food, once saying to *Southern Living* magazine, 'That's hard-times food in Harlem, not true Southern food.'"[93] In *The Gift of Southern Cooking* by Edna Lewis and Scott Peacock (2003), Peacock (who is white) writes in the introduction of the two chefs' shared Southern experiences steeped in a Southern agrarian life driven by the seasons and "a deep appreciation for the foods of our childhood."[94] The differences in their experiences, according to Peacock, are geographical (her from Virginia and him from Alabama), temporal (her coming of age in the 1920s, him in the 1960s and 1970s), and historical (Virginia was influenced by French and English cuisines, Alabama by "'black Irish,' Native American, Caribbean, and African influences").[95] Whatever differences their races might have made in their identities, the common Southern-ness of the chefs is what binds them in friendship and collaboration. The cookbook is "not a comprehensive compendium of Southern cooking," according to Peacock, but it is meant to represent the dishes "we love the most and believe are staples of the Southern table,"[96] drawn from the pair's experience and research as founders of the Society for the Revival and Preservation of Southern Food.[97] The primary rhetorical exigence of the book is to represent a distinct Southern cuisine.

There are many other cookbooks by African American writers who strategically choose to represent themselves and their cuisines as Southern: Nicole Taylor's *The Up South Cookbook: Chasing Dixie in a Brooklyn Kitchen* (2015), Robbie Montgomery's *Sweetie Pie's Cookbook: Soulful Southern Recipes from My Family to Yours* (2015), Barbara Smith's *B. Smith Cooks Southern-Style* (2009), and Delilah Winder's *Delilah's Everyday Soul: Southern Cooking with Style* (2006). Many of these titles combine elements of Southern and Soul, and all are written by authors who purposefully identify with the South.[98] Nicole Taylor, for example, writes in her introduction about a desire in her twenties to distance herself from "country" Southern food and identity in favor of urban, haute cuisine.[99] It wasn't until she moved out of the South to Brooklyn, New York, that she reconnected to her Southern-ness through homesickness and her podcast, *Hot Grease:* "I began to understand that birthing a meal and saying grace with my Southern drawl connected me to the tree limbs of my being."[100] Taylor's claim to Southern identity is purposeful and key to the exigence of the cookbook. Like Taylor, Barbara Smith came to understand her Southern identity by living outside of the South. Smith writes in *B. Smith Cooks Southern-Style* that she grew up without really thinking about Southern identity, realizing only after traveling the United States and Europe as a fashion model that her family's traditions had more in common with the South than her southwestern Pennsylvania birthplace. Even though her family moved from Virginia to Pennsylvania long before she was born, the family had maintained its Southern identity, cuisine, and character.[101] While the label "soul food" was applied by others to Smith's New York restaurant, Smith denies that it was her intention to represent that cuisine.[102] For Smith, claiming a Southern identity is a purposeful choice, one that connects her to family heritage and a global history. Southern food "blankets me in comfort," Smith writes. "It makes me the happiest gal from southwestern Pennsylvania."[103] Dora Charles's *A Real Southern Cook: In Her Savannah Kitchen* (2015) claims *"Real Southern"* in her title as a purposeful choice. Charles makes a clear distinction between "Real Southern country food" and "fancy city cooking" and between "black Southern food" and "white Southern food."[104] Though she recognizes that "black and white alike" share tastes for "cornbread, bacon, greens," black Southern food is superior not for the abstract qualities of soul but in the concrete differences in seasoning and flavor.[105] Charles could claim a national or global soul food, but she is purposefully claiming membership in a Southern identity in which the black Southern experience is the more authentically Southern. It also tastes better. Charles's choice to align herself with "real" and "true" Southern identity is, in part, a bold power grab, defining herself and her cuisine as more real, more true, more Southern, and demonstrably better tasting than her former white Southern employer, Paula Deen, whose name has become almost synonymous with (white) Southern food. Charles's cookbook fits into this study because the author's rhetorical purpose is to define and claim a distinct Southern cuisine, and that choice is significant in itself.

Finally, I chose texts to include in the sample by thinking about the intended audience of the cookbook. The audience is a vital part of the arguments in this book. They are the readers being persuaded to perform the recipes, to adopt certain definitions of Southern cuisine, to be welcomed or excluded from Southern identity. More importantly, as part of the rhetorical situation, the audience as imagined by the author has enormous force on the shape of the argument that the speaker makes to accomplish the speaker's purpose. After all, it is the audience that must be convinced; therefore, the audience's particular biases, preferences, tastes, prior knowledge, abilities, world views, understandings of self, and group loyalties all must be accounted for in the structure of the argument.

For this study, the importance of the audience means first that a text must have a sizable popular readership. The goal of this rhetorical study is to gain an understanding of how these arguments might affect lived experience, and a real audience is required. It was not important to me that the audience be confined to the geographic South, only that the audience be personally invested in the performance of Southern-ness, wherever they may be. To find texts, I relied on "Best Southern Cookbooks" lists from Southern branded publications and bookstores. I looked at the catalogs of reputable publishers and imprints like Ten Speed Press, Artisan, and Andrews McMeel, who specialize in Southern cookbooks. I leaned on celebrity chefs who had been on popular television shows like *Top Chef* and *Mind of a Chef* or chefs who owned and operated popular restaurants in Southern metro areas. I also sought out authors with multiple cookbooks or large blog followings and online communities. In addition, I also wanted trustworthy speakers who were approved by scholarly audiences, so I was drawn to chef-authors with ties to the Southern Foodways Alliance and, to a lesser extent, cookbooks published by university presses. Similarly, I leaned toward in-network texts, if you will, approved by other reputable chef-authors and food historians; a book jacket blurb by John T. Edge, Nathalie Dupree, Frank Stitt, or Virginia Willis caught my attention. Each of these criteria spoke to the possibility of a wide and numerous audience — both popular and critical — that would be likely to read and act upon the arguments in the cookbook.

Thus, this study skews toward thick, glossy cookbooks with pages of full-color, artistic photography, written by professional writers or celebrity chefs with white-tablecloth restaurants. The criteria I've chosen for selection ensures the "literariness" of the cookbook. The genre of the commercially published chef cookbook contains a great deal of writing surrounding recipes and cooking instructions. These criteria also ensure a sample of literary cookbooks that prioritize reading and storytelling over utility and information. They all contain a similar balance of narrative text to instructive text and a similar conventional structure that gives preference to story. I've chosen to examine a subset of literary cookbooks because they rely on storytelling, especially autobiographical storytelling, as their most common strategy for contextualizing recipes and convincing audiences. The quality of the writing is certified through the institutional approval of reputable presses, professional editors, and, in some cases, skilled ghostwriters and coauthors. These professionally authored and commercially published books are well-written and well-edited. Most of the texts in this sample are responding to similar rhetorical situations within the constraints and affordances of similar literary generic conventions, making it easy to identify patterns across the body of texts. It is the uniformity that makes the deviations all the more significant, recognizing purpose and strategy in choices to submit to or subvert convention.

Come to Supper: An Invitation

If this were a cookbook introduction, this is the part where I would invite you to take this book into your kitchen and make it your own. Likewise, I invite you to join me in the work of bringing the study of food and food writing into literary studies. Perhaps the most significant contribution of this project to the field of literature is to theorize a literary canon that is as diverse in genre as it is in authorship. Reading cooking instructions as literary and rhetorical texts can contribute significantly to the diversity of texts in the literary canon. In 1993, John Guillory claimed in *Cultural Capital* that the debate over the literary canon had advanced the work of women and people of color in positive ways, but framing the debate in terms of *writers* included or excluded from the canon misplaced the focus on the talent of individual authors rather than on the faults of the system of education as a whole. Guillory argued that it is "the school, and the institutional forms of syllabus and curriculum" by which cultural capital was "preserved, reproduced, and disseminated over successive generations and centuries."[106] The problem of the canon is really "a problem of access to the means of literary production and consumption" through schools that "distribute cultural capital unequally."[107] Cookbooks can offer an antidote to this particular exclusion by focusing on a diversity of genre. The kinds of cultural capital required to compose a cookbook do not necessarily come from schools but from families; culinary knowledge moves in domestic spaces rather than public institutions, making entrance into the marketplace easier than, say, literary fiction. The widespread use of ghostwriters and professional coauthors makes this entry even easier, allowing the voice of the auteur to enter the conversation, even without experience or skill in sustained writing for commercial publication. Though certainly white male authors still dominate this genre, today's chef-authors represent a diversity of class and capital not easily found in other literary genres. Studying the cookbook as literature could bring a diversity to the literary canon that few other genres can.

Teaching and writing about the texts of cooking instruction — cookbooks, recipes, periodicals, blogs and databases, manuscripts and collections — offers opportunities for conversations about the cultures and networks of exchange that arise around these woman-centered texts. A study of food writing — published and archival, professional and ordinary — invites a theory-rich environment to study texts that have gone uninvestigated, with the added benefit of contributing to the diversity of the canon. I argue that teaching middlebrow food writing like the cookbook is a means of bringing not just racial or ethnic diversity to the classroom, nor simply gender or sexual difference, but a diversity of genres for students to read, write, and savor.

To be sure, there are real problems in Southern cookbooks. These are texts that systematically, on the sentence level, across the entire genre, erase human actors from the history of slavery. They may prioritize pleasure over any other concerns, especially the costs of time, labor, and cash that may be out of reach for even the average cookbook reader. They may advance restrictive binary gender roles. They may take credit for and pecuniary benefit from the contributions of others and are in no way obligated to make any exchange of capital for those contributions. They will say just about anything to make themselves appear to be authentic, without regard to historical accuracy. But in my opinion, the only appropriate answer to a scholarly monograph that points out only these flaws — a book that declares cookbooks to be racist, sexist, culture appropriating, and shallow — is to say, "Thank heaven, I don't read cookbooks," or as Cognard-Black and Goldthwaite understood in the silent protests of their colleagues, "You English folk will teach anything and call it literature."[108] It is easy to point out the shortcomings and flaws of cookbooks, especially if you read them apart from their rhetorical situations and intended purposes, but that way of reading and criticism does not provide any incentive to keep studying them.

I want you to read cookbooks, teach them, and write about them. Throughout this book, I do not shy away from critiquing cookbooks for language and rhetorical strategies that are exclusionary, reductive, essentializing, or culturally violent. But alongside that critique, I will always attempt to discover a reading of the text that highlights the cookbook as meaningful and significant, subversive and creative, with the potential for resistance and liberation. It is my intention to build on the work that has come before me to show what cookbooks can do, to imagine a way of understanding cookbooks as both entrenched in convention and creatively subversive.

—CHAPTER ONE—

HISTORICAL NARRATIVES

Using History to Revise Southern Identity

> Food adventurers tend to operate on the assumption that we really can sort out the authentic from the inauthentic ... I've come to think that the very idea of authenticity is both confused and confusing.
> —Lisa Heldke, *Exotic Appetites: Ruminations of a Food Adventurer*[1]

> It all depends upon how you define "traditional." Did it have to be served in the region in antebellum days ("before da wah?")? Before World War II? Before Jimmy Carter made the South cool? Before the turn of the 21st century? Does it have to be something your grandmother cooked or your grandfather loved to eat?
> —Robert Moss, *The Fried Green Tomato Swindle and Other Southern Culinary Adventures*[2]

THERE'S A CAST-IRON POT on a stone block outside the "Gateway to the Islands Visitor's Center" on St. Simon's Isle, Georgia. The stone block reads: "In this pot the first Brunswick Stew was made on St Simon Isle July 2, 1898."[3] The pot stands as a monument to the founding of a dish that transformed over a century from a hunting camp staple of squirrel and onion stew to a barbecue side dish of tomatoes, chicken, barbecued pork, lima beans, and corn. The specific contents of the stew and the occasion for eating it varies throughout the South, just as the story of its origin varies.

St. Simon's is home to only one such memorial to the first pot of Brunswick stew. Just to the southeast of St. Simon's, in Brunswick, Georgia, the annual

"Brunswick Rockin' Stewbilee" includes a stew cook-off, a 5k fun run, a "Pooch Parade," and a craft fair.[4] This festival to celebrate the origin of Brunswick stew gives festivalgoers the opportunity to reenact that first pot of stew and to reestablish the place of Brunswick, Georgia, in the origin story of Southern cooking.

Still another location makes the same claim to the original founding of Brunswick stew. To the north of St. Simon's, in Brunswick County, Virginia, six roadside historical markers tell another story of the origin of Brunswick stew:

> According to local tradition, while Dr. Creed Haskins and several friends were on a hunting trip in Brunswick County in 1828, his camp cook, Jimmy Matthews, hunted squirrels for a stew. Matthews simmered the squirrels with butter, onions, stale bread, and seasoning, thus creating the dish known as Brunswick stew. Recipes for Brunswick stew have changed over time as chicken has replaced squirrel and vegetables have been added, but the stew remains thick and rich. Other states have made similar claims but Virginia's is the first.[5]

Even though these three physical markers and reenactments tell contradictory histories of the founding of a traditional Southern dish, they all make claims of authenticity based on historical origins.

According to Josee Johnston and Shyon Baumann, authenticity is often defined in foodie discourse by comparing a dish to "a set of established standards, conventions, or traditions." This historical precedent demonstrates to the consumer that "the authentic food has stood the test of time and been deemed timelessly appropriate rather than an ephemeral food fad, [and] that it is true to its origins and has maintained its integrity."[6] The idea of historical "firstness" is probably the most common understanding of *authentic*: first and oldest, a long-running tradition, or a continuous custom. In some ways, all origin narratives have an element of firstness in them, always a claim to originality or invention, always set in the past (before printing and before this reading). But in this chapter, historical narratives are distinguished by their narratives of the distant past, to the origin of a public or community tradition, not just a creative person's recipe.

Implied in the claim to firstness is also the claim to continuity. Even if the recipe provided represents an innovation with the traditional dish, the connection to the first historical dish establishes the appearance of integrity, as Johnston and Baumann argue. Recipe headnotes that use origin narratives set in the historical record as claims of authenticity give the illusion of an unbroken arc from a historical origin to the present manifestation of a cultural tradition. Readers are assured that the recipe printed below the narrative is a direct, authentic descendent of this first, historical event, regardless of its evolution or innovations. Therefore, readers can conclude that cooking this recipe in their homes is a true performance of a real Southern identity that is continuous with the past.

This chapter uses origin narratives of Brunswick stew as a case study to map the rhetorical function of historical evidence in recipe headnotes as strategies for making arguments about authenticity. In order to certify the recipe as a script for an authentic performance of Southern identity, cookbooks that include recipes for Brunswick stew almost always have to deal with the controversy of the origin story, sorting out in the recipe headnotes whether the author believes in the primacy of the Georgia or the Virginia claim, or whether choosing a side even matters. I draw on origin narratives from thirteen books with recipes ranging from Raymond Sokolov's *Fading Feast: A Compendium of Disappearing Regional Foods* (1979) and John Egerton's classic *Southern Food: At Home, on the Road, and in History* (1987) to Matt and Ted Lee's *The Lee Bros. Southern Cookbook* (2006) and Matt Moore's *Southern Gentleman's Kitchen* (2015).[7] The sample also includes cookbooks from women like Nathalie Dupree (1990) and writers of color like Dora Charles (2015), who approach the historical narrative in markedly different ways from their white male counterparts.[8] Each narrative makes a reference to the historical origins of the first dish of Brunswick stew, often for very different purposes. Though all the historical narratives suggest that having an origin in the distant past makes the recipe authentically Southern, each emphasizes a different combination of factors that define authenticity.

Through a comparison of narrative structures, linguistic revisions, and factual variations in the narratives, I identify five distinct approaches to history and authenticity. These five approaches grow increasingly wary of the historical narrative as accurate or useful for convincing readers that the performance of the recipe is worthwhile. Narratives from Nathalie Dupree's *New Southern Cooking* (1990), Paula Deen's *Southern Cooking Bible* (2011), Faye Porter's *At My Grandmother's Knee* (2011), Christy Jordan's *Come to Supper* (2013), and Dora Charles's *A Real Southern Cook: In Her Savannah Kitchen* (2015) narrate the historical origins of Brunswick stew, but also begin to throw doubt on the ability of the historical narrative to be an adequate measure of authenticity.[9] These narratives acknowledge the uncertainty of the project of writing food history and the unreliability of the historical record. I argue that this changing attitude toward history reflects a discomfort with the Southern past, particularly its history of slavery, racial discrimination and violence, class conflict and income disparity, and repressive gender identities.

History and Southern Identity:
The Rhetorical Value of Age and Tradition

Southerners have a thing about history. In an essay on "The New Generation of Women Who Are Redefining the Southern Belle" from *Garden & Gun*, Allison Glock traces the root of Southern distinction to an awareness of history: "Southern women, unlike women from Boston or Des Moines or Albuquerque, are leashed to history. For better or worse, we are forever entangled in and infused by a miasma of mercy and cruelty, order and chaos, cornpone and cornball, a potent mix that leaves us wise, morbid, good-humored, God-fearing, outspoken and immutable. Like the Irish, with better teeth." In reply to criticism that Southern women are too sweet, amounting to "disingenuous cream puffs," Glock explains, "When you are born into a history as loaded as the South's, when you carry in your bones the incontrovertible knowledge of man's violence and limitations, daring to stay sweet is about the most radical thing you can do." The burden of Southern history is bone deep, according to Glock, and it shapes the identity of Southern women in profound ways. And yet, Glock finds that the shaping force is altogether positive. She plans to move her family "back home" to the South: "I want my children to know they belong to something bigger than themselves. That they are unique, but they are not alone. That there is continuity where they come from. Comfort too." For Glock, Southern history means community, continuity, and comfort. It also means cooking: "If nothing else, I want them to know how to make biscuits. And to not feel bad about eating a whole heaping plate of them."[10]

The historical narrative as an authentication strategy may have a special relationship to a quality of historical awareness widely acknowledged to be particular to Southern identity. The importance of the past in the present is encapsulated in the oft-quoted-until-cliché line from Faulkner's *Requiem for a Nun*: "The past is never dead. It's not even past."[11] Like Faulkner's history-haunted characters, Eudora Welty, too, remarks in her essay "From Where I Live" that the Southerner's penchant for storytelling is connected directly to the Southerner's experience of history through the "never-ending recital" of "lifelong and generation-long stories" passed down through families: "History had happened in the front yard or come up into the house," Welty explains, and these historical stories become "a family possession, not for a moment to be forgotten, not a bit to be dropped or left out — just added to."[12] Both Faulkner and Welty emphasize the past's lasting influence on Southern identity through narrative and storytelling.

The historical narrative in contemporary cookbooks is designed to appeal to this particular archetype of the history-minded Southerner who makes up the imagined audience of the New Southern cookbook. However, as Lily Kelting argues in "The Entanglement of Nostalgia and Utopia in Contemporary Southern Food Cookbooks," the Southerner's characteristic obsession with the past is often paired simultaneously with an erasure of historical fact. Kelting writes about the role that nostalgia plays in the discourse of New Southern food as a response to the "loaded history" and "incontrovertible knowledge of man's violence and limitations" that Glock describes. The result is "an anti-historical fantasy past" caused by "an active disengagement" with history that allows readers to visualize "a peaceful agrarian South."[13] This disengagement is made possible by "the erasure of the labor of slaves, sharecroppers, and black domestic staff,"[14] but it appears to be in the service of a progressive agenda of reconciliation "through the creative and potentially healing acts of cooking and eating."[15] This Janus-faced rhetoric —"offer[ing] both a nostalgic gesture and a forward-facing one"— characterizes one of the central tensions of New Southern food that continues to play out in arguments of authenticity.[16] History is important to Southern identity. *Traditional* is an easy synonym for *authentic*. And yet, some parts of Southern history are hard to look at and keep up your appetite.

The connection between the South's relationship to history, identity, and food can be seen in the following episode from journalist Tracy Thompson's 2013 book *The New Mind of the South*. In a chapter called "Shadow History," Thompson investigates the apparent paradox of Southern identity: a concomitant obsession with Old South history and near pathological denial of civil rights history. The "Shadow History" Thompson describes is the "darkness" of racial violence running below the surface of the sanitized version of Southern history glorified in events like Civil War reenactments. Thompson describes attending the national convention of the United Daughters of the Confederacy to observe and to interview individuals actively invested in the public performance and remembrance of Southern history. She found that when she asked people at the convention what it meant to be a Southerner, she got two reactions: "Most of the conventioneers I cornered looked baffled; the rest immediately veered off into the subject of cooking, as if they could explain the whole concept of Southern-ness that way."[17] Thompson sees the conventioneers' discussion of food as a non sequitur, more evidence of the illogical leaps that characterize the history-obsessed and history-denying Southerner. She dismisses food as an inadequate explanation of identity and an obvious dodge.

The conventioneers' choice to answer Thompson's questions about identity with a discussion of food is not off topic at all. In fact, talking about food actually proves Thompson's point: Southerners like her history-obsessed interviewees use food talk to maintain a color-blind and violence-free historical narrative. John Egerton suggests that inclusiveness is a defining feature of food in the South, praising food's ability to "unlock the rusty gates of race and class, age and sex" and "cut across the dividing lines of race and class, age and sex, politics and religion and geography."[18] Where discussions of Southern identity — like those surrounding Civil War reenactments — have privileged middle- and upper-class white male hegemony as the norm, discussions of the history of Southern food are uniquely positioned to value the contributions and voices of Native Americans, African Americans, women, and the poor. Food talk is not likely to provoke any objection from one's audience, or accusations of racism, classism, sexism, or lost cause-ism.

When placed beside Thompson's conclusions about Southerners and their characteristic obsession with history and simultaneous "lack of historical awareness," history-minded cookbooks are particularly apt for analyzing Southern food lore.[19] Southern cookbook writers use their introductions to reference the long history of Southern cuisine or to honor regional heritage through cooking. Damon Fowler opens *Classical Southern Cooking* (2008) with an anecdote about his outburst at a dinner party when another guest dismissed Southern cooking as not a real cuisine. The guests "guffaw" at the suggestion that fried chicken is a culinary art. Fowler "exploded": "Hell, yes, fried chicken! Every great cuisine in the world has it. What's the matter with it? And what's the matter with us? Why are we so fascinated with other cuisines and so insecure about our own? What's wrong with our culinary heritage?"[20] Fowler's response is to pen *Classical Southern Cooking*, a historic cookbook based on nineteenth-century sources. Similarly, James Villas "exclaimed one day, in [his] typically florid and shameless way" to his editor that he had "come to the conclusion that Southern cooking is not only the one legitimate cuisine in this country, but what I've written about so far is just the tip of the iceberg."[21] Villas places the beginning of Southern foodways at the founding moment of the American experiment, at the moment that pigs got off the English ships at Jamestown and the settlers encountered corn grown by the Powhatan Indians.[22] The "hog and hominy" reputation of Southern cooking has a specific point of origin, as old as America itself. Villas concludes that the heritage of Southern cooking "must be generally respected and preserved at all costs" and eschew "gastronomic novelty just for the sake of novelty."[23] For writers like Fowler and Villas, the South has a rich and proud history worth recording and preserving — a process that includes recording the history of foodways and memorializing that history through the performance of Southern cooking. The presence of historical narratives throughout Southern cookbooks certainly speaks to Southerners' particular interests in history as described by Faulkner, Welty, Glock, and Kelting, but the variability of these narratives and the readiness to repeat them without documentation also demonstrates Southerners' tendency to approach their own history uncritically, as stories "not for a moment to be forgotten . . . just added to."[24] For Southerners, reflecting, selecting, deflecting, and revising history for political ends is by no means a new concept. Southerners are not alone in their revision, but theirs has been remarked upon widely.

History and Rhetoric: Telling an Authentic Past

In this chapter, I argue that when recipe writers narrate the origins of a recipe as historical, they are using the historical narrative as a rhetorical strategy to convince an audience of the recipe's authenticity. The evidence that a recipe was created and used in the distant past is meant to prove that the recipe is useful for performing "real" Southern identity in the present. Rhetorician and philosopher Hayden White has famously argued that histories, by their very nature as narratives, are necessarily rhetorical. In his landmark text *Metahistory*, White defines "history" as "a verbal structure in the form of narrative prose discourse that purports to be a model, or icon, of past structures and processes in the interest of explaining what they were by representing them."[25] He distinguishes written history from "the past," suggesting that any narrative of the past is a poetic representation and not an objective reflection of historical fact. White argues that chronology and causality are not inherent in the facts but must be imposed upon them by a narrator. Writing history requires a "selection and arrangement of data from the unprocessed historical record in the interest of rendering that record more comprehensible to an audience of a particular kind."[26] The process of writing history begins with the "chronicle," the unprocessed historical record made up of documents and "events" without form or order. The historian makes the evidence into "story" by giving the events order and causality, "a discernible beginning, middle, and end," all while thinking about the effectiveness of that narrative on the audience.[27] White argues that historians make a series of authorial choices that are rhetorical and political:

"The ideological dimensions of a historical account reflect the ethical element in the historian's assumption of a particular position on the question of the nature of historical knowledge and the implications that can be drawn from the study of past events for the understanding of present ones."[28] In other words, the rhetorical choices evident in historical narratives demonstrate a historian's understanding of who creates knowledge and how that knowledge is exchanged for power. All historical narratives are rhetorical constructions.

I draw on White's vocabulary to read recipe origin narratives that rhetorically deploy evidence from the historical past. It can be easy to dismiss these brief passages in cookbooks as auxiliary, artless, conventional introductions. Yet any narrative of the historical past, as White explains, is laden with meaning. Reading historical origin narratives through the lens of rhetorical analysis gives a language for identifying, naming, and describing the choices of recipe narrative authors and the intended effects on their readers.

White has helped explain what is happening on the macro level of the narrative as a structure. Kenneth Burke offers another set of terms to explain what is happening on the micro level of language and word choice, and how those choices circumscribe the possibilities of interpretation. In his essay "Terministic Screens" from *Language as Symbolic Action*, Burke posits that language acts like a "screen" that directs attention "into some channels rather than others."[29] Burke offers the metaphor of photographs of the same objects taken through different colored filters. Though the objects remain static, each filter "revealed notable distinctions in texture, and even form." Like recipe histories, photographs appear to be "factual," and yet the most basic choice of composition — the selection of "terms"— necessarily reflects the ideologies of writers and shapes the expectations of readers.[30] Language choices set up "terministic screens," directing the audience's attention to particular conclusions and interpretations. Burke argues that every term has the potential to "invent" rather than "find" reality: "Even if a given terminology is a *reflection* of reality, by its very nature as a terminology it must be a *selection* of reality; and to this extent it must function as a *deflection* of reality."[31] The historical narratives under examination here are subject to the same complications; as they attempt to reflect what really happened at the origin of Brunswick stew, they select the details that best make their arguments and deflect attention away from unfavorable or uncomfortable subjects.

This is a fairly serious charge to level at cookbook writers: they are purposefully selecting evidence in the historical narrative to suit their particular purposes. But as White and Burke make clear, selection and deflection are an unavoidable part of the process of turning chronicle into story, of turning experience into language. Writers must use language to reflect, select, and deflect reality in order to generate a historical narrative that is useful for making arguments. In the introduction to *Composing Useful Pasts* — a collection of essays on history, narrative, and politics — Edmund Jacobitti echoes White when he argues against the traditional view of history as objective, dismissing the idea that "the historical facts are 'back there' somewhere, and objective historians and disinterested investigators can find them."[32] Jacobitti extends the arguments of White and Burke by suggesting that not only are historical narratives inevitably rhetorical but also variations in historical narratives are necessarily democratic. Jacobitti argues that rhetorical revisions in historical narratives assure that a "universal ideal" does not subsume and oppress other identities: "Unanimity about the past, in short, might well eliminate conflict in the present, but only by eliminating all but one view."[33] Variations in any historical narrative, then, are the natural outcroppings of a democratic society.[34] Critiques or counternarratives are always subversive, generating new knowledge and offering resistance to power structures that oppress.[35] In some ways, then, the variety of historical narratives — including their erasures, revisions, and obfuscations — could be read as political resistance, especially if we agree with Jacobitti that an "objective" history is only an unchallenged dominant history. Instead of charging cookbook writers with being unreliable historical narrators, we might instead come to think of them as rhetoricians using a conventional genre as a potential site of resistance to power.

Jacobitti continues to argue this point, drawing on Foucault's concept of genealogy to claim that historical origin narratives in particular are "not only arbitrary" but "suspiciously self-fulfilling."[36] Therefore, "all explanations that attempt to trace the origin of an event to a cause are untenable. All, in short, rely on a one-dimensional account of a multi-dimensional world where risk, contingency, and the instability of the human order are excluded or downplayed."[37] Even though all historical narratives are subject to the same criticisms, this does not discount their usefulness or suggest that we abandon the project of telling stories about the past. On the contrary, Jacobitti claims, "Arguing about the past, defining and defending our past, is a valuable and necessary part of defining ourselves in the present." Revision of the narrative is not a betrayal of an objective truth, but a rhetorical action that makes an argument for the political point of view of the narrator, a performance of identity.[38] The message of *Composing Useful Pasts* is twofold: first, no narrative of history should be accepted uncritically, and second, revising or countering narrative histories is not only good practice but also a citizen's mandate. Therefore, this study examines historical narratives not to adjudicate the "correct" story or even the most likely story. To the contrary, this study focuses on the *uses* of historical evidence: To what ends is history being applied? What goals does the writer of this history have in mind? What effect does the writer intend for this evidence to have on the audience?

The narratives of Brunswick stew that will serve as a case study in this chapter function as revisionist histories that constitute "useful pasts." The writers put their narratives to distinct political uses to define authentic group identity, and so their narratives will disagree on some of the basic facts. I argue that the revisions, alterations, erasures, and additions to the origin narratives of Brunswick stew reveal the political motives of the writers. Each narrative alters minor details and terms to select a useful history that will support claims about where the origins of authentic Southern culinary knowledge lie and what it means to claim a Southern identity.

History and Food Writing: Telling an Authentic Story

Food studies as a field is invested in the methods of cultural history as a source of knowledge useful for the present. But as food scholars know, there is often far more fancy than fact in historical food narratives. Andrew Smith argues that even beyond the South, stories about food are prone to distortions and revisions. Smith calls this kind of narrative "culinary fakelore": unverifiable stories "invented in modern times, for reasons other than historical accuracy, such as promotion of people, places, and products." Origin stories classified as fakelore may be loosely connected to enough facts to appear plausible but are unsupported by documented proof. Smith suspects that fakelore might be "inherent in all culinary histories," and likely extends from the passing of recipes through oral traditions. Fakelore convinces audiences because "the story rings true and is presented in such a way as to be difficult or impossible to disprove."[39] The audience has insufficient evidence (and frankly, insufficient motive) to prove or disprove the made-up narrative if it satisfies the requirements of narrative truth and meets the need for authentic performance.

In "False Memories," Smith outlines the conventions of narratives that will become fakelore. First, convincing fakelore solves a problem or explains a mystery. The narrative offers a plausible explanation for cultural phenomena. Second, Smith suggests that readers find fakelore simply "more enjoyable" than the historically "correct" narrative, and so the improbable story gets told and retold until the narrative becomes naturalized. "Finally," Smith says, "writers found the story attractive. As there was no primary source evidence, writers could — and did — embellish the story to give punch to their writing."[40] Because we are looking at origin narratives in genres where documentation of "primary source evidence" is not required or even strictly conventional (see more about citations in the next chapter), where entertainment is the primary purpose of the rhetorical situation, we cannot be surprised that a good story might be more likely to make it to print than a true one that lives up to scholarly scrutiny.

Fakelore, Smith argues, always has ulterior motives. Smith describes a particular type of narrative that seems to capture the motives behind Brunswick stew narratives: the fakelore narrative motivated by "political correctness or historical revisionism," characterized by the "undocumented attribution" of a recipe or food origin "to non-white males."[41] In Southern food writing, narratives like this typically give credit to African Americans and Native Americans for food innovations. These attributions, undocumented as they are, are convincing stories for contemporary readers and writers. After more than a century of silencing and ignoring African American and Native American contributions to any number of cultural institutions through narratives that deflected more than they reflected reality, these are "better" stories and feel truer and fairer. As useful pasts, these subversive stories resist hegemonic narratives. For white Southern writers, especially, it feels right and fair to place the founding of one of the South's best contributions to American culture in the hands of the oppressed.

Twenty-first-century Southern food writers are particularly invested in food as a unifying and equalizing force for Southern identity. Histories of Southern foods in New Southern cookbooks are more likely to advance a definition of Southern identity that grants many ethnicities equal access to ownership of Southern culture. In the era of New Southern studies, which seeks to examine the South outside of its typical North/South, black/white binaries, food histories are more likely to see the contemporary South as cosmopolitan, the result of a history of participating in global food systems. Such a narrative suggests that the South in the present wishes to be seen as postrace — that the South has always been a melting pot embracing Other cuisines and Other cultures. (Re)writing the stories of Southern cooking is one way that Southerners (re)define their Southern identity as a form of "collective, social self-narration, self revision."[42] The story of Brunswick stew provides an opportunity to see how writers negotiate race and power as they revise the origin of authentic culinary knowledge for political ends.

Recipes for Brunswick stew serve as an apt subject for a case study that interrogates the ways that recipe origin narratives construct and revise useful pasts. Even though it may not be as instantly recognizable a Southern food staple as gumbo or collard greens, Brunswick stew appears in contemporary Southern cookbooks with surprising regularity. Brunswick stew is traditionally a hunting camp staple, a thick stew of small game (usually squirrel or rabbit), tomatoes, onions, lima beans, and corn designed to cook slowly and feed a large group of people. In contemporary cookbooks, the recipe is often accompanied by a retelling of the stew's contested origins. In the *Foodways* volume of *The New Encyclopedia of Southern Culture*, Saddler Taylor remarks, "Brunswick stew has been the subject of more public debate than any other southern stew."[43] Brunswick stew, it is purported, was invented in either Brunswick County, Virginia, or Brunswick, Georgia, though a few narratives argue in favor of Brunswick, North Carolina. Today, the dish is a celebrated side for barbecue and the occasion for annual cook-offs and festivals in these three contested states. The narratives do not reach a consensus about when or where the stew originated, and yet the need to narrate the recipe's origin appears nearly universal.

I suspect that part of the need to narrate historical origins arises from the name of the dish. Unlike collard greens, the name "Brunswick stew" does not readily describe what is in it or how it is prepared. As Andrew Smith has suggested, fakelore arises when a mystery needs to be solved.[44] Why should it be called Brunswick stew when a name like "squirrel stew" or "wild game stew" would be more informative? In the absence of a descriptive title, the recipe writer must offer an explanation to encourage the reader to finish reading and, ultimately, to cook the recipe. Furthermore, Brunswick stew is a predictable spot to find fakelore because it is connected by name to a specific place, and a good narrative can be great marketing.[45] Any town called Brunswick is just as likely as any other county called Brunswick to have been the origin, and any chamber of commerce can craft a plausible story about how the simple game stew was invented in that place and throw a festival for boosting tourism and local pride. As the annual Brunswick stew cook-offs and festivals in Virginia and Georgia can attest, being the birthplace of any Southern dish is good business. Moreover, Brunswick stew seems to need a narrative because unlike gumbo, it is not consumed far beyond its fabled geographic origins in Virginia, Georgia, and North Carolina. So even though the name "gumbo" is even less descriptive than "Brunswick stew," gumbo needs considerably less narrating. Its popularity outside of Louisiana and outside of the South, for that matter, means that the name "gumbo" comes with a set of images and experiences common to readers with even the most basic familiarity with Southern cooking. Brunswick stew has no such store of common images in popular imagination. It needs a story.

Finally, Brunswick stew is a popular occasion for an origin narrative because the story offers the narrator a good opportunity for "political correctness or historical revisionism" and to attribute the origin to "non-white males."[46] Narrators are attracted to the possibility that they can write a narrative of a diverse South and attribute origins to African Americans and Native Americans. However, some narrators of Brunswick stew origins are anxious to avoid writing about race at all; their narratives write a different kind of history, one that erases raced characters from the narrative in order to tell a more palatable postrace story.

As a scholar of literature and rhetoric, I am not concerned with identifying an accurate historical account. It is not my goal to discredit cookbooks and recipes as useful documents for understanding history. On the contrary, I argue that when we read recipes as rhetorically constructed arguments for identity, we are able to see them as meaningful texts, purposefully authored by individuals with agency within a specific historic milieu and for a specific rhetorical use. When we read variations in the historical narrative, we can see these ruptures as rhetorical choices. The presence of fakelore in food writing suggests to me that food history is meaningful and persuasive to audiences who are attempting to measure the perceived authenticity and usefulness of performing a particular recipe — even when those narratives express doubt that the history is accurate. When recipe headnote writers choose to narrate the historical origins of a recipe, they invoke that history in order to make arguments about what makes a recipe authentic. Not every historical origin narrative serves the same purpose or operates on the same definition of authenticity. The sections below demonstrate five varying attitudes toward the inventions of history and authenticity, which become increasingly skeptical about the accuracy of historical origin stories and the value of fidelity to the original recipe.

Southern Exceptionalism and Old South Nostalgia

The narratives in this section argue that a dish is authentic by virtue of being first and being oldest, but Brunswick stew has a special authenticity by being connected to the antebellum South. Age and primacy of the claim is sufficient to make a particular version of Brunswick stew authentic, but being invented in the pre-Civil War era makes the dish particularly Southern. In popular imagination, the Old South represents a premodern era when the South was at its most "Southern." Put another way, this is the era when the South was most easily distinguished from the rest of the United States economically, politically, and culturally. Having an origin in the antebellum South suggests that the dish could not have been invented elsewhere, only under the specific conditions of that most exceptional imagined South.

These narratives endorse an antebellum origin story by arguing that the dish is innovated by an African American in the US South during the period of slavery. Though the accounts do not agree unanimously on this black inventor as an enslaved or free person, by connecting the recipe to slavery — an institution that seems uniquely connected to the South and not to the larger United States — the recipe becomes more authentically Southern. The particular representation of slavery and race in the Brunswick stew narrative suggests that this peculiar Southern institution was a kindly and creative slavery wherein slaves were not only allowed the freedom to innovate but also rewarded for their innovations with fame. By focusing on slaves or African Americans as historical innovators of culinary knowledge and founders of cultural traditions, these narratives make broad claims about what role African Americans can have in producing legitimate cultural knowledge. The antebellum origin narrative gives African slaves an important role in the foundation of Southern culture, but as we will see, the specific language used to describe slaves and their innovations (as terministic screens) can dramatically alter the value attached to these contributions.

One such narrative is built entirely on the premise that the historical origins of dishes are the sole determiners of authenticity. Raymond Sokolov is a journalist who has written several books about food in addition to columns for the *New York Times* and *The Wall Street Journal's* weekend edition. *Fading Feast: A Compendium of Disappearing American Regional Foods* (1979) is a collection of Sokolov's columns for the American Museum of Natural History's publication *Natural History* including histories and recipes for endangered American foods like Minnesota wild rice, "old-fashioned Yankee clambakes," and Hopi Indian cooking. The columns focused on "the specific reasons why regional foods are in trouble in our country," which Sokolov largely contributes to mechanized agribusiness, cultural homogenization, and widespread urbanization.[47] As Sokolov describes it, the situation is dire; as foodways sacrifice fidelity to their historical origins for innovation, the authentic traditions will "vanish." Sokolov continues, "The process is largely irreversible. Barring the advent of a totalitarian government on the order of the Khmer Rouge, we are not going to see significant numbers of people returning to the land. . . . History has taken its inexorable toll."[48] The thesis of *Fading Feast* is that historical precedence is the gold standard for authenticity; therefore, American food traditions are in serious danger of losing all authenticity as they move farther and farther from their historical roots.

The organizing principle of Sokolov's book at large is a concern for the death of historical authenticity. The suggestion in each chapter is that what

Americans know by these names — Brunswick stew, burgoo, Key lime pie, moonshine, and more — are only distant echoes of the real thing. Of Key lime pie, Sokolov writes, "Indeed, after some serious inquiry among local experts, I am now morally certain that virtually all 'Key lime' pies and drinks not prepared in private homes in the Keys are actually made with the juice of the Tahiti (or Persian or Bearss) lime, which is not a true lime at all."[49] Sokolov complains that moonshine, "along with so much else in our comestible folklore, is a casualty of efficient federal regulation, big business, and the homogenizing forces of urban civilization."[50] Sokolov's central argument is that these first and oldest dishes are the most authentic, declaring any modern innovations inauthentic meddling.

Sokolov's historical narrative of Brunswick stew offers a cinematic reading of the moment of origin:

> When Dr. Creed Haskins and several of his friends returned from a day's hunting in the woods of Brunswick County, Virginia, in 1828 or thereabouts, they found their loyal black retainer, Uncle Jimmy Matthews, stirring a stew he had concocted in their absence. They ate it, hesitantly at first, then smacked their lips and called for more. By then it did not dampen their appetites to learn that Matthews's thick and flavourful ragout was made from nothing more than butter, onions, stale bread, seasoning, and a passel of squirrels the same slave had shot that morning.[51]

Sokolov explicitly identifies Matthews as a raced and enslaved body. Matthews is a named character in the narrative, but he's still a flattened stock character, the kindly black "Uncle" and "loyal" slave. Later Sokolov identifies Haskins as "Uncle Jimmy's master" and Matthews as "his servant."[52] It is also significant that the sentences in this narrative are structured with Haskins and his hunting party as the active subjects.[53] The white characters "found" Matthews. They ate the stew with emotional reactions worthy of textual description. Their appetites are sated. Even "Matthews's thick and flavourful ragout" is the subject of a passive construction. It "was made," but in this sentence Matthews' agency is implied, not explicit. As terministic screens, the language choices in this narrative direct attention to Matthews as innovator, but the terms that Sokolov chooses to describe Matthews deflect attention away from his creative culinary knowledge onto the interests of the white characters.

In this historical narrative, Matthews is a character emplotted in Old South nostalgia for happy and loyal slaves whose culinary genius is instinctual and natural; his race is described in terms that deflect attention away from his individuality and agency. Matthews' "concoction" is not culinary knowledge as much as it is culinary instinct. Anthony Stanonis argues that in mid-twentieth-century cookbooks particularly, African American cooks were figured as accidental kitchen geniuses, unintelligible, stubborn, and instinctive.[54] Describing African Americans as divinely inspired or unintelligible reduces them from culinary innovators to stereotyped or anonymous characters who deserve only cursory credit. Not only is Matthews's credit for innovation undercut by the choice of terms, but Haskins's cultural power is also reified. Further in Sokolov's chapter, it is Haskins who gets credit for perpetuating the authentic Brunswick stew tradition. Though Matthews is identified as the innovator of the stew (and Haskins is accused of "eroding" the original recipe by adding wine), Sokolov reports that the "pure and authentic recipe" is handed down from father to son through the white Haskins family. It is Haskins's access to power structures of literacy, inheritance, and commercial publication that ensure the recipe gets preserved, canonized, and promoted. Sokolov's narrative advances an argument that Matthews's contribution to Southern culinary knowledge is limited to the accident of creation. The important cultural work of protecting authenticity is done by Haskins and his descendants.

The perceived authenticity of Brunswick stew is in danger because, according to Sokolov, "It is virtually never cooked according to the original recipe." Later "well-meaning cooks" further "domesticated" the wild game stew by adding vegetables. This inauthentic addition of vegetables is bemoaned by one Meade Haskins, "a descendant of Uncle Jimmy's master" who declared in 1907, "Vegetables are not in the original Brunswick stew. Those who prefer vegetables add them after the stew is done, in their plates." Sokolov's tone suggests the "improvements" to Brunswick stew are detrimental to its "authenticity" by taking it farther from its antebellum roots; the simple squirrel stew with onions was more authentic "before modern innovators turned it into a veritable succotash of corn and tomatoes and beans and whatnot."[55] So changed is the stew that it could almost go by another name: succotash. However, the "principal infraction against authenticity" according to Sokolov is the replacement of squirrel with chicken in the recipe. Sokolov recognizes that chicken likely tastes better than squirrel; nevertheless, he claims, "I would merely like to have the chance to taste the original dish. But I doubt I will, unless some hunter favors me with a brace of squirrels. They would have to be wild, woodland squirrels, of course, not urban squirrels that have fed on garbage."[56] Sokolov expresses doubt that an authentic squirrel can be found that would make an authentic stew, not only because of the urban landscape but also because of laws forbidding the sale of "uninspected game animals that have been shot in the wild."[57] However, Sokolov seems to suggest that authenticity is, in fact recoverable. If it were possible to get an "authentic" woodland squirrel, then Sokolov could cook the recipe provided by Haskins's heir and access a "truly authentic Brunswick stew."[58] The implication is that the ingredients called for by that first recipe are the final measure of authenticity, and those ingredients are directly connected to the conditions of slavery and the instincts of the slave who created it.

As a direct contrast to Sokolov's narrative, Matt and Ted Lee attempt to erase slavery from their narrative of the origins of Brunswick stew in *The Lee Bros. Southern Cookbook* (2006). Matt and Ted Lee, of *Lee Bros. Boiled Peanuts Catalogue* fame, made a name for themselves as mail-order distributors of Southern foods like boiled peanuts to displaced Southerners. In the introduction to the cookbook, the Lees describe themselves as displaced Southerners, having moved from Charleston, South Carolina, to Manhattan. Their homesickness drove them to great lengths to make their own boiled peanuts. The result was "a feeling of having cheated geography through food," creating an authentic delicacy in an inauthentic place.[59] The Lees marketed their boiled peanuts and other Southern-made goods to "expatriate southerners" like themselves, and they have been regular contributors in numerous food magazines since the late 1990s, including *Southern Living, Saveur*, and *Garden & Gun*. The brothers have set themselves up in business as purveyors of authentic Southern foods and goods; the success of their brand is based on their status as recognized experts and arbiters of Southern authenticity.

In their Brunswick stew narrative from *The Lee Bros. Southern Cookbook*, the Lees cite the Brunswick County historical marker (quoted early in this chapter), with some significant revisions: "According to the historical marker on highway 46 in Brunswick, Virginia, the town's namesake stew was invented by Jimmy Matthews, an African-American chef who in 1828 stirred up the first batch of the tomato-based chicken stew for a hunting party hosted by his employer, Dr. Creed Haskins."[60] This narrative makes a distinct departure from Sokolov's narrative, quite apart from suggesting that the first stew made by Matthews was not squirrel but a "tomato-based chicken stew" (which Sokolov explicitly identifies as an inauthentic corruption). But most significantly, the Lees figure Matthews as a "chef" and Haskins as an "employer." This elevation of status from "camp cook" in the historical marker to chef, from "loyal retainer" in Sokolov's story to employee, drastically changes the context of Matthews's contribution. The Lees ascribe to Matthews agency and cultural power. As chattel, his body and innovations were the property of his owner, as Sokolov's narrative and the Haskins's bequeathing and inheritance of the recipe document implies. However, as a "chef" (implying training and expertise) and as an "employee" (implying the power to sell his culinary knowledge to the highest bidder), Matthews is both the innovator of culinary knowledge and an agent of cultural power. According to the Lee brothers' narrative, this first batch of Brunswick stew is authentic because Matthews's knowledge and training as chef make him a trustworthy inventor.

Contrary to Sokolov's narrative of the recipe's movement through the Haskins family, the Lee brothers suggest that the culinary knowledge of authentic Brunswick stew passed through the Matthews family: "We should note that the current Brunswick Stew world champion, Henry Hicks, a tobacco farmer from Alberta, Virginia, claims tutelage from Theo Matthews, the great-grandson of Jimmy Matthews."[61] Matthews's authority is preserved into the present through the narration of the first recipe's movement through Matthews's family. The Lees' recipe does not use squirrel (only Sokolov suggests that one should), but they do seek "to honor the small-game tradition by using rabbit."[62] Honoring the tradition means honoring Matthews's position as first expert originator of this canonized "pan-southern classic."[63]

The Lees' addition of the title of "chef" to Jimmy Matthews gives him a unique status as an authentic source of culinary knowledge, representing a rupture in the narrative with real potential to resist the hegemonic story of white supremacy. However, the Lees' particular variation of Matthews as African American chef seems to strain credibility. This historical narrative is suspect because the details provided in it are simply not evident in the source they cite. If the Lees only read the roadside historical marker, what other document told them Matthews was African American? The highway marker does not provide any language that would indicate the race of any of the characters in the Brunswick stew origin story (an erasure that deserves more exploration in a moment). Even though Matthews is not clearly figured as a black slave in the historical marker, he is explicitly identified as black in the cookbook. The addition of Matthews's race back into the narrative suggests that the Lees have consulted some other uncited source apart from the historical marker, or they have in some way intuited Matthews's race from the marker's silence. Either way, explicitly identifying Matthews as African American suggests that his race is relevant to the Lees' narrative and to the argument they are making. In their attempts at political correctness and historical revisionism, the Lees have ascribed to Matthews the ability to generate new, authentic culinary knowledge and exercise cultural power and simultaneously inscribed the language of a racial hierarchy upon him. The suggestion is that the audience would be more convinced that the recipe is authentic if it was invented by an antebellum chef who is black than by a camp cook whose race is unclear.

Though these two narratives from Sokolov and the Lee brothers seem to be diametrically opposed in their view of the value of the culinary innovations of African Americans in Southern cooking, they are actually quite similar in their attitudes toward race and authenticity. Giving Jimmy Matthews the credit for inventing a dish that is central to authentic Southern identity suggests that African American identity, knowledge, skills, and experiences are not only included in real Southern identity but also central to it. Giving Jimmy Matthews credit for the origin also suggests that slavery is central to the real Southern identity. Sokolov embraces this and uses the history of slavery to mark the peculiar Southern-ness of the recipe. However, the idea that slavery is central to the Southern experience is a prospect that causes some narrators, like the Lees, to strategically avoid language that would clearly mark Matthews as a slave, to the point that the Lees and the marker they cite rely on undocumented fakelore to paint a more favorable picture of the Southern past that covers over slavery while preserving the concept of authenticity.

First Americans and Prehistoric Authenticity

For the two narratives addressed in this section, the concept of authenticity is still measured by age, but both narrators attempt to identify a "prehistoric" narrative: an even older origin that predates Jimmy Matthews's 1828 hunting camp stew. Both John Egerton and Saddler Taylor argue that Native Americans in the South deserve a share of the credit for having traditional one-pot game stews since time immemorial. At one point in the writing of this chapter, the subtitle of this section was "Authenticity Times Infinity," a private joke for myself, playing on a child's game of one-upmanship. Egerton and Taylor "win" the contest for finding the first origin by placing the origin before recorded history, the earliest possible origin in a history so distant that no one can effectively dispute it. Race and ethnicity still play an important role in both Egerton's and Taylor's narratives because both suggest that African Americans and Native Americans can share credit for inventing Brunswick stew equally. At any rate, Euro-Americans and white Southerners have little or no right to claim credit.

Like *Fading Feast*, John Egerton's *Southern Food: At Home, on the Road, and in History* (1987) is more like an encyclopedia of Southern foodways than a cookbook. The first section, "A Gastronomical View of the South," offers an extended discussion of the historical and social contexts of Southern food; the second, "Eating Out," is a survey of Southern restaurants. Only the last of three sections, "Eating In" provides recipes. Like Sokolov, Egerton is also concerned about homogenization threatening authentic Southern foodways:

Is Southern food, like the South itself, losing its distinctiveness and its identity in the smothering embrace of modern American culture — or could it be that when the last vestiges of Southernness have faded into oblivion, there will still exist somewhere in the region a few more steaming bowls of black-eyed peas and fried okra and turnip greens, a few more cuts of genuine country ham, a few more hot buttered biscuits, a few more slices of pecan pie, a remnant of surviving Southerners to enjoy them?[64]

Egerton's question suggests that Southern identity may soon "fade into oblivion," but authentic Southern foodways may be the solution to saving it. In an increasingly urban South, Egerton says, "Fast is overcoming slow, artificial is overwhelming real, and new is putting old in jeopardy."[65] There is a need to recover the historical origins of Southern foodways to combat this homogenizing force that threatens to undermine the perceived authenticity of Southern food.

In the narrative preceding the recipe for Brunswick stew, Egerton summarizes and paraphrases Sokolov's account with an academic-style citation, but Egerton purposefully revises Sokolov's language describing Matthews's race. The "Uncle" appellation is dropped, as well as the language of the "loyal retainer." Matthews is still figured as a slave, but the language is indirect. Egerton does not go so far as the Lee brothers in erasing slavery, but instead of using the word *slave* to identify Matthews, Egerton identifies Haskins explicitly as "his master." What remains is the same outline of Sokolov's narrative: "A black cook named Jimmy Matthews concocted a squirrel stew for his master, Creed Haskins, in Brunswick County, Virginia, in 1828." However, Egerton concludes his narrative of Brunswick stew with the suggestion that there is another explanation that predates the Virginia story: "It seems safe to say that Indians were making stews with wild game long before any Europeans arrived, and in that sense there was Brunswick stew before there was a Brunswick."[66] The first and oldest innovators of Brunswick stew, according to Egerton, are actually Native Americans. Egerton may be engaged in the invention of fakelore here; without documentary evidence, he creates a narrative that solves a mystery, fills a silence in the chronicle, and offers a satisfying ending that validates the contributions of marginalized communities in the South.

Egerton's choice to locate the origins of Southern food culture in African American and Native American cuisines in the story of Brunswick stew is consistent with his rhetorical purpose throughout *Southern Food*. Throughout the book, Egerton highlights the contributions of marginalized characters in the history of Southern cooking. Egerton claims that most of the staple foods of the Southern diet came "from Africa with the people in bondage. . . : okra, black-eyed peas (also called cowpeas), collard greens, yams, benne seed (the mystical and luck-bringing sesame), and watermelons."[67] Southern cooking is inseparable from slave culture; "the hospitality and cuisine of the South reached its apex" at the same moment that the Southern states experienced "explosive growth in the slave population." Even though Southern cooking is inseparable from the shame of slavery, Egerton argues, "to throw out the superlative dishes" of the South because they were made possible by slave labor "would be to ignore the creative genius of generations of black cooks."[68] On the whole, Egerton's rhetorical purpose is in line with epideictic rhetoric, meant to praise the contributions of African Americans. I quote at length to illustrate the laudatory tone of the narrative:

> Blacks caught in the grip of slavery often exhibited uncommon wisdom, beauty, strength, and creativity. The kitchen was one of the few places where their imagination and skill could have free rein and full expression, and there they often excelled. From the elegant breads and meats and sweets of plantation cookery to the inventive genius of Creole cuisine, from beaten biscuits to bouillabaisse, their legacy of culinary excellence is all the more impressive, considering the extremely adverse conditions under which it was compiled.[69]

Though Egerton does preserve the verb "concoct" from Sokolov's narrative in his own description of Matthews's innovation,[70] his stated rhetorical purpose is to counteract stereotypes of black cooks as "voodoo magicians."[71] Egerton's narrative is proudly revisionist, offering a necessary correction to the racist narratives that silenced African Americans and Native Americans as innovators of culinary knowledge. Until "more recent times," Egerton claims, the presence of black cooks in Southern kitchens "was virtually ignored in cookbooks and other places of public record," except where they were portrayed as "simple-minded" and "accidental" geniuses, "not to be taken seriously." Egerton praises contemporary cookbooks that have attempted to "give full credit" to the "many creators" of Southern food. However, Egerton sees this work as ongoing: "The comprehensive history of black achievement in American cookery still waits to be written . . . [African Americans] and all other Americans need to see the story fully told."[72]

Reading Egerton's Brunswick stew narrative in this context gives added significance to his choice to revise Sokolov's terms in favor of purposefully anti-racist language. Egerton uses Matthews's role in the innovation of a Southern tradition as an opportunity to shift cultural power to all African Americans.

Extending the origin even further into pre–recorded history to Native American foodways is consistent with the epideictic mission of Egerton's text and results in a power sharing between the two people groups. Egerton's narrative opens up the possibility for authentic Southern identity to include African and Native Americans as cofounders of culture and tradition.

Similarly, Saddler Taylor explicitly fills the silences about race in the language of the historical marker and extends credit to Native Americans for inventing Brunswick stew. In his entry for Brunswick stew in the *Foodways* volume of *The New Encyclopedia of Southern Culture*, after directly citing the narrative on the historical marker, Taylor points out that the marker is missing "important" information about Jimmy Matthews's identity and about the origin of Brunswick stew: "It is important to note that Jimmy Matthews was African American. That fact, combined with the understanding that Native American cooking traditions also influenced these early camp stews, reminds us that Brunswick stew resulted from a synthesis of shared food traditions."[73]

Though the historical marker speaks with the official voice of the state as an approved monument, it appears not to record all of the "important" details, but to organize and select those details into a rhetorical history. In the marker's story, where the language of race and slavery are absent, the origin of Brunswick stew is untainted by the possibly toxic history of slavery. But by reiterating that Jimmy Matthews was African American, and by drawing on Native American traditions, Taylor is able to tell a story of Southern history where ethnic minorities synthesize their food traditions peacefully and organically. Elsewhere in *The New Encyclopedia*, Wiley Prewitt also credits Native Americans for "probably creat[ing] the forerunner of Brunswick stew and burgoo" in their traditional stews of game meat and vegetables "in hunting camps and communal dinners."[74] Prewitt and Taylor both suggest that Brunswick stew may be a literal and figurative melting pot of ethnic traditions.

If these dishes, with their long histories of organic mingling of ethnic traditions (as presented by Egerton, Taylor, and Prewitt), are indeed considered authentic, then by extension the authentic South is *not* the Jim Crow South of segregation and racial violence. Nor is the authentic South the antebellum South of slavery. Instead, the authentic South is one that predates racial divisions. In this version of Southern history, free and equal exchange of traditions between ethnic groups is the oldest and most authentic South; slavery and segregation are aberrations in that story. This suggests that the South was once peacefully cosmopolitan and could be so again. Performing the tradition of Brunswick stew is an effective method for performing and inventing a cosmopolitan and racially diverse Southern identity.

Genealogy and Southern Obsession with History

Perhaps the most common theme in headnotes about Brunswick stew is the disagreement about the origin stories. Though the preceding narratives have focused on the primacy of the Brunswick County, Virginia, claim, Georgia and North Carolina origin stories are also common. When headnotes with historical origin narratives tell multiple origin stories, the writers often conclude, as Marilyn Moore does in *The Wooden Spoon Book of Home-Style Soups and Stews*, that "The question will never be resolved — it's one man's word against another's." With the absence of any conclusive documents, the disagreement between the stories is impossible to settle. "In the meantime," Moore writes, "we can all enjoy a good mess of this controversial dish."[75] This particular structure (everyone disagrees about the origin, but who cares because it's delicious) is repeated across the sample. This narrative pattern questions whether the historical record is capable of providing any clues about the authenticity of a particular version of Brunswick stew. Indeed, headnotes about the contested origin stories suggest that the search for origins — and particularly the stubborn disagreement over origins, despite a lack of evidence — is an authentic characteristic of real Southerners.

For example, James Villas includes recipes for Brunswick stew in two of his many cookbooks: *The Glory of Southern Cooking* (2007) and *Pig: King of the Southern Table* (2010).[76] Both headnotes suggest that the disagreement over the origin story is unresolvable and typically Southern. Like Sokolov and Egerton, Villas, too, is concerned with cataloging the dishes peculiar to the South before these authentic traditions become extinct. Villas begins *The Glory of Southern Cooking* by explaining the goal of the book:

> to canvass the food traditions of every single state in the South [except Texas], try to clarify the similarities and differences among most of the best-known classic dishes, expose numerous area specialties that remain obscure and could even be on the verge of extinction, and generally document, in recipes and headnotes, the most important factors inherent in this unique style of cooking.[77]

Villas states explicitly that the headnotes where I have been looking for origin narratives have a specific rhetorical function: to identify and stratify distinguishing features of Southern food. In other words, Villas explains that the narratives in headnotes are meant to tell us what makes Southern food authentic.

In the Brunswick stew narrative from *Glory*, Villas outlines the arguments for origins in Georgia, North Carolina, and Virginia. First, Villas explains,

"Georgia crackers are fully convinced that the lusty stew was created in Brunswick, Georgia, in 1898, at a July Fourth celebration." This particular bit of fakelore locates the origin in a community practice that seems a quintessential image of Southern experience. The pejorative "cracker" suggests that only the poor white residents of Georgia believe this story, and even though "the original pot" has been set up as a monument "to make the claim official," it would be foolish to believe the story.[78] Villas implies that this historical narrative is not reliable.

Villas has little to say about the North Carolina origin except that the dish is traditionally served with Carolina pork barbecue even today. Without more documentation, that narrative is similarly spurious. Villas confirms that "only Virginians have documents to prove" their origin story (though he does not indicate where those documents are or what they contain), and he asserts "the stew can be traced back to 1828 when a certain 'Uncle Jimmy' Matthews first prepared it in Brunswick County for a large hunting party." Villas undermines each of these narratives by insulting Georgia "crackers," demeaning "Uncle Jimmy" with a diminutive nickname, and setting up his own recipe as the best version available: "Well, I've eaten Brunswick stew everywhere, but all modesty aside, I still think it's hard to beat the one I've been making for my Brunswick stew parties thrown maybe three times a year, where guests eat only stew, salad, and cornbread, and drink beer."[79] This narrative implies that while it seems clear that Brunswick stew is an authentically Southern tradition with a long history, the historical narratives themselves are generally unreliable for authenticating the particular recipes. However, Villas suggests that searching for — and arguing over — historical origins is something common among Southerners. Villas opens his headnote by claiming, "It seems that I've spent a lifetime investigating the origins of Brunswick stew, not to mention cooking and eating it."[80] That a person would or could spend a lifetime in such a project is presented as something only a real Southerner would care to do. As Villas explains in the preface, the South is the only region of the United States to develop a distinct cuisine, and "comparisons with other American styles are almost ludicrous."[81] Even if the histories are not in agreement, no other region can point to distinct dishes or authentic histories like the South can.

Villas also includes a recipe for Brunswick stew in his 2010 cookbook *Pig: King of the Southern Table* with a narrative that similarly recounts the disagreement over the origin story and emphasizes present practice as authentic.[82] The recipes in the two cookbooks are nearly identical, with only minor changes in the amount of water called for (one quart less in *Pig*) and the time required to sauté the onions and celery (two minutes in *Glory*; five minutes in *Pig*). The narrative in *Pig* also acknowledges all three origin narratives, noting, however, that while "arguments can flare" over the true origin, "Overwhelming evidence points to Virginia as the true home of the glorious dish." Villas does not mention Matthews at all as the original innovator of the stew in *Pig*. Instead, Villas highlights the vehemence of the disagreement. Virginia, Georgia, and North Carolina all "still hold very serious annual Brunswick-stew cook-offs," demonstrating how intensely these states believe in their own origin stories. The "debates" about the authentic origin, ingredients, and proper serving of Brunswick stew, according to Villas, "are endless."[83] Again, there seems to be no objective value to any of the historical narratives; all are equally suspect. But what appears to be truly Southern is the intensity of the interstate rivalry and the stubborn belief in these different origin stories.

Like the narratives from Villas, Matt Moore highlights the disagreement in the historical narratives and the foolishness of the Southerner's typical stubbornness in *A Southern Gentleman's Kitchen:* "Though folks in Brunswick County, Virginia believe they were first to create this dish, I'm here to settle the score. This once squirrel-based stew was proudly created and perfected in Brunswick, Georgia. Well, at least that's my story and I'm sticking to it."[84] In this humorous headnote, Moore purports to have the definitive proof of the authenticity of his historical narrative, only to reveal that he has no better evidence than those who claim the Virginia story is true. This gently combative and humorously stubborn position on history is reminiscent of the gentlemanly dueling traditions and intense pride of place that characterize the South of popular imagination. What makes these recipes for Brunswick stew authentic is not their sound historical narratives but their entanglement with a long-running and stereotypically Southern feud over historical facts.

Improving on the Past and New Southern Cuisine

One of the most prevalent challenges for the writers of New Southern cuisine is to reconcile the newness of it to traditional authenticity as firstness or continuous customs. The historical narratives in these headnotes are markedly different from the ones described above in their attitudes toward changes in traditional dishes. Where Sokolov mourned the loss of the squirrel in Brunswick stew, the writers examined in this section express relief that the dish has evolved over time. Rather than holding the original recipe as a gold standard, these historical narratives treat the first stew as an oddity to demonstrate that this present version is improved without losing its authenticity. The purpose of recalling the historical origin is to distance the present iteration from the less sophisticated past and yet maintain a link to the authentic tradition as a new chapter in Brunswick stew's long history.

Paula Deen's Southern Cooking Bible offers an example of negotiation between historical authenticity and current innovation. Deen narrates origins in the past, but she also updates culinary knowledge, suggesting that fidelity to origins may not be as authentic as continued innovation. Deen writes in a letter to the reader from the dust jacket sleeve that the recipes in this book are simultaneously "classic dishes" that "showcase the diversity and ingenuity of Southern cuisine" and "brand-new" recipes. Every recipe, then, has two potential origin points: the "dish" may have originated in the past, but the method of preparation — the "brand-new" recipe — is original with Deen. Narratives in this cookbook tend to follow the same pattern of linking to an authentic past and demonstrating thoughtful updates. Though Deen acknowledges culinary knowledge-makers from the distant past, learning about the historical innovators of Southern cuisine causes Deen to "hold my head a little higher. I am just so proud to count myself among them."[85] Deen identifies herself as both a recipient of Southern cooking knowledge and an authentic generator thereof. The decision to establish herself as an inventor of culinary knowledge affords Deen a significant level of cultural power to innovate with recipes and create new dishes while maintaining authenticity. Because she is a celebrity chef with a recognizable Southern brand, she has the ethos to make this argument that the historical standard is inferior to her more authentic innovation.

Deen's headnote for the Brunswick stew recipe begins with a very brief acknowledgment of the Georgia-Virginia contest, which she dismisses quickly: "Wherever it got its start, it's a soul-satisfying combination of tangy, sweet, and smoky flavors." Deen casts doubt on whether or not a historical origin can even be reliably established. The inclusion of the contested origins in the narrative suggests that the historical origin is still relevant, though it is not necessarily an indicator of authenticity. Deen does not rely solely on the history of the origin to argue for authenticity. Rather, her description of the flavor and convenience of the dish is what will convince the reader to go to the kitchen: "My version comes together quickly, since I use rotisserie chicken along with bacon and barbecue sauce, but it tastes like you've been simmering it for hours."[86] Deen relies more on her own ethos as celebrity chef than on the origin of the dish in history to mark the recipe as legitimate culinary knowledge and authentically Southern fare.

Dora Charles, author of *A Real Southern Cook: In Her Savannah Kitchen* and a former long-time employee of Deen, follows a similar narrative pattern, dismissing the controversy and emphasizing her own tastes and expertise. Charles, who is African American, uses her cookbook's introduction to describe her relationship with Deen, which began long before Deen became famous for her Savannah restaurant Lady and Sons and Food Network shows, and before she became infamous in the summer of 2013 for using a racial slur, eventually resulting in her firing from the Food Network in 2016. According to Charles, the chef-author began working for Deen when "Paula was running a restaurant at Best Western on the south side of Savannah" called "The Bag Lady."[87] Charles and Deen "really hit it off" and discovered they had much in common in the ways their grandmothers taught them to cook.[88] Charles describes her loyalty to Deen, reporting that she turned down offers for "two and three times my salary" from other restaurants.[89] Implicit within the introduction is the suggestion that Charles may share responsibility for Deen's success; Charles and her family did the cooking while Deen and her sons were front of house and in front of the camera. Charles also implies that Deen may not have recognized or compensated Charles's contributions. Charles and a fellow long-time cook nicknamed Jellyroll wonder aloud why they haven't been invited on one of Deen's famous "Paula Deen Cruises," and Charles reports that when she left her job after twenty-two years, she had been promoted to manager "at $18 an hour instead of $10, but things were not the same."[90] Throughout the introduction, Charles's tone is diplomatic, balancing criticism with praise, and withholding comment on scenes that readers would potentially find offensive. When Deen asks Charles and Jellyroll to dress as Aunt Jemima on two separate occasions, Charles writes that they declined, without further explanation.[91]

The narrative strategy that Charles uses to emphasize her own ethos in the Brunswick stew headnote is in line with her diplomatic distancing from Deen in the introduction. Charles's rhetorical purpose throughout the book is to define her own identity as *A Real Southern Cook.* The source of Charles's authentic Southern identity is her family lineage and inherited knowledge and skills, which were present long before Charles was employed by Deen. According to Charles, "In fact there was always a fabulously good cook in my family, going right back to slavery, when both sides of my family labored on plantations in the Lowcountry."[92] Charles defines herself as the heir to a domestic historical narrative rather than a public one, and even though that narrative is tied to slavery, Charles writes that she is "proud to have a place in this long line of good cooks" who have learned "know-it-in-your-bones, no-recipe kind of cooking 'cooking by ear.'"[93] With all of this focus on Charles and her family as authentic sources of culinary knowledge, it is no surprise that in the headnote for "Chicken Brunswick Stew," Charles makes no mention of the dish's origins in the antebellum South. Instead she uses her own tastes and preferences as benchmarks for measuring of authenticity. Charles writes:

> This is one of those famous Southern dishes people fight over. Is it from Brunswick, Georgia, or Brunswick, Virginia? Does it have tomatoes in it — and squirrel or pork? Does it have to cook all day and night? Some of the versions with everything that walks around tossed into them are too much for me. I like it with just chicken, which is the one essential meat — corn is the other essential. There's a tradition in some areas that it goes with barbecue, which seems like overkill. But it's very good, so maybe it goes with everything.
>
> You can serve the stew by itself in a big bowl or over rice or grits. It's a great dish for picky eaters, like my grandson Keo, who can't get enough of it even though he usually hates onions and peppers.

Like Deen, Charles opens the narrative by describing the contested origins, and while she does not dismiss these histories as inaccurate or untrustworthy, she does not take any time to answer those frivolous questions. Charles's quick turn from historic controversy to her own taste suggests that the historical debate has no influence on her choice of ingredients or procedures. What influences her choices are her own taste (what she likes and what is "too much" for her) and her family's approval (in the form of Keo, the picky eater). Charles shows no loyalty to the tradition of serving stew with barbecue, but is willing to agree if the flavors are right.[94] In Charles's narrative, history and tradition are not sufficient motivations to cook or valid evidence for establishing the argument of authenticity; instead, Charles's ethos and her own tastes — those of a "real Southern cook"— should be sufficient to convince an audience that the recipe is a performance of authentic Southern foodways.

In addition to the headnote narrative, Charles's Brunswick stew recipe offers another example of the chef-author using her own ethos as a marker of authenticity. The recipe includes "1 tablespoon Dora's Savannah Seasoning," a blend of Lawry's Seasoned Salt, salt, black pepper, and garlic powder that Charles keeps on hand to season many dishes.[95] The recipe for "My Savannah Seasoning" is in a section titled "Some Things You Have to Know How to Make to be a Good Southern Cook."[96] This essential knowledge for sharing in Southern identity is original with Charles, according to her naming practices; to be a "Good Southern Cook" means learning from a "Real Southern Cook." Charles could have called for each of the ingredients for the seasoning mix separately in the recipe, but by declaring this mix a kind of proprietary ingredient, Charles further puts her own individual stamp on this Brunswick stew, disregarding historical or traditional authenticity and placing herself as the authority over authenticity.

Like Deen and Charles, Christy Jordan also distances her recipes for Brunswick stew from the "original" historic squirrel recipe. Jordan is the author of several cookbooks and the recipe blog SouthernPlate.com. In her 2013 cookbook *Come Home to Supper*, Jordan includes a recipe for "BBQ Joint Stew." In the headnote, Jordan explains that she chooses not to call her recipe Brunswick stew, though it is very similar in ingredients and preparations to other recipes by that name:

> At the first sign of chill in the air, BBQ joints around here start cranking out this delicious stew. Many people refer to it as Brunswick stew, but *traditional* Brunswick stew used to have rabbit or squirrel in it — most modern versions don't for obvious reasons. . . . So, I call it "BBQ Joint" Stew to avoid the looks of fear that crop up from time to time when Brunswick stew is mentioned.[97]

Jordan suggests that while the historical game stew known by the title "Brunswick stew" might be authentically Southern, it is also backward, outdated, and fear-inducing. Even though merely mentioning the traditional connection preserves a link in the chain of authenticity, Jordan distances her "BBQ Joint Stew" from the historical origin. Jordan supports her argument for authenticity by connecting the recipe instead to barbecue, an equally authentic Southern cuisine and essentially Southern experience. The second half of the headnote explains that real Southern "BBQ joints" make this stew "because it helps them use up any leftover shredded pork and chicken they may have. By mixing in their signature sauce and whatever vegetables they have on hand, they can turn out a flavorful, filling stew unlike any other."[98] Jordan's recipe maintains its authenticity by keeping a close connection to the equally historic barbecue tradition instead of the hunting camp.

The three preceding narratives deny that the distant historical origin is the most relevant factor for authentication. All of the writers mention the historical origins and traditional recipes in order to establish a historical precedence for their new recipes. Though these narratives erase Jimmy Matthews as an innovator and historical figure, Deen, Charles, and Jordan each endorse another individual or group as innovators of authentic culinary knowledge. Deen identifies herself as an authentic Southern innovator. She has the authority to determine that the historical recipe needs updating, and the ethos to update without losing authenticity. Charles, too, asserts her own authority and declares that authority comes from her family's historic ties to the South and lineage of good cooks. Similarly, Jordan marks the traditional stew as authentic but unappetizing; her own version, borrowed from traditional barbecue, maintains authenticity while distancing itself from even the name of Brunswick stew. It is possible, then, to read these women's endorsement of their own access to culinary knowledge through a feminist lens. All three speak with the authority of experts of Southern cooking with the ethos of professional cooks and writers. Each writer chooses to narrate historical origin stories in order to supplant them by endorsing other sources as more authentic. In all three cases, the historical origin narrative is used to question the reliability of history to determine authenticity. The authority to narrate Southern history of white male narrators like Egerton, the Lee brothers, and Villas — with reputations as journalists, food critics, scholars, chefs, and taste makers — is in some ways assumed. Therefore, these white male writers seem to have more faith in the historical narrative (with its cast of all male characters in the prototypical male setting of the hunting camp) to establish a convincing argument for authenticity. I contend that the particular rhetorical approach practiced by these male cookbook writers is not available to cookbook authors with less direct access to hegemonic identities. Deen and Jordan, as white women writers and professional cooks, simultaneously disavow the masculine historical narrative and claim their own ethos as authentic cultural arbiters. Charles, as a black woman writer and professional cook, claims a space for herself as an individual and for black Southern cooking under the aegis of real Southern cooking.

Doubting History and Feminist Ways of Knowing

In the final section of this case study, I look at narratives that continue to distance Brunswick stew from its origin while maintaining the recipe's authentic links to the distant past. Like Deen, Charles, and Jordan, the three female cookbook writers described in this section suggest that the masculine hunting camp history is insufficient for establishing authenticity. Instead of relying on the broad historical narrative, these narrators focus in on the family and family history as the most authentic link to the past. In *Quick-Fix Southern,* Rebecca Lang mentions again the contested origin story: "Ask a Southerner about the origins of Brunswick stew, and you'll start quite the historical debate." She then goes on to dismiss this debate as unsolvable, focusing instead on the origin of the recipe in families and the line of culinary inheritance: "No matter where it came from, family recipes are passed down and sometimes even the pots in which they bubble. I am now the proud keeper of my grandfather's handmade stew pot."[99] Instead of convincing readers that the recipe is authentic by drawing on the larger historical narrative of the very first Brunswick stew, this group of narrators uses smaller domestic histories to make that argument.

Another example of a historical narrative that privileges the feminine family over the masculine hunting camp comes from Nathalie Dupree's *New Southern Cooking.* Dupree is perhaps best known for her public television series from the late eighties and nineties, "New Southern Cooking." However, Dupree also has training from the Cordon Bleu in London and experience as the chef and owner of a restaurant, the founder and director of Rich's Cooking School in Atlanta, and a prolific food writer. In 1990, when a new edition of *New Southern Cooking* was published, Dupree was already widely recognized as a leading authority on authentic Southern cooking. Dupree has been a lasting figure in Southern foodways as one of the founders of the Southern Foodways Alliance and winner of the Craig Claiborne Lifetime Achievement Award by the SFA in 2004.[100]

Dupree's cookbook presents two contending histories for the origin of Brunswick stew (neither of which mention Jimmy Matthews as an innovator) in order to benefit from a connection to both a spurious but entertaining public history and a more reliable family story. In the headnote for her recipe for "Abercrombie Brunswick Stew," Dupree explains that either the stew was named for the town of Brunswick, Virginia, or it was "named for the Earl of Brunswick, who visited the Deep South before the War Between the States. He observed that a succulent pork was being served to guests on the lawn while an equally succulent stew was being served to laborers in the backyard. Like many an Englishman, he preferred the stew to the grill."[101] The recipe itself, Dupree reports, comes from her friend Jimmy Bentley, who inherited the recipe from his ancestors with the surname "Abercrombie." The "Earl of Brunswick" narrative suggests that the dish's origins precede its name or written record. The humble stew was fed to "laborers," separate from "guests" who ate the superior barbecued meat, and it went without a special name until the English gentleman "discovered" this hidden treasure and gave it his title. The origin "in the Deep South before the War Between the States" is strategic, as is Dupree's choice to call the Civil War "the War Between the States." These choices mark the recipe as arising from the unique Old South experience, even if the realities of slavery are masked by the term *laborers.*

Although Dupree gives space to this account of how the dish got its name, the headnote suggests that this specious antebellum origin is mere "legend." Dupree indicates that it is more likely that "Brunswick stew apparently received its name from Brunswick County, Virginia." The retelling of the "Earl of Brunswick" legend is meant to contribute to the authenticity of the recipe by establishing age and connecting to distinctively Southern experiences, but the origin of the tradition is only one authenticating factor. In addition, Dupree chooses to name the recipe for the Abercrombie family, emphasizing that what makes the recipe authentic is its history in a single family, passing down the "old-fashioned basic Brunswick stew" recipe through generations. The historic origin of the dish's name is an unlikely legend, but readers can be assured that the recipe provided is an authentic one with a confirmed pedigree in the Abercrombie family.

Though Charles argued that her cooking knowledge in general came from women, this is the first story of Brunswick stew in particular that suggests women alone might be responsible for maintaining the tradition of Brunswick stew (even Lang inherited her stew pot from her grandfather). Though there are many other cookbooks and scholarly studies invested in crediting women for kitchen innovations, most narratives about Brunswick stew are highly masculinized in the hunting camp or barbecue pit. Because the recipe comes from the "Abercrombie side" of Bentley's family, it appears to have come to Bentley through female relatives (assuming that Bentley's male relatives share his surname). The implication is that age and history are still important to establishing authenticity, but an authentic history may be a private and domestic story, not a public one. Dupree resists the metanarrative of Brunswick stew as a masculine invention and custom by placing the origin of an authentic recipe in the family home rather than the hunting camp.

Faye Porter goes a step further than Dupree in crediting women and domestic traditions with the historic origin of Brunswick stew. Like Dupree, Porter names her recipe after a particular family: "Bott's Brunswick Stew." Porter's 2011 cookbook *At My Grandmother's Knee: Recipes & Memories Handed Down by Women of the South* is devoted to recording the movement of recipes between grandmothers and granddaughters in Southern families. I will examine Porter's book in more detail in the next chapter on citation narratives, but here, at the end of this chapter on historical narratives, Porter's Brunswick stew narrative provides a final example and a fitting transition. Porter's narrative for "Botts's Brunswick Stew" demonstrates the limits of the historical narrative as an authenticating strategy. Instead of discussing the controversial and conflicting historical origin stories of the recipe, Porter cites the history of this recipe in a single family from Georgia. According to the headnote, "Botts's Brunswick Stew" is a recipe submitted by Shelli Hegler of "Lowrenceville [*sic*], Georgia." Hegler's recipe, like the citation narratives that will be the subject of the next chapter, is named for the originator, her great-grandmother, Rosa Mae Long

Botts, who prepared the stew "for the annual Christmas barbecue." Contrary to the story of Brunswick stew as a hunting camp staple, Hegler presents stew-making as a task for women: "While the men slow-cooked the Boston butts over hickory coals just outside the field barn, the women would be getting the Brunswick stew, side dishes, and desserts ready for 'the feast' that took place around two o'clock."[102] The narrative makes no mention of a historical origin outside of the family, nor does the headnote make any suggestion that Hegler's family's Christmas traditions are typical of the region.

The choice not to narrate the historical origin suggests that for Porter's rhetorical purposes and intended audience, that kind of masculine public history is inappropriate for establishing authenticity. In this instance, age and tradition are still important for marking the recipe as authentically Southern, but Porter is focused on the family and the women of the South, both of which are excluded in the historical origin narrative like the one on the official highway historical marker in Virginia. The historical narrative of Brunswick stew as cited and repeated in contemporary cookbooks is a strictly masculine affair tied to the hunting camp. If recipe narrators like Porter and Dupree want to attribute culinary knowledge to women, they will have to employ a different kind of narrative that eschews the historical in favor of some other measure of authenticity. Porter erases the hunting camp history and, instead, uses the stories of an individual family to show the recipe's authentic matrilineal genealogy through what I will describe in the next chapter as a citation narrative.

Implications: Toward a Conclusion

White's *Metahistory* is helpful here in the final moments of this chapter, in reminding us that histories are not objective or transparent; no emplotment of the chronicle is without visible markers of ideology and argument. White draws these conclusions from an examination of supremely trained and world-renowned historians and philosophers. We cannot expect *more* historical objectivity from people trained as journalists or chefs (or the ghostwriters and cowriters who collaborate with them). I do not point out these issues with the narratives to chastise any of the writers examined here for not doing their proper homework. It is important to remember the rhetorical situation they are writing in. The cookbook is largely figured as a document for entertainment and practical use. Furthermore, as Jacobitti argues, a multiplicity of narratives creates a polyvocal history with the potential to generate a more democratic discourse. Instead of looking for a single authoritative historical account of the one authentic Brunswick stew recipe, this chapter has focused on exploring the reasons why writers of recipe headnotes decide to tell the historical origin stories of this one stew with such regularity — and what it might mean to choose another narrative strategy for authentication.

The variations in the many historical narratives provided here seem to support specific interpretations of history's ability to verify authenticity. Though all the narratives in this chapter argue that age and tradition are a large part of what makes a recipe authentic, they disagree on precisely which history is most useful, and to what uses history can be put. For some authors, the Virginia Brunswick stew origin story proves the dish is authentically Southern because it comes from the antebellum Old South of the imagination, when the South was at its most Southern as a distinct region. Raymond Sokolov emphasizes the origin of Brunswick stew as the innovation of a slave, another peculiarly authentic Southern experience. And although Matt and Ted Lee purposefully erase Matthews's slavehood while maintaining his ethnicity, they suggest that his invention is authentically Southern because of his unique status as an antebellum "African-American chef," marking the Old South as surprisingly cosmopolitan and progressive. John Egerton, Saddler Taylor, and Wiley Prewitt use their narratives to share credit equally among African American and Native American innovators. By giving marginalized characters credit for the invention of authentic Southern food traditions, these authors use their privileged positions to endorse marginalized people groups as part owners of authentic Southern identity.

Still other narrators use historical narratives while simultaneously expressing doubt that history is useful for authentication. James Villas and Matt Moore suggest that the real historical origins may not be knowable, but arguing about historical origins against sound reason is essential to the Southern personality. Paula Deen, Dora Charles, and Christy Jordan use the historical narrative to connect their modern recipes to authentic traditional origins while also distancing their recipes from those less desirable original versions. Their narratives negotiate the tension between creating a new cuisine and maintaining traditional authenticity. Finally, Rebecca Lang, Nathalie Dupree, and Faye Porter disconnect from the public historical narrative of the male-centric hunting camp altogether in favor of a woman-centered history of familial ties and feminine innovation. They redefine which story of the past (and which past) is most useful for arguing authenticity. These narratives describe the historical origins of Brunswick stew but bypass (perhaps forget or erase) Matthews in favor of a shorter history, one that recognizes that the origin story is contested, and that true origin in the distant past probably cannot be documented anyway. Instead, these narratives use the historical past as a screen to throw the present into sharp relief, showing the more cosmopolitan, more abundant, more progressive present.

The historical origin narrative may only work rhetorically for a specific combination of author, audience, and subject. Authors like Sokolov, Egerton, Villas, the Lees, and the institutional authorial voice of the roadside historical marker in Virginia might be more likely to use historical narrative as an authenticating factor because they have access to that history as authorized (white and male) speakers. To use history as an appeal assumes that the speaker sees himself as an agent in or of that history. Put another way, the speaker sees himself reflected in that narrative: *this is my history, the story of me and mine.* I use that masculine pronoun purposefully, for it takes a significant measure of cultural power to gain access to literacy and authorship, to the chronicle, to the cultural and academic capital of plots, to commercial publishing venues, to marketing apparatuses. An even more significant measure of privilege is required to be able to use this access to grant credit of knowledge and access to power to another individual or people group. Narrating history or citing an innovator is a transfer of power, but it requires a surplus of power to manage it.

For the historical narrative to work as authentic, the reader or audience should similarly identify with the narrative in order to be convinced that it is valid, meaningful, and authoritative, and to be convinced that having a historical origin makes the recipe authentic. The imagined audiences of Southern cookbooks are individuals who somehow identify as Southerners or have some investment in the practice of Southern identity through cooking and eating. A kinship between author and audience is assumed, even if it is only through a benign curiosity. For a historical narrative to be convincing to a reader, it must be familiar to the reader as a "story of us."

Finally, and perhaps most important for an "entertainment" genre like the cookbook, the author and audience must agree that the history (or this particular version of it) is *pleasurable.* Not only should the parties see themselves represented in the narrative, but they also should see themselves represented well, in a manner they are comfortable seeing themselves. Pleasure is at the center of all cookbooks, whether it is the pleasure of cooking, of eating, of sharing, of remembering. And here, the pleasure of representation, of seeing oneself represented as an agent of cultural power and heir to culinary knowledge, is chief among the many pleasures of a cookbook. This focus on pleasure explains why the ability of the historical narrative to authenticate foodways always reaches a limit. For a great many Southerners, black and white, the history of the South is not pleasurable. The stories do not represent all Southerners pleasantly; that racial-binary formation of Southern-ness does not represent *all* Southerners, for that matter. This leads writers to erase the history of slavery or obscure it in euphemisms or complicated sentence structures. It leads them to share credit widely to tell the pleasant story of the peaceful melting pot, or to focus on the pleasant family story rather than the potentially unpleasant public history of the South at large. The remaining chapters in this book explore the many other rhetorical strategies that recipe headnote writers use when history fails to be an effective argument for authenticity.

CHAPTER TWO

CITATION NARRATIVES

❧

Recording Provenance to Prove Authenticity

> Recipes are indeed a creative process, for both the writer and
> the user. Many people read recipes and cookbooks for enjoyment,
> so writing style is almost as important as cooking reliability. . . .
> The headnotes on recipes provide an especially good
> place for the author's voice to shine through.
> —Ostmann and Baker, *The Recipe Writer's Handbook*[1]

> If I may steal the old joke about the Hungarian recipe that begins
> "First you steal a chicken . . . ," then the first direction for
> writing a cookbook is, first you steal a lot of recipes.
> —Karen Hess, "Recipe for a Cookbook: Scissors and Paste"[2]

I REMEMBER WHEN I first discovered that my great-grandmother did not invent angel biscuits. I had finally decided I wanted to learn how to cook. I had settled the battle between my fear of being seen doing anything "feminine" and my absolute homesickness for the foods of my childhood. If I wanted to eat angel biscuits again, I was going to have to bake them myself. I got in the habit around that time of carrying a notebook and a pen with me when I visited relatives. I would raid their recipe collections, copying down recipes for anything that sounded familiar. I copied recipes written on index cards, on the backs of restaurant receipts, on deposit slips torn from checkbooks, on tithing envelopes they kept in the backs of the pews in the church where I grew up.

Like a good researcher, I tried to keep track of where I got the recipe. If it had a name on it, I dutifully copied that name, too. In my notebook, I would try to document the source I was looking at and the circumstances of my collection: "Jamie Jeffers' Sour Cream Pound Cake. Mom's recipe box. Index card. Circa 1975." I copied "Aunt Signa's Wheat Bread" from my mother-in-law's recipe box. It came with a written warning that the recipe was *not* to be shared; the Swedish aunt had remarked as she dictated the recipe, "Vee keep it in zee family, ya?" The recipe writer had preserved the dialogue, complete with accent, in writing. This I also dutifully copied. If there was no name, I would ask where the recipes came from. Most of the time, the collector could give me a name, a story about the woman who gave it to her, a story of a time the dish was made and served. It was not often that the origin was a mystery. I took notes while the people who had fed me talked about the people who had fed them.

When I was ready to learn how to cook, I went to the source I thought of as the most authentic: my people. Their tastes were like my tastes. Their experiences had been like mine. Their available resources were very like mine. I knew that their collections would be tried and true, and even if they were not timeless (my grandmother, Jo Welty, *loved* trendy Jell-O salads), they represented identity for me: my class, my region, my religion, my race, my time, and my place. As I wrote down my family's recipes, I documented their provenance, the record of that recipe's movement from the "original source" to myself. To me, these stories of exchange were a life story, a biography of the network of women I valued. If anyone asked for my recipes, I could show them a straight line between me and the authentic source of culinary knowledge, perhaps generations behind me.

One of the first recipes that I collected was for Grandma Taylor's angel biscuits. Angel biscuits became the symbol of nostalgia for me. My father, Eddy Helms, ate biscuits and peanut butter with syrup for breakfast every single morning when I was a kid. All week long, he ate store-bought biscuits, cracked from their cardboard cylinder and baked on a cast-iron griddle in the oven. But on weekends, we made "Grandma Taylor's" biscuits. We'd mix up the dough on Saturday night to rise in the refrigerator overnight and be baked Sunday morning. My mother didn't make many things from scratch — and I purposefully avoided any knowledge of cooking — but I did like rolling the biscuits and dipping the dough in bacon grease before setting them up to bake. Angel biscuits were one of the few foods of my childhood that I thought of as being real family knowledge, made with real ingredients.

Not long after I started collecting recipes, I was looking through my husband's grandmother's recipe collection and found that she, too, had a recipe for angel biscuits. She had clipped it from a newspaper. Not only did my Grandma Taylor not invent "Grandma Taylor's Biscuits," but the recipe was so widely circulated, syndicated, clipped, and pasted that anyone's great-grandmother could have had it. To find the thing that I thought was a private family practice in a place so public as a newspaper undermined the authority of both cooking women: no inventors here, I thought, merely collectors. If angel biscuits belonged to everyone's grandmother, I thought, then angel biscuits belonged to no one. The public, mass distribution of angel biscuits revealed that the only recipe I thought of as really from scratch was as available to the world as the cylinders of store-bought biscuits.

I could no longer point to a direct line of provenance between my great-grandmother and me because the line went *everywhere*. Instead of a single, direct, unbroken line, it was more like a map of networks with many lines intersecting in public space. At first I felt a kind of betrayal. I had been naïve to think that my great-grandmother, a West Texas farmer's wife in the 1920s, had invented an original recipe for biscuits; but no one had tried to disabuse me of this fiction. The recipe had lost some of its authenticity by being in the public, but as I explored *authenticity* in this project, I came to see that angel biscuits had always maintained their constructed authenticity through storytelling, and through storytelling, I could construct whatever version of authenticity most comforted me. If I wanted, I could leave the record as it was in my notebook, and I could let anyone who saw it believe, as I had, that my Grandma Taylor was a great culinary innovator. Not only was *authenticity* as a category fragile and constructed, it was also resilient and relatively easy to reconstruct. Now when I tell the story of angel biscuits, it is a story about me claiming my inheritance of culinary knowledge and taking my place in a network of cooking and writing women who represent the authentic knowledge, skills, and abilities of my people.[3]

The record of exchange that I documented in my own notebooks has a parallel in the recipe headnotes of published cookbooks. The citation narrative is a form of origin narrative that credits a prior author for innovating or contributing a recipe to the cookbook. Like the historical narratives examined in the previous chapter, citation narratives argue that a recipe is authentic because of its age and relationship to cultural traditions by describing its employment in the past. However, unlike historical narratives, citation narratives do not suggest that the individual being cited invented the first version of this *dish*. Instead, the individual is cited as the source of the *recipe*. Though the source may be credited with creative additions to the recipe or developing the most superior version of the dish, the source is textual, rather than traditional. In other words, the citation narrative traces the provenance of a recipe text rather than attempting to identify the first innovator of a cultural practice, as the historical narratives of Brunswick stew do. For this reason, citation narratives tend to have relatively short histories, rarely tracing origins beyond a few generations of grandmothers and great-grandmothers, and almost always involve networks of families and known acquaintances.

Citation narratives often accompany recipes with titles like "Bott's Brunswick Stew" and "Abercrombie Brunswick Stew" examined in the previous chapter.[4] Those narratives focused on the movement of recipes through family histories rather than public histories. They credited known individuals for providing the text of the recipe to the cookbook author. Citation narratives like these demonstrate an uneasiness with history as a method of authentication. Porter and Dupree used the citation narrative to indicate age and traditional Southern identity without invoking the problematic history of slavery, the troubling nostalgia for the antebellum South, or the masculine hunting camp. Instead, they tell pleasurable stories of families inheriting and bequeathing knowledge. This domestic history is an effective rhetorical strategy for cookbooks whose rhetorical purposes are epideictic — meant to celebrate or praise Southern identity and culture. The citation narrative deflects attention away from a complicated history of the South at large by directing attention toward the simpler story of a much smaller network.

Chef-authored New Southern cookbooks tend to focus on the chef's innovations and original creations; therefore, they are invested in the ethos of the chef and cookbook writer as a carefully constructed source of authentic culinary knowledge. Acknowledging that the recipes in a chef's cookbook might be collected rather than created could undercut the chef's image as an authority. However, just as my first-year composition students learn to repeat to me each fall, citing sources can increase the writer's credibility, demonstrating the writer's investment in ethical and professional research practices. The citation narrative acknowledges the source of a text using a method that is ethical and professionally approved, even if it is informal and optional. But more importantly, the citation lends ethos to the cookbook writer by establishing a reputation for both the recipe contributor and cookbook writer as so-called authentic sources of knowledge. Where the recipe has been and who has owned it is part of the valuation of authenticity.

Moreover, the citation narrative situates both individuals (the cookbook writer and the recipe contributor) in a network of exchange. Recipes move freely, as this chapter will demonstrate, because of their exemption from copyright protection. Recipes exist in a culture of copying where texts and ideas move easily between individuals, between the public and the private, between the published and the unpublished. The publication of a collection of recipes is a kind of authorship that is necessarily collaborative, and the citation narrative validates this collaborative authorship as a necessary and preferred method of knowledge transfer. Both the network and the method of exchange are validated in narrative as sources of supposedly authentic culinary knowledge. Rather than seeing the compiling of recipes as mere collection, I have come to see the movement of recipes as something that makes recipes potentially subversive, dangerous, and exciting. Recipe collectors use citation narratives to write a story about a network of family and friends. The citation narrative is a story of authentic Southern cuisine that often features ordinary women as authors and authorities. Telling the story of a recipe's movement from the private kitchen of an ordinary cook to the published cookbook of a professional chef and writer valorizes the movement of cultural knowledge through informal and unpublished domestic networks over the movement through formal and published public networks.

Authenticity and Provenance: Fixing Meaning and Value through Citation Narrative

I connect citation to the concept of authenticity through *provenance*, a term borrowed from the art world. In art history, museum curation, and art dealing, *provenance* refers to the record of a piece of art's movement from the artist's possession to the present owner or exhibitor through deals, sales, gifts, and, often, thefts. Art historian and biographer Alex Danchev offers a meditation on the utility of provenance in an article for *Journal for Cultural Research:* "The provenance of a work of art is in the first instance a summary life story, an outline biography."[5] The official outlines, Danchev argues, are a rhetorical and political narrative "shaped, and reshaped, for a purpose" into "a narrative arc, a dramatic arc, a mythic arc."[6] That purpose is "authentication," and the narrative of provenance "attests that the work is genuine, that it is what it seems . . . and not an imitation. In a word — the key word — the provenance is a proof of authenticity."[7] But in art, and in life, Danchev suggests, authenticity is largely a fiction, a selection of details that deflect reality as much as they reflect it.

I use the term *provenance* in particular because of its connection to the marketplace. Not only does provenance refer to the chain of ownership and document money exchanged, but the provenance also determines the market price of an object. As proof of authenticity, the provenance is a certificate of market value. In cookbooks, the narrative of a recipe's movements can similarly serve as proof of authenticity. And though recipes tend to move without the exchange of cash in informal networks, the publication of a recipe in a cookbook moves it into the marketplace of economic capital. When the recipe moves from the gift economy to a market economy, the provenance is evidence of the recipe's authenticity and value. The citation narrative is also the method by which contributors are "paid" for their recipes in the form of cultural capital through public acknowledgment of credit.

Narrative appears to be the chosen method for assigning, transferring, and protecting the ownership of culinary knowledge in the form of recipe when it enters the marketplace. The narrative is a stopgap measure that attempts to fix meaning through the citation of origin and the explanation of the network of exchange. In *Who Owns Culture? Appropriation and Authenticity in American Law*, Susan Scafidi explains that the need to construct and certify authenticity arises when a cultural product — like folk art or a recipe — moves from exchange within a cultural group into the public marketplace. When recipes are exchanged informally between mothers and daughters, family members, or friends, or within religious, ethnic, or geographic communities, the shared values of the community protect the recipe's meaning. Meaning is agreed upon orally, informally. As an example, Scafidi describes the process of giving a rosary to a godchild. The buyer, seller, giver, and receiver of the rosary all agree upon the meaning of the object and the significance of the transaction: "Since this exchange occurs among group members who already share the same culture and jointly 'own' its cultural products, however, it does not involve the transfer of identity, although it may reinforce beliefs, aesthetic preferences, practices, or values that the parties hold in common."[8] When rosaries (or recipes) move outside of the family unit into the public marketplace, they become accidental property, and suddenly the meaning is at the mercy of an audience that may not share the values or know the meaning agreed upon by the collective culture. The recipe could lose its cultural value and authenticity through mass production, distribution, imitation, and innovation. To protect against the perceived loss of authenticity through cultural appropriation of a community's or individual's work, the recipe needs interpretation for the public. A narrative is required to fix the meaning for an audience that may not be able to appreciate it otherwise. In short, the citation narrative is a notice to the reader or recipe performer that the recipe has a particular value, already agreed upon by insiders of a particular cultural group and authenticated by this explanation of ownership and origin. My family's recipes didn't need written stories while they lived in my mother's recipe box, but if I were to take these recipes to a cookbook or blog, they would require "a recommendation, a context, a point, a reason to be," as Susan Leonardi so eloquently observed.[9]

The cookbook narrator plays a key role in the determination of a recipe's value and authenticity. If provenance is evidence of a network of cultural exchange, then the cookbook author is a hub in that network where power is concentrated. To borrow a term from Pierre Bourdieu's *The Field of Cultural Production,* cookbook authors are like "art traders." They give cultural and market value to otherwise free and anonymous recipes through narrative. Bourdieu suggests that texts are created and valued collaboratively and the image of the author as "the first and last source of value of his work" does not account for the other hands that carry a text from author to market, transforming a work into a cultural commodity that can be exchanged for economic capital.[10] These intermediaries may include art dealers, publishers, and editors. The cookbook author plays a similar role, moving the cultural product of a recipe from informal domestic exchange into the public market for sale. Bourdieu argues that "the cultural businessman" is the person who "exploits the labour of the 'creator' by trading in the 'sacred' and the person who, by putting it on the market, by exhibiting, publishing, or staging it, consecrates a product which he has 'discovered' and which would otherwise remain a mere natural resource."[11] Provenance and the practice of citation is the process by which a recipe or a painting is assigned "sacred" status, or authenticity. As editor and dealer of recipes, a cookbook author is invested in maintaining the "creator" status of the recipe contributor through citation of provenance. Through the citation narrative, a cookbook writer is able to "consecrate" the "natural resource" of ordinary recipes into authentic culinary knowledge because of the writer's ethos and accumulation of capital. As Bourdieu argues:

> The art trader [in this case, recipe compiler] is not just the agent who gives the work a commercial value by bringing it into a market; he is not just the representative, the impresario, who 'defends the authors he loves.' He is the person who can proclaim the value of the author he defends . . . and above all 'invests his prestige' in the author's cause, acting as a 'symbolic banker' who offers as security all the symbolic capital he has accumulated (which he is liable to forfeit if he backs a 'loser'). This investment, of which the accompanying 'economic' investments are themselves only a guarantee, is what brings the producer into the cycle of consecration.[12]

In other words, the cookbook writer's act of bringing ordinary recipes from ordinary cooks to market under the imprint of the writer's name as cookbook author depends on the writer's own accumulation of knowledge, power, and capital. The act of authorship under the law makes possible the authorship of ordinary recipe contributors through the norms of cookbook publication. All depends on "a magic act" performed by the author where the "ready-made article" of the ordinary recipe is transformed into "an object whose market price is incommensurate with its cost of production."[13] The magic act, I would argue, is performed in the citation narrative, where the writer and readers —"the universe of celebrants and believers"— come to an agreement about the "meaning and value" of the recipes in the tradition of recipe exchange.[14] The process of constructing authenticity, in this case, is a complicated exchange of many kinds of capital in the appearance of an innocuous paragraph about a cookbook writer and her great-grandmother's recipe for angel biscuits.

Authenticity and Ownership:
Intellectual Property in Law and in Practice

As a recipe enters the marketplace through publication, it also becomes subject to intellectual property laws. Though the text of recipes cannot be copyright protected, I argue that the citation narrative recognizes recipes as intellectual property in opposition to the law.

The cookbook as a whole text is protected by copyright in the same way that a whole novel or anthology is protected; the individual recipes (lists of ingredients and procedures), however, are not considered literary expression and so may be appropriated without infringement. However, the norms of cookbook publishing suggest that people in the food writing industry *do* recognize the rights of recipe innovators to own their intellectual property by establishing the citation narrative as an informal convention for giving credit. As Jason Mazzone explains in *Copyfraud and Other Abuses of Intellectual Property Law*, problems occur when there is a "gap" between laws and norms, "between the rights that the law confers and the rights that are asserted in practice."[15] In Mazzone's formulation of the "gap," the primary problem is copyfraud — a case of an author "overreaching" and claiming rights that the law does not confer, usually in the form of collecting a fee for work that by law should be free in the public domain. In my own work, however, I do not see this gap as a problem but as a site of meaning making. Because no law or governing body regulates how, when, or why a cookbook writer should give credit for a recipe, then the choice to cite is, indeed, a *choice* that reflects a rhetorical purpose.[16]

Perhaps the best way to define contemporary intellectual property law in the United States is to start with a list of items that are protected. According to Edward Samuels in *The Illustrated Story of Copyright*, "books, drama, dance, music, sound recordings, pictures, photographs, sculpture, architecture, movies, and computer programs" are copyrightable. The text of the copyright statute that governs contemporary cookbooks asserts that copyright protection extends to "original works of authorship fixed in any tangible medium of expression."[17] From this statute, Samuels identifies two factors required for protection: fixation and originality.

"Fixation" requires that the work be recorded in a perceptible way. The statute leaves the manner of recording wide open to include methods of recording or viewing that have not yet been invented. For the purposes of recipe copyright, the requirement for fixation means that the recipe must be in the form of alphabetic text, be it born-digital or paperbound. Originality, Samuels dramatically understates, is "the more difficult concept."[18] The current statute does not define specifically what constitutes originality, but Justice Oliver Wendell Holmes's decision in a 1903 Supreme Court case defines originality as the unique thumbprint of a single author: "the *personal* reaction of an *individual* upon nature. *Personality* always contains something *unique*. It expresses its *singularity* even in handwriting, and a very modest grade of art has in it *something irreducible*, which is *one man's alone*. That something he may copyright."[19] My added emphasis exaggerates the depiction of the solitary author genius who generates creative works that are neither derivative nor imitative, that are imbued with the author's identity and personality, and that could only be created by that person in his or her unique experiences and contexts.

Recipes fail both tests of copyright eligibility. Though most recipes do eventually get written down in "fixed" form, John Whiting reminds us that recipes are often in circulation orally long before they are codified in text.[20] By then, the first "authentic author" is generally lost to time, and the "fixed" form is necessarily derivative of these oral forms. Originality is hard to measure in recipes, too, because recipes in general are combinations of established practices and procedures. My innovative recipe for an exciting soup may contain flavor combinations that are novel, but these ingredients will be subjected to cooking techniques that apply to all soups. More often than not, recipes do not bear the unique thumbprint of a single author, but instead reflect the practices and preferences of a culture or a community. A recipe is a collaboratively authored project, even if some of those collaborators are invisible or long forgotten.

In addition to fixation and originality, two other factors are at play exempting recipes from copyright protection; Samuels explains that copyright does not apply to "works of utility" or "facts." Copyright protects elements of creative expression, distinct from strictly functional elements (which can be patented),[21] and facts, which "do not owe their origin to an act of authorship" and cannot be "original."[22] Recipes are often seen as works of utility, written formulas for making a product. By this argument, the form of the recipe — standardized measurements, lists of ingredients, and straightforward imperative prose instructions — emphasizes the recipe as fact rather than literary expression. The results of mixing yeast with warm water and flour are not dependent on authorial creativity but on scientific principles.

Recipes belong to a category of cultural works that are excluded from copyright protection. In the introduction to *The Construction of Authorship*, Martha Woodmansee and Peter Jaszi argue that cultural works like recipes, "improvised works," "folklore," "items of cultural heritage," and "works of the oral tradition" operate under a very different set of values than those protected by copyright; these collaboratively authored and community-owned products "are valued chiefly for their fidelity to tradition rather than their deviations from it."[23] In other words, these works are valued as authentic when they are connected to a distant past or enacted in community rituals, and originality may actually decrease the recipe's value in certain rhetorical situations. The values of copyright law are not consistent with the values of recipe writers and users.

The citation narrative implicitly refutes the exception of recipes from copyright protection. Where the law values only fixed textual forms, the citation narrative emphasizes the value of movement and multiplicity. Often, citation narratives describe the recipe's movement as atextual; the recipe may pass through oral traditions or through physical demonstration long before it is documented and published. These narratives valorize informal exchange of culinary knowledge as superior to fixation through formal publication. Where the law values only original creations of single authors, citation narratives articulate the value of traditions that are collectively owned and relatively unchanged over time. At the same time, citing another recipe author suggests that originality in a recipe is possible and that recipe creators are, in fact, authors.

But most of all, the recipe headnote in general, and the citation narrative in particular, marks the recipe and the cookbook as literary expression. In the twenty-first century, recipes for utility are available for free online. Databases of searchable recipes are available on smartphones and tablets that cooks can take into the kitchen. Services like Pinterest will hold the recipes found online in digital recipe boxes that can be made public for friends and family and strangers to follow and share. When I want to cook something new, I go online for a recipe I can *use*. I go to cookbooks for authorial personalities that I trust or enjoy. Cookbook writers establish their personalities as unique, individual authors and personas in the recipe headnotes and paratexts. These are the parts of a cookbook that are undeniably protected by copyright law as fixed, original, and literary. It is significant, then, when cookbook authors use these literary headnotes to recognize the contributions of other authors of recipe text.

The practice of the citation narrative, I argue, is a reaction to the limits of copyright law. The law recognizes recipe innovation and cookbook writing as two completely separate actions with completely separate guidelines and definitions of authorship. In practice, however, these actions are valued as equal. Jaszi reiterates in "On the Author Effect: Contemporary Copyright and Collective Creativity" that neither the law nor the definition of authorship are inevitable, and when the definition of authorship under the law prevents new structures from protecting works with alternative models of authorship, alternate structures emerge outside of the law.[24] To make up for the gap between the legal view of authorship and the cultural value of culinary innovation, the community of food writers and cookbook publishers have developed informal norms for citing the sources of recipes in narrative headnotes.

Handbooks of advice for cookbook writers and bloggers offer insight into how the cooking instruction industry establishes norms and conventions for dealing with the collaborative nature of recipes and the values of copyright law. The handbooks suggest that good professional practice means giving credit to recipe innovators, even though the law does not require it. *Recipes into Type: A Handbook for Cookbook Writers and Editors* by Joan Whitman and Dolores Simon (1993) acknowledges that "most food writers make use of recipes that are not their own invention."[25] Similarly, *The Recipe Writer's Handbook* by Barbara Gibbs Ostmann and Jane L. Baker (2001) and *Will Write for Food: The Complete Guide to Writing Cookbooks, Blogs, Reviews, Memoir, and More* by Dianne Jacob (2010) both address how writers should treat recipes that come from other sources.[26] All three handbooks address issues of attribution and citation, demonstrating norms for handling intellectual property.

First, the handbooks suggest that the citation narrative is a strategy that protects a writer from prosecution for copyright infringement. All three handbooks advise writers to cite their sources because the law is not entirely clear on the status of recipes. In *Recipes into Type,* Whitman and Simon acknowledge that a writer cannot always know where every recipe in their collection "originally" comes from and that the finished cookbook "may well contain instances of unwitting plagiarism." In all cases, when the source is known, the authors advise the writer to "give credit to the originator, preferably in the headnote."[27] Ostmann and Baker also acknowledge that "the legal position on the ownership of recipes is somewhat murky," but that "in the broadest sense recipes are ideas" and therefore not eligible for copyright protection.[28] However, they argue, "the exact wording of the recipe procedure" can be protected. Thus, "copying a recipe verbatim would be a violation of copyright."[29] This particular interpretation of the law demonstrates an understanding that the language of a recipe is the original work of an author, even if the idea of a dish is in the public domain. However, Ostmann and Baker acknowledge that their advice is not based entirely on the law but on "professional courtesy" and "the general rule of thumb."[30] The main concern is not legal but ethical and professional. Dianne Jacob's *Will Write for Food* is considerably more alarmist in its treatment of copyright law than either of the handbooks examined so far, using imperative forms and powerful, active verbs. The threat of legal action against a cookbook writer is more evident in passages like these:

> If you're using other writers' recipes, it is essential that you give credit. Whatever you do, don't post a recipe exactly the way it appears and claim it as your own.[31]
>
> It's best to credit Judy and explain her significance in the headnote.[32]
>
> When in doubt, give credit, and you'll create fewer problems. . . . Even if you've completely reworded the recipe, to be safe, say where it came from.[33]
>
> If your Aunt Helen handwrote a recipe for angel food cake on an index card and doesn't remember where she got it, do an online search and see if you can determine the original author. Aside from that, all you can do is tell people about Aunt Helen and her recipe, so no one thinks you've stolen it.[34]
>
> To the question, "How do I protect my recipes?" the US government answers: A mere listing of ingredients is not protected under copyright law.[35]

The language choices here suggest an urgency and a fear: whatever you do, don't open the door to accusations of copyright infringement, and by all means, protect yourself. The threat does not seem to come from the law itself but from the industry and its critics. Therefore, the thing to be "protected against" is not legal action but the loss of the cookbook writer's ethos and credibility. The citation narrative protects the image of the cookbook writer as an original and creative authorial persona who shows appropriate deference for the works of others in the professional community.

The handbooks further suggest that because the cookbook writer is invested in maintaining a reputation as an original author, the headnote is an opportunity to entertain the reader and display a unique authorial voice. A citation narrative functions as both an entertaining story and evidence of the author's ethos by situating the author in relationship with authentic sources of traditional culinary knowledge. Ostmann and Baker consider the exchange of recipes to be a "part of the pleasure of cooking and sharing credit should be a natural part of writing about cooking."[36] Citing another source, then, connects the writer to experiences that would be familiar to readers in their own cultures of recipe exchange. Ostmann and Baker advise that readers are likely to be entertained by reading a citation narrative: "Readers like to know about a recipe, where it comes from, what makes it special. This information easily can be included in a headnote and can help draw the reader into the recipe."[37] Readers are connected to an author and a recipe by being made to feel as another node in a network of recipe exchange. Jacob also suggests that the headnote is a "chance to draw readers into the recipe" and to "set a mood, give the recipe a personality, or tell a story."[38] The point, Jacob argues, is to entertain readers. Moreover, the citation narrative establishes the credibility of the cookbook writer. Ostmann and Baker make clear that a citation is not the enemy of ethos: "Acknowledging that an idea came from someone else or was inspired by another recipe doesn't make your work any less original — and might even give it credibility."[39] The original "author's voice" can "shine through" in the way the narrative is told, even as the author acknowledges that the recipes come from other sources.[40]

The author's ethos is not compromised by a citation, because the citation lends authenticity to the recipe and authority to the writer. Whitman and Simon suggest using a citation in a headnote or title when the name of the source might "mean something to the reader" or "lend authenticity" to the recipe.[41] If the recipe comes from a famous chef or renowned restaurant, that story will add a feeling of authenticity to the recipe. Though Whitman and Simon warn that "unless the contributor is a celebrity," the citation may "give the reader a sense of being shut out" of a private network,[42] I argue that for Southern cuisine in particular, narratives of the family are especially effective for making arguments of authenticity. The names of the contributors may not be recognizable to readers, but the figures of grandmothers and mothers in the home kitchen are likely to be powerful reminders of traditional foodways. Giving credit for a recipe idea or text is a rhetorical strategy for establishing ethos for the writer and authenticity for the recipe through the figure of the authorized contributor.

Citation Narratives: A Case Study

The following case study examines authors' particular, recurring citation strategies for arguing authenticity. Each author records the provenance of a recipe from a particular contributor to the cookbook writer, but each does so to highlight a different kind of authenticity. While most cookbooks use occasional citation narratives in combination with other rhetorical strategies, for the books examined in depth in this chapter, the citation narrative serves as the primary rhetorical strategy, or is a motif that organizes the entire text. The writers of the cookbooks make few claims to their own originality or innovation in the kitchen, as these authors are not professional chefs. Instead, they act as collectors, editors, and storytellers. The headnotes in each are formulaic and consistent throughout the text, each headnote following a similar pattern of citation.

The citation narratives argue that the recipes are authentic because of their provenance. The contributor is validated as an authentic source of knowledge, and in the process, the writer is marked implicitly as a knowledgeable and connected source as well. The narratives also imply that the recipe has moved through authentic processes of knowledge making and exchange: learning at Grandmother's knee, inheritance, archival research, network exchange, and collection. The citation narratives argue that authentic Southern recipes come from ordinary innovators through informal networks of exchange.

Validating Grandmothers as Sources and Inheritance as a Method of Exchange

I started this chapter with a very cute story about my great-grandmother, about the women in my family and their recipe collections. Besides being true and cute and an apt introduction to the practice of citation, this story also happens to connect me to a network of authorized sources of culinary knowledge: mothers, grandmothers, and great-grandmothers. An introduction to a grandmother figure is almost a uniform convention of cookbook introductions. In the second paragraph of *Bon Appetit, Y'all*, Virginia Willis claims, "My part on the old and complex story of Southern food began in my grandmother's country kitchen, with its walls made of heart-of-Georgia pine."[43] Willis goes on to credit her grandmother, Emily Louise Wingate Baston (Meme), and her mother, Virginia, for providing the basic instruction and motivation for her cooking. Willis argues that her mother and grandmother validate her authenticity both as a cook and as a Southerner: "A love of fresh, home-cooked food and a tradition of unconditional hospitality have always been guiding values in my family — I see them as a testimony to our Southern heritage. I spent much of my childhood in the kitchen with Meme and Mama, absorbing those values and acquiring skills I would later develop into a profession."[44] Willis's book, subtitled *Recipes and Stories from Three Generations of Southern Cooking*, uses this authenticating connection to mother and grandmother as an organizing principle.

Even when the cookbook is not organized around family history, grandmothers show up in introductions with surprising regularity. In the second paragraph of the preface to *Smoke and Pickles*, under the heading "What I Cook Is Who I Am," Edward Lee introduces his grandmother as an influence.[45]

Sean Brock introduces his grandmother in paragraph five, but still in the first page of the introduction.[46] John Currence thanks his mother in the first two paragraphs:

> I grew up in a New Orleans house where cooking was an immense part of the daily landscape. My mother, who was a full-time history teacher, made hot breakfasts, packed us lunches, and cooked supper every day. . . . Watching her in the kitchen I learned a strong work ethic . . . I observed selflessness, and I came to understand the importance food and eating together play in the role of a healthy family life.

The third acknowledges summers spent with grandparents growing vegetables.[47] Brock and Currence use their mothers and grandmothers as further evidence of their rural, Southern roots. And even though Ed Lee's grandmother is Korean and living in Brooklyn, his connection to her is evidence of a traditional, domestic culinary knowledge. For these professional, male chefs, speaking to cooks at home, this very first authenticating move of the narrative is a significant one.

Grandmothers represent a traditional, premodern, domestic culinary knowledge, connected to Johnston and Baumann's definition of authenticity as "historical tradition" and "simplicity."[48] A grandmother's culinary knowledge is likely to come from inheritance, reflecting a "simpler time" before industrial agriculture and mass-produced convenience foods. While Willis, Lee, Brock, and Currence are all formally trained chefs, their institutionalized culinary school knowledge is inauthentic in comparison to the lessons learned from grandmothers and mothers.

Southern chefs are not alone in this figuring of the grandmother as the seat of authenticity. The first of Michael Pollan's famous "Six Rules for Eating Wisely" is "don't eat anything your great-great-great grandmother wouldn't recognize as food."[49] This claim is both a reference to the authenticity of the distant past and a gendered claim (did our great-great-great grandfathers not think of food, too?). Our great-great-great grandmothers are the solution to our food problems, but Pollan argues it is because our mothers are the source of the problem. Mothers should be responsible for maintaining a healthy food culture by "[teaching] us what to eat, when to eat it, how much of it to eat, even the order in which to eat it." But in Pollan's opinion, mothers have failed to compete with advertising and dubious nutritional science.[50] In this context, a cookbook writer's citation of grandmothers as contributors of recipes is a link to an authentic source of culinary knowledge.

Faye Porter's 2011 cookbook *At My Grandmother's Knee: Recipes and Memories Handed Down by Women of the South* uses the citation narrative exclusively in headnotes. Each headnote describes a recipe's movement from a grandmother who innovated and perfected the recipe to a granddaughter who keeps the tradition alive through practicing the recipe. The granddaughters contribute the recipes to Porter's collection along with stories and memories of their grandmothers. The narratives in Porter's cookbook argue that authentic culinary knowledge comes from grandmothers and moves unchanged through systems of inheritance and experiential learning.

To compose *At My Grandmother's Knee,* Porter collected recipes and stories from many contributors, all listed alphabetically in the "Contributor's Index" at the end of the book. Some are recognizable food writers like Tammy Algood (author of *The Complete Southern Cookbook*, 2010; *The Southern Slow Cooker Bible*, 2014; *Sunday Dinner in the South*, 2015, among others) and Patsy Caldwell (coauthor of *Y'all Come Over*, examined further in this chapter).[51] It is unclear from the text of the book how Porter found contributors to collect the recipes, but many of the granddaughters are from Nashville, where Porter lives, suggesting that she collected them from among her acquaintances. Each narrative contains quotations from the granddaughter contributor, which suggests that Porter interviewed each contributor, or perhaps collected written narratives with each recipe. *At My Grandmother's Knee* is structured upon familial networks of recipe exchange and inheritance, and its narratives consistently emphasize grandmothers as authentic sources of culinary knowledge. The argument is that these recipes are good for readers to perform authentic Southern identity as welcome members of the family network described in the narrative.

The headnote for "Fried Green Tomatoes" is representative of the cookbook's narrative style, form, and content:

> **Sarah Smith** (Tupelo, Mississippi) was named for her grandmother, **Sarah Langston** (Saltillo, Mississippi). She and her siblings called their grandmother Mammy. Mammy had a small garden where she grew most of the vegetables for her family to eat. Sarah shares that tomatoes were grown and sold as a source of income. "When we were little we would pick a few green tomatoes that 'forced' grandmother to fry us up some fried green tomatoes," Sarah says. "Like most women trying to feed a farming family, she always cooked meals in large quantities. There were always three hot meals a day served around the Langston house."[52]

Like this one, all headnotes in Porter's collection identify a city of origin for the contributor and the innovator and a description of the kinship relationship between them, including each grandmother's unique endearment. Identifying the hometown of the women is evidence of their Southern identity and a common strategy for authenticating the recipe as truly Southern. Each recipe has at least two contributors whose names are presented in boldface type: the Grandmother who innovated the recipe and the Granddaughter who shared it with Porter.[53] About one-third of the recipes in *At My Grandmother's Knee* have the innovator's name in the title (i.e., "B.B.'s Turnip Greens," "Ham a la Mamie").[54] Most have a quote from the granddaughter, usually giving an anecdote about the grandmother, a memory, or a description of her character. Not all narratives are related directly to the dish as in "Fried Green Tomatoes." The narrative for Sara Fay Wasson's "Broccoli-Chicken Casserole" makes no mention of the casserole. Instead, Wasson's granddaughter describes how Wasson was "a classy, sophisticated lady" who "was always in the best clothes and beautifully groomed."[55] The narratives are invested in verifying the ethos of the Grandmother as an authentic source of knowledge and in reifying the system of inheritance as an authentic method of knowledge exchange.

One of the longest headnotes in the collection, the narrative for "Blackberry Jam," highlights the Grandmother's culinary knowledge and her importance as a character in the transfer of authentic traditions and cultural identity:

"Putting up jam" with Granny, **Alma Mae Hughes Davis** (Clintwood, Virginia), was a summer tradition as far back as **Michelle Fleming** (Nashville, Tennessee) can remember. Heading together to the berry patch behind her house, Granny would carry a stick to scare off snakes. Michelle recalls stuffing her mouth with berries when Granny wasn't looking — but somehow she always knew what her granddaughter was up to. Once back at home, Granny would cover Michelle's briar scratches and bug bites with pink calamine lotion. Michelle says that Granny included her in everything she did — planting and picking vegetables, berries, and flowers; rolling dough and cutting biscuits with a juice glass; sewing and quilting; art and music; and summer camping trips to Myrtle Beach, Tweetsie Railroad, and Gatlinburg. Granny broadened her world and shared her love for Appalachian culture.[56]

Davis, the Grandmother, is both the holder and transmitter of vast cultural knowledge, including medicine (calamine), agriculture (planting and picking), cookery (biscuits), fashion (sewing), crafts (quilting), art, and music. The scaring off of snakes suggests both a knowledge of the natural animal world and a hint of the supernatural one. It is through Davis that the Granddaughter Fleming receives an education in the geography and culture of Appalachia. As the authentic source of knowledge, Davis becomes a powerful agent for defining regional identity for Fleming, and, by extension, for Porter and Porter's readers.

Though the narrative gives little information about the specific recipe for black-berry jam, the record of provenance gives evidence that the recipe is authentic because the source is authentic. So is the method by which Fleming learns the recipe: at her Grandmother's knee.

These two arguments — that Grandmother is the source of authentic knowl-edge and that her knowledge can be inherited through recipe collection — form the basic structure of Porter's cookbook and all of its narratives. In the intro-duction, Porter credits Grandmothers as the sources of love, traditions, memo-ries, friendship, guidance, and family legacy. Grandmothers hold special knowl-edge about making do, a skill at the heart of the Southern metanarrative.[57] Grandmothers transmit their specialized knowledge through demonstration, oral tradition, and text, which is then practiced by their progeny. Practicing the knowledge and passing it to another generation increases the authenticity of the recipe, connecting it to an idealized past that the recipe reader can access through reading and through the performance of the recipe. Porter describes one family who uses the occasion of cooking the Grandmother's recipes to maintain the Grandmother's cultural authority through storytelling.

> **Jenny Lewis** (Nashville, Tennessee) shares that her mother inherited her mother's ability to cook and bake. While Jenny and her mom baked all kinds of pies at Thanksgiving and Christmas, Jenny's mom would relate stories of Grandma Wolfe, **Nora Virginia Wolfe Houldershell** (Moorefield, West Virginia), and how she dried fruit (with clothespins on a clothesline on the porch) and never threw anything away.[58]

Lewis and her mother practice Houldershell's culinary knowledge ritu-ally, using the opportunity to reify the grandmother's authenticity through storytelling. Similarly, Leigh Willhoit Doucet explains that even though her mother "lost her battle to breast cancer in 2001," she will maintain the chain of inherited knowledge with her own daughters: "While they will never know her personally, I hope to impart to them so much of what she taught me."[59] It is important to Doucet that her children recognize their grandmother as the original source of culinary knowledge, and teaching them her recipes will allow them to "know her" and maintain the cultural traditions of Southern cooking.

Narratives of provenance like the ones in *At My Grandmother's Knee* argue that the recipes are authentic because of the superior knowledge of Grandmothers and the reliability of knowledge transferred through inheri-tance and experiential learning. Most importantly, the cookbook is built on the assumption that these authentic recipes are available for readers outside of the family network to perform. Even if the reader does not have a Southern

Grandmother herself, that reader can benefit from the authentic knowledge of many Grandmothers, as the reader is invited to join the familial network of recipe exchange. Moving recipes to the public marketplace does not undo their authenticity because the narrative interprets the recipes' meaning. The market value of the recipe to be purchased in this published cookbook is established through the citation narrative. And Porter's value as author and collector is made clear in her storytelling.

Validating Professionals as Sources and Research as a Method of Exchange

While Porter's narratives centered on the Grandmother as an authentic source, and inheritance as an authentic method of exchange, another group of citation narratives focus on the professional cook as an authentic source and research as an authentic method of knowledge transfer. While not exactly a citation narrative that gives credit for a recipe text, a common form of headnote used by chefs credits another source for inspiring a recipe. The chef-author still presents the recipe text as an original innovation, but acknowledges another source for offering an idea incorporated in the recipe. In *Afro-Vegan,* Bryant Terry credits other cookbooks for some ideas. One of the ingredients in Terry's "Date-Sweetened Almond Milk" is "inspired by [Rosamund] Grant and [Josephine] Baker's recipe in *The Taste of Africa,*" but Terry maintains credit for the rest of the recipe.[60] Terry decides to add ginger to a recipe for pickled green beans after reading a recipe for "gingered pickled carrots" in Hugh Acheson's *A New Turn in the South.*[61] Similarly, in the headnote for "Vanilla Spice Ice Cream," Terry credits two sources for concrete contributions to the recipe. According to Terry, "My buddy Matt Halteman suggested that I use white beans in this ice cream to give it a creamier consistency." White beans are listed as the first ingredient. Further in the headnote, Terry explains that he was inspired to create a recipe for a milkshake using this ice cream (which is provided on the same page) after seeing a recipe for a milkshake in Edward Lee's *Smoke and Pickles.*[62] Though Terry shares credit for some of the ideas that go into the recipe, on the whole, he is still taking credit for the text of the recipe and the overall idea of the dish.

What Terry is highlighting in these narratives is his own ethos as a scholar immersed in a network of cuisine. Contrary to the view of the singular author codified in copyright law, Terry presents his connectedness to others as evidence of his authority. As Terry writes in the introduction, quoting the African American artist Romare Bearden, "The artist has to be something like a whale swimming with his mouth wide open, absorbing everything until he has what he really needs." Terry admits that this quote "has guided me through the process of writing this book over the past year," and also notes that "Bearden's stunning collages are a major inspiration for *Afro-Vegan*."[63] These statements from the introduction, combined with his use of citation and "inspiration" narratives, validate cookbooks written by professional chefs as viable means of finding authoritative recipes. The logic of the argument is something like this: if cookbooks are sources that professionals like Bryant Terry can draw on and maintain credibility, then readers of Bryant Terry's cookbook can expect to do the same.

This same kind of formula organizes cookbooks based on historical cookbook research, like Damon Fowler's *Classical Southern Cooking* and Nancy Carter Crump's *Hearthside Cooking*.[64] In each of these cases, the author or editor at the center of the cookbook is presenting recipes collected from other sources. The citations are part of an argument that is meant to convince readers that these recipes are authentic and good for performing a continuous Southern identity. Fowler's cookbook, for example, is marketed on the flyleaf of the 2008 revised edition as "rooted in meticulous scholarship, a passion for good cooking, and a deep love for the unique culture of the South."[65] Fowler draws from nineteenth-century cookbooks — primarily Mary Randolph's *The Virginia Housewife*, Lettice Bryan's *The Kentucky Housewife*, Sarah Rutledge's *The Carolina Housewife*, and Annabella Hill's *Mrs. Hill's New Cookbook* — to represent "a kind of golden age for Southern cooking."[66] Fowler cites these sources throughout the cookbook, and sometimes cites *their* sources, as in the case of "Annabella Hill's Curry Powder," which, according to Fowler, is nearly identical to William Kitchiner's recipe in *The Cook's Oracle*.[67]

Fowler and Crump's citations of professional cooks and writers are not necessarily optional, as in the case of other chef-authored cookbooks. These two examples in particular purposefully blur the lines between academic research and popular cooking instructions. As Sandra Oliver writes in the foreword to the second edition of *Hearthside Cooking*, Crump wrote the first edition at a time when "academia did not yet deign to regard food history as a topic worth serious research and writing about, but writing a cookbook was perfectly alright."[68] In the preface, Crump describes her own struggle for recognition of foodways in scholarly communities beginning in the 1980s and the role of "current food-history scholarship" in shaping the contents of the revised edition.[69] Because Crump is trained as a scholar and is writing in order to make a space for food in academia, her citations are part of her ethos as scholarly researcher and her work's reputation as part of a recognizable academic field. Crump draws on archival and published sources in the narrative introductions to recipes and cites the name of the historical contributor; she also uses end-notes and includes a bibliography divided into "Reference Works," "Primary Sources," and "Secondary Sources." This kind of academic citation, governed by professional bodies and regulated by institutional peer review is not an exact equivalent to the kind of informal narrative systems of citations that are the focus of this chapter. However, they do demonstrate an identical motivation for the speaker and effect on audience — establishing the author as an ethical and authoritative researcher who can be trusted to provide authentic culinary knowledge.

Like the historical cookbooks discussed above, edited community cookbook compilations like *A Gracious Plenty* and *The Southern Foodways Alliance Community Cookbook* published by the SFA, as well as *The Southern Living Community Cookbook* edited by Sheri Castle, offer another example of research-based cookbooks where the authorial voice of the cookbook is acting as editor, citing and contextualizing sources in narrative. As Porter does in *At My Grandmother's Knee*, the author of the headnotes and narrative text in these compilation cookbooks does not take credit for any of the recipes and does not pretend to offer any original recipes. Books like this can be created because of the free movement of recipes outside of copyright law and in the public domain, but a cookbook that collected these recipes without citation would have a hard time establishing relevance. As in the case of the academic histories of Fowler and Crump, this kind of cookbook constructs its authenticity from the perceived authenticity of its sources. Citing sources does not undercut the author/editor's credibility; citation is the *source* of their authority.

Joan E. Aller's *Cider Beans, Wild Greens, and Dandelion Jelly: Recipes from Southern Appalachia* is a kind of compilation cookbook like those described above, but instead of collecting historical recipes exclusively, Aller collects recipes from the cooks and owners of inns and bed-and-breakfasts throughout Appalachia in order to represent the cuisine of the region where she lives. Aller herself is positioned as a semiobjective researcher. In the author biography on the book's dust jacket, Aller is described as "an artist and trained community volunteer" who "has always dedicated herself to preserving beauty, culture, and tradition." Though the "Introduction" makes clear that Aller lives in Southern Appalachia full time, it is also clear that Aller moved to the region from elsewhere.[70] Aller explains that she looked around her "place" in "a mountain hollow on a bad dirt road" and began "to feel a little wistful for the past and fretful about the future of this beautiful and peaceful place."[71] Aller saw signs that "the modern world" was changing the region, for better and for worse, and that there was a need to "capture" the history and identity of rural Appalachia before it was lost. Aller works as a historian and documentarian by researching, interviewing, photographing, and documenting the recipes and food traditions of Appalachia in order to combat stereotypes of the region with more authentic narratives (in her opinion).[72] The collection is built on the arguments that the cooking professionals at inns and bed-and-breakfasts are authentic sources of culinary knowledge and regional history, and that research is a valid method for recipes to move and maintain authenticity. As representatives of the traditions of the rural past, as well as trained and paid cooks, these sources can provide recipes that reflect the cultural foodways of the region and that will reliably guide the home cook through the performance of the recipe. As a trained and experienced documentarian, Aller is a responsible researcher who maintains the authenticity of the recipes she receives by carefully recording their provenance through citation narratives.

Aller's narratives are unique in this sample for their explicit invocation of the reader as the final destination in the provenance. Aller's headnotes identify the reader as "you," and encourage the reader not only to perform the recipes as provided but also to improvise with them and customize the ingredients according to the cook's tastes. Aller does not often appear in the text as a recipe innovator herself. Instead, her role is editorial. Aller is present as an editor in every headnote, inviting the reader with an imperative clause to get in the kitchen and play with the recipes in her book. After describing the recipe's origin in the distant past or in current practice, Aller offers "you" hints for preparing or suggestions for altering the recipe. The implication is that the reader is a node in the network of exchange described in the book, and, like Aller, the reader may come to the book as a researcher. Whether the reader is a native Appalachian or an adopted one like Aller, the narratives validate the reader's method of knowledge acquisition as authentic — especially readers not native to Appalachia. Aller suggests that acquiring knowledge of Southern food traditions from a cookbook is just as authentic as acquiring it at Grandmother's knee.

Aller explains in the "Acknowledgments" that she solicited recipes from friends and from the owners of inns and bed-and-breakfasts throughout the region.[73] Aller's narratives follow one of two patterns throughout *Cider Beans*. She consistently identifies the source of the recipe either in the specific inn or B and B or in the historical traditions of the four groups to settle and influence Appalachian culture: Native Americans, Melungeons (a group of migrants of unknown origin, perhaps Spanish Muslims), Africans, and Europeans.[74] The second pattern is nearer to the format of the historical narrative described in chapter 1 of this book. The recipes in that pattern are authentic because of their historical pasts, but like the citation narratives in Aller's book, these also indicate Aller's textual research methods, implying that research is an effective method for identifying authentic Southern recipes.

The narrative for "Oven Baked Blueberry French Toast" in the "Breakfast" chapter is an example of the first pattern that follows the conventions of the citation narrative:

> This recipe, from the Cripple Creek Bed and Breakfast Cabins in Crockett, Virginia, was handed down from the owner's grandmother. Cripple Creek is situated in the Blue Ridge Mountains on 35 acres of wooded hills and rolling pastures dotted with wildflowers, blackberry bushes, and apple trees. I just love blueberries, so I hope this recipe from Cripple Creek will become one of your favorites![75]

The headnote does not identify the source of the recipe by name, but Aller suggests that the recipe is authentic to the region because it is cooked in the Cripple Creek Bed and Breakfast. Aller borrows a technique from Porter by arguing that the recipe is further authenticated by its origin with the grandmother of the owner. The narrative implies that the recipe has been authenticated through the traditional means of transmission through inheritance. That Aller acquires the recipe through research does not diminish its authenticity. In fact, the narrative suggests that this authentic past can be recreated through, perhaps, a stay at the bed and breakfast or through making this recipe multiple times until it becomes a favorite. Aller does not suggest that she has an intimate relationship with either the owner of the bed and breakfast or the owner's grandmother. Instead, Aller seems to come into possession of the recipe through research, asking the owner to share the text of the recipe. This pattern of a four-step provenance recurs throughout Aller's book: the recipe moves from an innovator to a bed and breakfast representative, to Aller, and then to the reader. For example, Aller acknowledges that the owner of Clay Corner Inn in Blacksburg, Virgina, got the recipe for "Freezer Coleslaw" from her grandmother. The unnamed owner "was kind enough to share" the recipe with Aller. Aller implies that she has made the recipe herself and suggests that the reader will, too.[76] The recipe is authentic because of its connection to the past and through the ethos of its contributor, and neither Aller nor the reader can undermine that authenticity.

Other recipes, following the second pattern of narrative described above, demonstrate Aller's research methods in archives. In the desserts chapter of *Cider Beans*, Aller provides a recipe for "Melungeon Wedding Cake" that was "found in a diary from the 1860s." Aller provides excerpts from the diary text: "Take the whites of 14 eggs . . . 1 cup butter, beaten to a cream . . . 2 cups sugar . . . finely Sentamon [*sic*]. Mix 3 teaspoons of yeast powders with 3 cups flour. Mix all thoroughly, add favoring [*sic*] to suit. Bake 1 hour."[77] Aller reports that she tried to make the cake using the recipe from the diary, but found that the conditions of the modern kitchen are different from "back in 'the good old days.'" Though Aller practiced the recipe as it was written, she provides the "modern baker" with instructions involving an electric mixer and more readily available ingredients and reflecting modern tastes, such as frosting.[78] This narrative demonstrates Aller's methods of finding authentic recipes. First, she researches in archives for primary source documents. The narrative suggests that she consulted at least two recipes: the one from the 1860s diary quoted above and another "original translation, by a family member" that specified brown sugar.[79] It isn't clear from the narrative what is meant by "original translation" or of what family the translator is a member, but the implication is that the diary entry was copied or "translated" by a relative of the first recipe writer, and Aller used both recipes to develop a third recipe suitable for the modern kitchen. The second step in Aller's process, then, is experimentation through performing these historic recipes as they would have been performed by women "in the good old days." Aller's investment in recreating authentic recipes is physical as well as academic; she has beaten the batters "by hand" in addition to reading about them. Finally, Aller is an eater. She reports, "I found myself sneaking into the kitchen to get just one more tiny piece."[80] Her knowledge of the recipe is intimate and complete. Describing this process of literary, historical, and scientific research and experimentation assures the reader that Aller is a credible researcher as well as a skilled cook who can be trusted to preserve the authenticity of this recipe. The reader is also authorized to perform the updated recipe, confident in its provenance. Though the modern version is changed significantly, its origin in the distant past and the researcher's ethos preserve its authenticity.

Unlike the "Melungeon Wedding Cake," Aller's recipe for "Mountain Fried Steak" is represented as unchanged from its original textual source. Aller makes it explicitly clear that the recipe, "attributed to Josephine Watt Case, who was born in 1870," is printed exactly "as it was given to me." Aller quotes Case, who wrote, "1 pound of steak. Get round steak, because it is the best for this. Pound the steak so that it will be tender for little children and those that don't have good teeth." Aller's only alteration is a "note" at the bottom of the instructions suggesting that vegetable shortening makes a "fine" substitution for lard.[81] The narrative suggests that Aller came to this recipe through archival research, rather than through inheritance. Though Aller shares no intimate network with Case, the transmission of Case's knowledge to Aller and her readers is direct and authentic. Aller as researcher presents the text in its most authentic state: as she found it in the archive.

Aller's citation narratives offer a model for acquiring culinary knowledge that can be replicated by almost anyone seeking authentic Southern culture. This appeals especially to travelers and visitors to the South, who seem to be Aller's target audience (as Aller is herself). Through travel, cooking, eating, and reading, anyone may become a part of the story of Southern foodways as the owner of authentic knowledge that has a verified provenance. Aller's explicit invocation of the reader emphasizes the reader as an authorized owner of this knowledge. Having purchased the book, the reader is instructed to take ownership of the recipes and customize them to his or her own tastes, convinced that the recipe's provenance and the researcher's ethos will certify the dish's authenticity for a performance of Southern and/or Appalachian identity.

Throughout *Cider Beans*, Aller presents herself as a researcher, collector, and experimenter, connected to a vast network of archives and food professionals. Aller's position as narrator, rather than innovator, offers a model of collaborative authorship that runs counter to the principles of copyright law. Aller makes no claims to the originality of the recipes; instead, her claim to intellectual property rights come from the act of curation and the literary expression that knits the collection together through headnotes. And yet, Aller's meticulous, consistent, and purposeful insistence on citing sources (an optional exercise, both by legal and industry standards) suggests that Aller prizes the innovation of recipes as a valid form of authorship requiring recognition. Giving credit to cooking professionals and archival sources validates the recipes in *Cider Beans, Wild Greens, and Dandelion Jelly* as authentic Southern Appalachian cultural knowledge.

Validating Readers as Sources and Online Networks as Methods of Exchange

In the same way that the cookbooks described above rely on familial networks of inheritance and professional networks of research to obtain authentic recipes, the cookbooks examined in this section depend on networks of readers in online communities as a source. Recipe blogs may be a relatively recent invention of the twenty-first century, but they descend from a much longer tradition of magazines and other publishing entities soliciting recipes from readers. As a historical example, in the 1880s, Estelle Woods Wilcox and her husband, Alfred, were Minneapolis-based publishers of a successful household magazine, *The Housekeeper*. They used recipes from the magazine's readership to publish *Buckeye Cookery*, an expansion of a community cookbook celebrating the American centennial edited by Wilcox for the First Congregational Church in Marysville, Ohio, in 1876. The Wilcoxes continued to revise and publish *Buckeye Cookery* for nearly three decades. They even rebranded *Buckeye Cookery* under the title *The Dixie Cook-Book* and released it through an Atlanta-based publisher, L. A. Clarkson & Company, from 1883 to 1893, highlighting the contributions of Southern based readers in a special "Popular Dixie Dishes" section.[82] Even today, *Southern Living* magazine and cookbooks collect, publish, and cite reader contributions. *No Taste Like Home: A Celebration of Regional Southern Cooking and Hometown Flavor*, written by Kelly Alexander for *Southern Living*, includes recipes from "readers, chefs, and locals-done-good in each region" of the South. All contributors are cited. Chef and local celebrity recipes are accompanied by a quotation, a photo, and a short biography. Reader recipes are not so clearly marked. Recipes with the heading "A Recipe from a Local" are followed by a name and a location. For example, Dorothy Roberts of Hiawassee, Georgia, contributes recipes for "Butternut Squash Bake" and "Roasted Winter Squash."[83] Since Roberts is neither a chef nor a celebrity (so far as a Google search can be trusted), it is presumed that she is a reader. A recipe from Athens, Georgia, chef Hugh Acheson is given the same heading, "A Recipe from a Local," but the attribution makes his identity clear by calling him "Chef Hugh Acheson" and listing the name of his restaurant, Five & Ten.[84] In both magazine-related cookbooks, past and present, the editors use citations as an argument for the authenticity of their recipes. These citations are evidence that readers have a relationship with the magazine, and that the magazine can draw on a network of real people who really live in the South. The names of recipe contributors are not likely to be familiar to readers, but the presence of a named contributor connotes a personal authenticity. What matters most in these citations is location, suggesting that readers trust "a local" and a home cook to give them a recipe that will work and will accurately represent place in order to perform an authentic place-based identity.

Like cookbooks published by magazines, cookbooks based on blogs depend on a network of readers connected by digital subscriptions rather than postal ones. In *Will Write for Food*, Dianne Jacob offers "practical and realistic advice" for readers who "like to blog as a hobby" and want to learn "how to approach editors."[85] Jacob offers a full chapter on how to "Get Published with a Food Blog," including advice for turning a recipe blog into a cookbook. For Jacob, a blog is "quite simply . . . the easiest way to jump into being a food writer. Jump in and publish your first post within an hour." Without editorial "gatekeepers," bloggers can be fast, innovative, trendy, and fun.[86] But Jacob returns often to the key difference between blogs and other kinds of writing: audience response and interaction. Jacob writes of her own blog, "It's been so much fun to write whatever I like, and satisfying to get a response.... I've been delighted and amazed by the response and my new community online."[87] She describes a blog as "a conversation with readers" and a "platform" to give a writer "visibility to readers" and "move forward in your career." A blog with a readership demonstrates to potential publishers that the cookbook would also find a viable audience.[88] The defining feature of blogs and the cookbooks that come from them is interaction between writers and readers, a feeling of membership in a community. Citation narratives in cookbooks connected to blogs often emphasize this feeling of community, sharing credit with readers in a way that may both authenticate a recipe and authorize a writer.

Stacey Little's *The Southern Bite Cookbook* is based on his popular blog, SouthernBite.com. The cookbook combines some of the strategies of Porter and Aller but with a unique twenty-first-century online twist. Like Porter, Little invokes the family and the familial network as the source of his recipes. The cover claims that the book contains "more than 150 irresistible dishes from 4 generations of my family's kitchen." On the blog, Little describes himself as "a true Southerner coming from a long line of amazing cooks" whose goal is to provide blog followers with easy, "authentic" Southern recipes for busy families.[89] In addition, like Aller, Little also gets some of his recipes from outside the family network. Little's collection is different, however, in that many of his recipes come from a digital network of readers who are connected to Little only through the shared digital discourse of the blog. The relationship between Little and his contributors is not unprecedented. Many cookbooks, especially those compiled and published by magazines, often include recipes solicited by the magazine publishers and contributed voluntarily by readers. The citation narrative "pays" the contributor for their intellectual property in the form of cultural capital, simultaneously providing evidence of the cookbook writer's power as a central hub of a network of cooks and validating this method of solicitation and contribution without remuneration as an authentic and fair means of recipe movement.

Little is unique among the cookbook writers in this chapter because he also freely innovates and improvises with the recipes he receives from contributors. Though Little does want to be recognized as a creative cook, he also is heavily invested in arguing for the authenticity of his recipes as traditional and historical. Little negotiates a balance between these two rhetorical purposes through citation narratives that clearly separate Little's innovations from those of his family members and reader-contributors. Little's ethos benefits from being a powerful part of a knowledgeable network and an innovator in his own right. The citation narrative demonstrates both of these characteristics in a single paragraph.

Authenticity is a central and recurring term in Little's cookbook and on his blog. Little defines authentic Southern food as "the resourceful use of local, fresh ingredients," but he does not shy away from using convenience foods like frozen or canned vegetables or "condensed cream of chicken soup."[90] Little explains in the introduction to the cookbook that he started the blog, *Southern Bite*, to "share my restaurant reviews and musings," but after posting a recipe increased the traffic to the blog, Little made it "one of his life's missions to document the recipes that have been passed down through the generations." The blog and the cookbook, Little says, are his way "to share my family's food with the world."[91] Like Porter, Little is interested in preserving the inheritance of authentic culinary knowledge innovated by previous generations; however, unlike Porter, Little consistently asserts himself as coauthor and innovator as he simultaneously cites others for their authorship and innovation.

The narratives cite a textual contributor, but they also describe how Little has changed the recipe to make it his own. In most of the narratives, Little gives credit to a family member or a blog reader who gave him *a* recipe, but he will make clear that the recipe *as it is presented* has been significantly changed, enough to make it Little's creative work and intellectual property. Still, Little shares ownership with the contributor explicitly. At the end of the book's introduction, Little thanks his readers, family, and friends for their loyalty to his blog, arguing, "This is *our* book. It's not just my work; it's the collective work of the folks who came before me, the readers who have submitted recipes, and the folks that came before them too."[92] Little's narrative suggests that no recipe is truly original knowledge and that there are always innovators who "came before" and will come after. Though Little demonstrates a commitment to ethical citation by giving credit to others, the headnotes also suggest that Little's ethos as New Southern home cook is supported by his connection to a wide digital and familial network of innovators who "came before."

Little distinguishes between recipes that come from readers and those that he has innovated himself or inherited from family in page design and narrative form. Recipes contributed by readers are formatted to be immediately and visually distinguished from other recipes. Each recipe contributed by a reader is marked by what looks like an old recipe card at the top of the page announcing "Reader Recipe," followed by the title, the reader's name, and the city of residence or origin. The headnote then describes the relationship between Little and the contributor and a narrative of how the recipe came to be. Some head-notes describe the changes that Little has made to the recipe.

The headnote for Donya Mullins's recipe for "Slow Cooker Party Mix," the first reader recipe in the cookbook, does not give evidence of alteration: "This recipe is from one of my blogger friends, Donya. She took the standard recipe for a party mix and adapted it for the slow cooker to save a little time. This method frees you up if you're scrambling last minute to get things ready for a party or get-together."[93] The narrative makes clear that Little is a member of a network of bloggers. As Little validates the authenticity of another Southern blogger's creations, he simultaneously offers evidence of his own authenticity as a peer. Mullins is credited with the innovation; she "adapted" the standard recipe to make it novel. And though it appears that Little shares the recipe as it came to him, the message is that the innovations of bloggers, like Mullins — and by extension, like Little — are not threats to authenticity. The citation narrative serves to validate the online network as an authentic community and its inno-vators as authentic knowledge makers.

Little's editorial presence is more prominent in the reader recipe "Mississippi Roast." Little explains in the headnote that Vicki Kleppelid of Ridgeland, Mississippi, sent the recipe to him after her sister-in-law made it for her. The provenance of the recipe moved through familial networks first before moving online. The headnote provides evidence of Little's innovation on the recipe: "I even strained the broth in the crockpot and reduced it down on the stovetop in a saucepan to make a delicious gravy." The recipe itself does not give instructions for this step, suggesting that the text of the recipe — the ingredients list and action steps — are as the reader submitted them, but Little models for the cook-book reader how he has innovated and altered the recipe, and how the cook-book reader might do the same. Little offers another innovation for the recipe, suggesting in a call-out box at the bottom of the page that the roast could be served in a recipe titled "Weeknight Leftovers: Pot Roast Po-Boy Sandwich."[94] Though Kleppelid is credited as a contributor and her sister-in-law's recipe text appears to be transmitted unchanged, Little offers two options for innovation that suggest that a recipe as a text is not the exclusive property of its innovator. In *At My Grandmother's Knee*, Porter's narratives suggest that the oldest form of the recipe is the best, and that cooks should strive to make their products look and taste as much like the grandmother's as possible. In *The Southern Bite Cookbook*, by contrast, Little implies that recipes are ever-evolving, welcoming the cook's improvisation and innovation. The citation narrative models this attitude toward recipes as intellectual property.

Another reader recipe offers a good example of Little's stance on the muta-bility of recipes. Even before the recipe for "Sausage and Cheese Pie" has come to the contributor, Dru Lovett, Little explains that it is "one of those recipes that has been passed around, altered, and updated."[95] The informal movement of the recipe demonstrates the freedom that cooks have to alter the recipes that come to them and the authenticity of the informal network of exchange. Though the recipe is widely available, each cook's version is authentic because it reflects that cook's particular tastes and creativity. Similarly, Little's recipe for Brunswick stew also shows evidence of having been "passed around, altered, and updated," which serves to increase its authenticity through provenance and creative innovation. The headnote reads:

> Everyone has a different recipe for this hearty stew, sometimes called Camp Stew. My version is a combination of a recipe from a famed lunch-room lady from Luverne, Alabama, and another family recipe that is gen-erations old. The type of meat varies by recipe. Some include chicken, pork, beef, and even wild game.[96]

Little credits three sources for the recipe provided here. First, there is the abstract ideal recipe that everyone has access to as members of the same cul-ture. Brunswick stew (as the previous chapter illustrated at length) has an active presence in the Southern imagination, and while the particulars of the formula may vary, a communally owned Brunswick stew recipe exists prior to Little's text. Second, Little acknowledges a debt to a text from an unnamed "famed lunchroom lady" from Alabama. He does not provide enough information to identify her, nor does he mention her more specifically on the blog. The spe-cifics that he does provide highlight both her Southern-ness and her expertise in cooking. It is significant, however, that she is not a "chef" but a "lunchroom lady," a professional food service position that evokes both nostalgia and simple home-style cooking. The third source, an inherited family recipe text, similarly authenticates the recipe as "generations old" and suitable for cooking at home. Despite these three citations, Little still claims ownership of the recipe that is provided in the cookbook. "My version is a combination," Little writes. The act of combining received textual sources with communally held ideals is a valid act of authorship that allows Little to take ownership of the culinary knowledge he is sharing.

Little demonstrates in these citation narratives that while recipes are neces-sarily derivative, they can still be authentic *because* of the networks from which they derive and the organic and inevitable creativity of individual cooks. The provenance, then, is not a list of owners who have maintained the integrity of the recipe, but a list of owners who have each left an individual imprint on the recipe. Integrity and faithfulness to tradition are not the primary indicators of authenticity in these narratives. Rather, authenticity extends from the movement of recipes in networks — familial and digital — and the innovations that accrue as the recipes move. Little's introduction and headnotes suggest that the continuous movement and joint ownership of recipes are inevitable, and that recording the movement of the recipe invites the reader to join the network of owners and innovators.

Validating Archetypes as Sources and Experience as a Method of Exchange

The final cookbook examined in this chapter is in a category of cookbooks unlike many others. While the most literary cookbooks tend to have much in common with autobiography, memoir, and literary nonfiction, *Y'all Come Over: A Celebration of Southern Hospitality, Food, and Memories* by Betsy Caldwell and Amy Lyles Wilson (2013), situates its recipes in relationship to short, fictional narratives. *Y'all Come Over* follows on a successful formula Caldwell and Lyles have perfected in two previous collaborative efforts, *Bless Your Heart: Saving the World One Covered Dish at a Time* (2010) and *You Be Sweet: Sharing Your Heart One Down-Home Dessert at a Time* (2012).[97] All three books are divided into sections based on entertaining occasions, most of them events connected directly to sterotypical Southern experiences, including Fourth of July parties, college football game day, Sunday dinner with the preacher, and church potlucks. The narratives suggest that the authentic sources of Southern culinary knowledge are characters in the form of Southern archetypes, and the authentic movement of these recipes is through essential Southern experiences.

The pattern of stories and recipes is the same in all three cookbooks. At the beginning of each chapter is a two-page spread with a fictional narrative about the citizens of Luckettville, a small Southern town "so Podunk" that the new preacher "couldn't even find it on an old Rand McNally atlas, and you can forget about GPS."[98] Each narrative follows one fictional citizen of Lucketville, usually female, preparing to entertain at least one guest for a meal. The recipes for the dishes described in the story are provided in addition to several other recipes suitable for the occasion. The fictional narratives often identify a fictional recipe innovator; one of the characters from Lucketville has created the recipe. However, the recipe headnotes often contradict the fictional narrative, identifying another real-life contributor. I argue that Caldwell and Wilson use this citation strategy to emphasize the origin of the recipes in Southern culture at large over their origin with any individual in particular. As the authors seek to capture the mind of the South in fiction and food, it matters less who innovated the recipe than how it is involved in the practice of authentic Southern identity. In other words, the provenance — the narrative of a recipe's creation and movement through networks — is the primary factor in determining authenticity. Even if the documented provenance is fictional, it reflects the real movement of recipes in typical Southern communities.

It is clear from the first words of the introduction to *Y'all Come Over* that the authors are invested in representing the authentic Southern experience: "In the South, it seems there is no shortage of reasons for throwing open your doors and inviting friends and family over for a bite to eat."[99] The entertaining occasions and recipes included are meant to reflect the customs and foodways of the South as a whole. The narrative for "Family Fireworks" captures the Southern custom of Fourth of July barbecue celebrations and some comic Southern stereotypes like old women in "loud clothing" and big earrings, alcohol-free punches for "a God-fearing yet fun-loving family," and the characteristic Southern humor: "Even if you pay your taxes in full, love your neighbor as yourself, and limit your swearing to two curse words a week, sometimes bad things do happen to good people. 'Even God blinks,' Irma says, 'so you might as well be prepared.'"[100] The foods for the fireworks party are recognizable dishes from the Southern canon (barbecue chicken, smoked pork, deviled eggs, rum punch) and a few with a twist on canonical ingredients (barbecue peanuts, corn and roasted peanut salad).[101] In the narrative, each of these dishes is credited to a contributor from the fictional Muller family. The recipes appear in the pages following the narrative, and while a few of the headnotes for this section identify a real contributor, they all emphasize the regional origin of the recipes. In the note for "Blackberry Lemonade," the author explains, "Blackberry picking in the South has got to be one of the hottest and hardest activities there is. But this drink is so delicious it makes up for it."[102] Blackberry picking and lemonade drinking are identified as quintessentially Southern experiences. Similarly, "Summer Peach Cheesecake Ice Cream" is based on seasonal Southern ingredients: "Fresh peaches in the South are at their best around the Fourth of July. This is one great way to take advantage of them."[103] "Southern Fried Dill Pickles" have no named contributor, but the title sufficiently marks the recipe's origin in the South. Though Joe Fowler is identified as "the king of hush puppies in our circle," it is not explicitly clear that the printed recipe is his original text. Instead, the headnote emphasizes that "Hush Puppies" are familiar and popular at fish fries, another essential Southern tradition.[104] The fictional citations demonstrate that identifying the innovator of a recipe is a norm expected in cookbooks, but that in the end, it matters less that an individual created it than that anyone could employ that recipe in their performance of Southern identity. Blackberry lemonade, peach ice cream, fried pickles, and hush puppies belong to the Southern collective identity. The citation narratives in this chapter suggest that even in the cases where real individuals contribute recipe text, the real creators of these dishes are found in collective Southern culture and experiences.

The second chapter of *Y'all Come Over* similarly demonstrates the origin of recipes in essential Southern experiences. "A House Divided" is one of those "only in the South" stories of a married couple, Cammy and Toby, who are on opposite sides of an ages-old college football rivalry between Ole Miss and Mississippi State. They have found peace in their relationship by sharing cooking duties on game day. Cammy's contributions are based on "her favorite foods from childhood" with "her own spin on them." She makes "her trademark muffuletta sandwich," sweet potato chips, and "Touchdown Brownies," while Toby makes "Armchair Quarterback Soup," bacon-wrapped barbecue shrimp, and rhubarb cake.[105] The recipes and headnotes emphasize the collective Southern experience. Cammy's sweet potato chips are titled "Deep-Fried, Deep-South Sweet Potato Chips" with the one-word headnote, "Addictive!"[106] Cammy's individual contribution (fictional though it may be) is subsumed in the dish's Southern origins. Her muffuletta sandwich, too, is identified in the headnote as a Louisiana delicacy as well as her fictional creation.[107] The recipe text for Toby's "Armchair Quarterback Soup," Caldwell explains, was actually contributed by "a gentleman from Mississippi" that she and her husband met in San Antonio. While the headnote gives credit for the recipe to an individual, the story is evidence to support the claim that "everybody knows that Southerners are friendly."[108] The headnote suggests that while the recipe might be the innovation of an individual, it belongs to Southerners as a part of the common Southern experience. The fictional citation narrative emphasizes that authentic Southern recipes come out of essential Southern experiences and characters.

Throughout *Y'all Come Over*, the citation narratives are consistent with the book's overarching agenda for representing a collective Southern identity. Even though the narratives suggest that the recipes originate with a fictional individual, the titles of recipes like "Old-Fashioned Southern Fried Okra" and "Honey Brined Southern Fried Chicken" identify origins in Southern culture as a whole.[109] The shorter headnotes emphasize their Southern origins, too, describing salmon croquettes as "an old-fashioned Southern classic" and claiming that "all Southern women have several frozen salad recipes on hand" like "Frozen Apricot Fruit Salad."[110] The overall argument is that individual contributors do deserve credit for their innovations but that the ur-recipes belong to

all Southerners. The specific individuals responsible for innovations in knowledge are not as important as the cultural group that draws power from that
knowledge, employing it in the interest of the culture at large. Caldwell and
Wilson go through the motions of attribution by naming fictional innovators
and authors of recipes as they play with the conventions of the contemporary
cookbook, but the message of *Y'all Come Over* is that recipes are authorless and
originless in the traditional sense; rather, they have a thousand authors and a
thousand origins. The individual contributor does not argue as effectively for
authenticity as the story of the dish's origins in Southern culture at large.

Implications: Toward a Conclusion

This chapter outlines one of the basic premises of this project — namely, that
the origin narrative is an optional rhetorical exercise purposefully chosen to
have a specific effect on the audience, consistent with an overall rhetorical message of the book as a whole. The four categories of books examined here have
agendas regarding the value and authenticity of recipes based on the identities
of the individuals who contributed them and the methods by which they move
through informal networks to formal publication. Each style of citation narrative makes a different argument about who can create authentic knowledge
and how that knowledge moves in a culture. Faye Porter is invested in crediting the Grandmother figure with authentic culinary knowledge and valorizing
the process of inheriting culinary knowledge through experiential learning at
Grandmother's knee. Joan Aller validates the culinary knowledge of the professional cook through her network of bed-and-breakfast cooks and owners.
She gathers her knowledge through research and experimentation, empowering
the cookbook reader to bring her or his own culinary knowledge to the recipes
provided. Intellectual engagement with recipes through research and reading is
valued as highly as the experiential learning that Porter describes. Stacey Little
is invested in equating the familial network of recipe exchange with that of
the online community. The narratives in *Southern Bite* suggest that recipes
are not sacred documents to be passed unchanged, but instead are organic, living documents that change naturally as they pass through the hands of many
owners. Patsy Caldwell and Amy Lyles Wilson eschew the formal citation in
favor of fictional narratives, arguing that the culinary knowledge of the South
does not originate with any particular innovator or belong to any particular
practitioner. Instead, the authentic knowledge of Southern food grows out of
essential Southern experiences and is held among all members of the identity
group through shared experience and collective memory. The narratives of each

book and their formulation of the origins and movement of culinary knowledge fix the meaning of the recipe by determining who can exercise power to shape a culture, to open and close membership in the culture, to define and legitimate authentic cultural practice.

Though these cookbooks give examples of the power of narrative to interpret the meaning of recipes, it is important to recognize that the citation narrative is indeed a stopgap measure, not only because it fills a gap between laws and norms but also because it is a temporary fix. Narratives are in some ways truly inadequate when it comes to assigning ownership and giving credit. The narrative can be skipped, simply not read, and the provenance is broken. The narrative can be cut off when copying. Time itself can erode an origin narrative from its recipe. A better story can supplant the old one. The citation narrative is not a permanent solution to the perceived problem of the lack of legal protection for recipe innovations.

However, I would not be so quick to advocate for any change in the law. In fact, the erasure of a prior innovator by an author could be read as a subversive act of resistance to oppressive power. In her cookbook *Hallelujah! The Welcome Table*, Maya Angelou writes about copying recipes from the newspaper with her grandmother, whom she called Momma. Once a month, the local newspaper printed a "women's page" with recipes submitted by readers. The newspaper printed the names of the white women who contributed recipes. Angelou writes that "Momma knew all the names and the maids who worked for them."[111] This may be a vague suggestion that the maids might have been the real innovators and unacknowledged contributors of these recipes. Momma would copy the recipes from a borrowed paper — presumably without the white contributors' names still attached — and then she would cook the recipes for her family. The copied recipe became a family recipe: "Momma's version of wilted lettuce."[112] Angelou herself writes the story and shares the recipe, titled "Wilted Lettuce," with no contributor's name attached.[113] There is nothing especially transgressive about copying a recipe from the newspaper. But the copying of recipes takes on added significance for Angelou, who notes that though the recipe moved only one physical mile from the home of the woman who contributed it to Angelou's home, it crossed an ideological chasm between "the white part of town" and "the black area, which was still called the Quarters."[114] To emphasize the breadth and depth of that divide, Angelou titles this chapter, "Recipes from Another Country."[115] Angelou remembers wondering about the woman who contributed the recipe: "Would she think that a black grandmother was feeding her grandchildren the same dish she was offering to her privileged family? Would she resent the grandmother or just shrug her shoulders and say, 'Let them help themselves'?"[116] Angelou senses that copying the recipe is somehow taking power from the privileged, and if they knew it was happening, they might not approve. Her action of printing that recipe without a citation narrative may be an act of claiming power over knowledge that had been unjustly taken away. While my Grandma Taylor may have been given credit for inventing angel biscuits by grandchildren and great-grandchildren who didn't know any better, Momma *takes* credit. Angelou's narrative suggests that Momma's act of copying and collecting is a consciously subversive act of erasure, breaking the chain of inheritance, interrupting the record of provenance, and taking full ownership of the recipe as its new author.

The free movement of recipes outside of intellectual property law facilitates both constant innovation and the establishment of a canon of recipes. Because the alteration of a recipe is fair use (three changes makes it yours), there is almost no danger of litigation. Real innovation occurs when practitioners are not afraid of being sued or of having to sue to protect their intellectual property. At the same time, the freedom to share, exchange, and publish existing recipes (with or without citation) guarantees that a canon of tried and true, reliable recipes are widely available. It is the unprotected status of recipes that allows for them to quickly move through a culture and become canonized among a community of cooks. There is no cuisine without many practitioners simultaneously practicing and perfecting the same dishes. Sidney Mintz argues that the defining characteristic of a cuisine is plenty of cooks and diners arguing about the variations in recipes: "I think a cuisine requires a population that eats that cuisine with sufficient frequency to consider themselves experts on it. They all believe and care that they believe, that they know what it consists of, how it is made, and how it should taste."[117] What makes a cuisine, in Mintz's definition, is a cognitive awareness and public discourse on the subject. The fact that people talk about the proper preparation of a dish, and that everyone feels they are part owners of that knowledge, makes the dish part of the cuisine.[118]

The fact that the citation narrative has become so conventional is a sign that the cooking instruction industry does recognize the recipe as authentic culinary knowledge and intellectual property. Citation narratives, though informal and optional, do seem to suggest that the recipe text is not mere lists of instructions, works of utility, or derivative and unoriginal. Rather, the citation narrative indicates that the recipe is thought of in the industry as the "significant literary expression" of an individual author, working in concert with visible and invisible collaborators. The system of citation in narrative is not without flaws. What exists now is a kind of gift economy where recipe innovators are paid in cultural capital as often as they are paid in economic capital. The system favors those who already have a surfeit of cultural capital in the form of access to publication, facilitating their exchange of that cultural capital for (admittedly sometimes very small sums of) cash. As a white male writer, Little is a privileged editor who draws on the capital of others to support his claims of innovation. Porter and Aller, too, have a measure of privilege as authors that they use to highlight the contributions of other women innovators who are not professional writers.

While Scafidi acknowledges that "an assertion of authenticity may compensate" for the lack of exclusive rights, she also warns that a system that does not protect cultural products leaves marginalized cultures vulnerable to appropriation by hegemonic institutions.[119] The absence of a clear and uniform way of establishing ownership benefits those with most power already and ignores those without power. While Bryant Terry has access to the same kind of narrative strategy, he uses it far less often than white writers like Little, Aller, and Porter. He may have some privilege as a public figure and author of multiple cookbooks to share capital with the chefs and authors who inspire him, but the citation narrative is not the best choice for his rhetorical goals. As a writer of color attempting to represent a globally inflected African American cuisine, he gains the most ethos by connecting himself to a global and historical narrative that shares credit with a diasporic culture rather than to a single contributor. Terry is working against a tradition that withheld credit from black cooks and innovators as a group; his method of arguing authenticity similarly gives credit to groups rather than individuals. The citation narrative is a move toward formalizing the process of giving credit, but as the advice from *Recipes into Type* suggests, citing celebrity chefs still "means something" more to readers than citing ordinary innovators.[120]

The citation narrative is a strategy for arguing authenticity that reveals the collaborative nature of cookbook writing and recipe making, and the investigation of cookbook authorship practices could contribute much to rhetoric and composition studies. This extended description of citation narratives and copyright laws is not to argue that recipes need more, or less, or even different protections. Instead, I argue that the status of recipes under the law, particularly the law's vision of recipe authorship, simply does not match the scholarship on recipes or the practice of recipe writing in the public sphere. Woodmansee argues in "On the Author Effect: Recovering Collectivity" that the notion of The Author, "an individual who is the sole creator of the unique 'works' the originality of which warrants their protection under laws of intellectual property," may be codified by law, but it "is a relatively recent invention" and it "does not closely reflect contemporary writing practices."[121] Woodmansee argues that there is far more collaboration in contemporary writing practice than the law would suggest. In fact, Biagioli, Jaszi, and Woodmansee argue in *Making and Unmaking Intellectual Property* that "all new cultural production is inevitably not only collaborative but derivative."[122] Cookbooks, recipes, and other cooking instructions are not only inevitably collaborative but also often transparently so, using the evidence of their collaboration to authenticate alternative forms of innovation, authorship, learning, and teaching. The cookbooks examined in this chapter use narratives of a recipe's provenance to demonstrate a variety of networks for the movement of recipes and a variety of attitudes toward the recipe as text. Together, these cookbooks argue that authentic culinary knowledge is circulated rather than fixed, and that authentic creativity may not follow the same model of originality codified in intellectual property law. A cookbook writer's ethos is built on membership in networks of culinary knowledge.

The citation narrative is a method of network building that is intimately tied to personal identity. The following chapter takes up the question of originality and ethos again through an investigation of chef-authored cookbooks of New Southern restaurants and haute cuisine. These celebrity chefs are expected to make original innovations on classic and canonical Southern foods, suitable for sale and consumption in high-end restaurants. Headnotes accompanying these recipes must argue that the recipes provided are simultaneously authentic, with a solid reputation in the South, and original, bearing the creative stamp of a unique chef. Chef-authored cookbooks, like the ones examined in the next chapter, are too focused on the present and future trends for historical narratives to be useful. The chef's investment in creativity and originality means that the writer cannot afford to undermine his or her ethos as innovator by too often giving credit to another contributor for recipe text. Instead, the authors of these recipe headnotes (not always assumed to be the chefs themselves) must focus on the chef's person — Southern identity, experience, and credentials — in order to convince audiences that the chef is qualified to improvise with traditions without losing authenticity. Where this chapter focused on narratives that told the provenance of a recipe, the following chapter will explore narratives that tell about the pedigree of the chef.

—CHAPTER THREE—

PERSONAL NARRATIVES

Certifying the Chef to Represent Cosmopolitan South

> I've eaten some amazing food and seen some incredible places, but
> eventually I long to get back down South. I yearn for my people and
> my home, and especially for its food. It's me. It's a Southern thing.
> —Donald Link, *Down South: Bourbon, Pork, Gulf
> Shrimp & Second Helpings of Everything*[1]

> Can you separate a Bolognese sauce from the Italian
> arm that stirs the simmering pot?
> —Edward Lee, *Smoke and Pickles: Stories and
> Recipes from a New Southern Kitchen*[2]

I FOUND OUT THAT TEXAS, my birthplace, might not be in "the South" when I was in college taking a class in Southern literature. I was writing my term paper about Eudora Welty, and I had checked out from the library a book about death or funerals in the South, or something. I can remember almost nothing about it except that it combined in its analysis the works of Welty, William Faulkner, and Larry McMurtry — arguably Texas's most famous author. In the introduction, the author justified including McMurtry even though he mostly wrote Westerns and Texas was, this author suggested, not *really* in the South.

This was news to me. I was born and raised in the Texas panhandle on a cotton farm, in a cotton farming town. The most significant landmark of my childhood, the one thing that told me I was almost home, was a cotton gin, still functioning even now. I grew up in a town that was, and probably still is, racially segregated. Black families, almost without exception, lived quite literally across the tracks from the rest of the town. In my town, population 1,972, we were all working poor. My great-grandmother, Frankie Welty, who died in 1990, was enamored of all things Scarlett O'Hara and told a story of her family's own Tara, irrevocably lost. She also told an apocryphal story about some ancestor who was determined to go and fight in the Civil War. His wife did not want him to go. She dumped a plate of hot food on his lap in an argument. He immediately stood up, mounted his horse, and went straight to war to defend his honor and manhood against his wife and Northern aggression, and never returned. By the time I learned that Texas might not be the South, I had already decided that I was related to Eudora Welty. My mother's maiden name was Welty. Surely we were descended from the same set of Swiss brothers that Welty described on the first page of *One Writer's Beginnings*.[3]

Without really thinking about it before the age of twenty, I identified myself as a Southerner. I was a Southern Baptist, and I was studying at a Southern Baptist university. I do not remember anyone ever asking me to identify myself as a Southerner or not, but I remember that when I read that some people did not count Texas as Southern, I felt it as a personal challenge — a challenge to my person. So a few years later, when I was writing my master's thesis about Eudora Welty's short stories, I wrote in the introduction how very personally I identified with her and her world. Not only was I probably related to her (yes, I've said it three times now in print. If I turn around three times and throw salt over my shoulder, it will be true), but her people spoke the language of my people. When Welty wrote, "We in the South have grown up being narrators," I counted myself among storytellers.[4] It mattered to me that I should be able to call myself Southern. And I thought that it mattered to my argument in my thesis that my audience should know that I call myself Southern.

And here, in this present volume, I have done this identity work over and over again through story. In this analysis of narrative strategies, I would be remiss not to turn the scholar's gaze to my own narration. Not only have I outlined my claims to a Southern identity, but I also have outlined my connection to Southern food through stories of my birthplace, my childhood, my ancestry and family networks. In the preface, I narrated myself into a network of writing and cooking women in the South, inheritor of their texts and their culinary knowledge. In the introduction, I used my personal pronoun to show that I was so intimately acquainted with the cookbook genre that I could adopt its conventions for my own purposes. This move was a badge of my professional identity, and, as introductions do, this one narrated the development of my reading and thinking. I had to forgo the personal narrative opening in chapter

1 in part because (and now I hate to admit it) I have no personal relationship to Brunswick stew. We don't eat it in Texas. The first time I made it was while writing that chapter. I've only eaten it one other time, in a fast food barbecue chain restaurant in North Carolina. To reveal this personal *in*experience, at that moment, would be to reveal the fragility of my Southern-ness. Chapter 1 of a book about Southern authenticity is no place for such a revelation.

My narrative at the opening of chapter 2 is the longest in the book. Ostensibly, like the narrative that opens this chapter, it serves as an introduction to a subject, the practice of recipe exchange and citation. But the narrative is also personal. It narrates my personal memory, but more importantly, it is a story about my person, my personality. It certifies that I am an insider in the two communities I'm critiquing in this work: Southerners and food writers. I purposefully chose to narrate a story about biscuits, a canonical Southern food, to connect myself to Southern foodways. I described myself as a researcher and food writer, both curious and ethical. And then I admitted myself guilty of the same sin I was critiquing in this book and in that chapter: the selection of the narrative that most closely meets my rhetorical needs for authenticity, not necessarily the one that most closely matches reality.

And here I am doing it all over again. I needed to convince you, again, that I am a Southerner, even if my birthplace is on the margins of the South. This makes me qualified to comment on Southern-ness. Note, too, the markers of Southern distinction I've chosen to deploy: agricultural economy (specifically, cotton), small rural towns, segregation, working class values and poverty, great-grandmothers with Old South nostalgia, storytelling, a claim to Southern ancestry, Southern Baptists. I've needed to certify myself as Southern by selecting the version of the South that aligns best with my experience. But I also needed to personally align myself with the people I'll be critiquing in a moment who also use stories about themselves as evidence of their authenticity. We all have a need to establish our ethos in order to make arguments: *I am a writer you can trust. I am qualified to make these arguments. This story is the certificate of my authenticity.*

The Personal Narrative

This chapter examines a class of narratives that I'm calling personal narratives. While personal narratives do often turn up in recipe headnotes, they do most of their authenticating work in the longer textual elements of introductions, prefaces, and narrative interludes. I define the personal narrative in this chapter as a narrative that focuses on the authenticity of the individual chef-author, telling a story of that creator's experience or memory that will prove that the recipes created by that individual are authentic because of the creator's identity. The personal narrative is one that suggests that the recipes provided in this book are authentic because they come from an authentic source; the person providing the recipes is a certified creator or innovator of Southern culinary knowledge, licensed by his or her experience or identity. Personal narratives make the argument that who is cooking matters almost as much as what is being cooked or how.

The headnote and narrative elements of cookbooks are the author's claim to authorial identity and originality. While the voice and language of the recipe itself is purposefully standardized for easy reading, the headnote and introductions are opportunities for the cookbook writer to demonstrate his or her unique authorial identity, personality, and voice.[5] This is especially important for the chef-author who is marketing a very personal cuisine. Rather than representing the whole of the canon of Southern cooking — as, perhaps, John Egerton's *Southern Food* or Damon Fowler's *Classical Southern Cooking* have done — the chef-authored books examined in this chapter aim to present a one-of-a-kind experience, the kind of Southern food that is *originally* theirs, available exclusively at their restaurants and in the pages of their books.[6] Here, again, lies a central tension in New Southern cuisine: the speakers in the narratives need to prove simultaneously that their recipes are Southern (connected to long-standing traditions of a distinct community) and that they are New (connected to the original creativity and unique experiences of a single person). The person and personality of the innovator is of primary importance in determining the value of the recipe.

In some ways, this focus on the person of the innovator is a means to resist the cultural violence that conversations about authenticity can create. In her 2004 article for *Food and Foodways*, "Authentic or Not, It's Original," Meredith Abarca argues that labeling a recipe or dish as "authentic" discourages any further improvisation or innovation with that recipe, marking "other versions as questionable and consequently dismiss[ing] them" as not "real."[7] Here, Abarca is discussing ethnic cuisines whose authenticity is being judged and evaluated by cultural outsiders. Whether the label of authenticity comes from a cultural insider or outsider, the effect is a cultural violence, essentializing a people group and cutting off future growth and development.[8] Abarca defends the rights of cultural insiders to receive the food traditions of their forebears, filter those recipes through their own experiences, and add their original creative powers to the development of their own cultures. This is a resistance to culinary colonizers who prefer to see "authentic" cuisines as unchanging products of the past rather than dynamic cultures of the present.[9] Abarca calls for "a paradigm that addresses originality rather than . . . authenticity," that would allow writers and cooks to speak for themselves and not for their cultural groups: "To speak of original rather than authentic," Abarca argues, "the production always belongs to the person who creates it," which prevents the closure of cultural borders and "opens the door to cross-cultural, cross-generational dialogues."[10] Where conversations about authenticity can close off possibilities and exclude all but the narrowest of identities, a focus on originality allows for multiplicities, demolishes hierarchies, and empowers marginalized voices.

Certainly, the chef-authors of New Southern cuisine wish to be read as original and as owners of their innovations. Edward Lee, in *Smoke and Pickles*, introduces readers to "my cuisine" and "my culinary voice."[11] In a two-page spread of white, handwritten-style script, isolated on a plain black background, Lee declares in all capital letters: "WHAT I COOK IS WHO I AM."[12] The recipes in the book are an extension of Lee's personality, experiences, and identity. Similarly, Sean Brock and John Currence each open their cookbooks with a section titled "My Manifesto."[13] The manifesto sections lay out the driving principles behind each chef's personal culinary vision and practice. Brock goes a step further by encouraging readers to improvise with the recipes in *Heritage* to make their own cuisines. Of the twenty-two points in Brock's manifesto (all addressed as imperatives to the subject "you"), half are about making personal choices in the kitchen based on "your" identity and experience. Brock tells readers to "cook with soul — but first, get to know your soul," "cook from the hip," and "listen to your tongue; it's smart."[14] Brock instructs the reader directly: "I want you to find and gather ingredients in your own region and make these recipes your own."[15] Cooking should flow from your identity (your soul, instinct, taste) and reflect your geography. Novelty and innovation are not hindrances to authenticity; rather, novelty and innovation are what make the recipes valuable to readers as culinary capital that they can use to distinguish themselves from other individuals and to distinguish Southern cooking from other cuisines.

Even though New Southern cookbooks emphasize originality and invention, they do not forget authenticity entirely. Within the pages can be found historical narratives that connect recipes to a distant past as evidence of authenticity. Brock includes a recipe for "The Charleston Light Dragoon Punch 1792," modified from "the original recipe" found "at the South Carolina Historical Society" and accompanied by a narrative about the militia's involvement in the Civil War.[16] New Southern cookbooks also include citation narratives that share credit as an argument for authentic Southern-ness, as I briefly introduced at the end of the last chapter. Currence describes tracking down the recipe for chocolate chess pie. According to Currence, the pie was served at Walker's, a "meat and three" diner in Farmville, Virginia, but made by women from a local church: "The local Baptist church ladies . . . were surprisingly forthcoming with their secret."[17] The narrative connects the recipe to "essential" Southern experiences (meat-and-three restaurants, Baptist church ladies selling pies, recipe exchange in a female network, the potential *not* to share outside the network) and identifies the source of the recipe (ordinary women) as authentic culinary knowledge makers.

Implicit in both kinds of narratives, however, is an underlying argument about the chef-author's ethos. Brock and Currence are both identified through their narratives as trustworthy sources enmeshed in authentic Southern knowledge and experiences. They are in touch with Southern history and networks of culinary knowledge. The personal narrative redirects attention away from arguing about the authenticity of the recipes — which readers are encouraged to see as new, original, and innovative — toward the authenticity of the chef-author-innovator. These chef-centric cookbooks have to explain to readers how the original innovations of a single chef still fit into a recognizable Southern cuisine. Though these cookbooks often use memories and personal narratives to establish the chef's ethos as original, the marketing of the cookbook is still pointed toward representing Southern regional cuisine at large. To maintain this balance — with originality and novelty on one hand and group membership and regional distinction on the other — chef-authors point to their own authenticity as chefs and Southerners as the foundation of their cuisines. If their original recipes flow from their distinct personhood — and if their personhood is distinctly Southern — then it follows that their recipes will represent authentic Southern cuisine and identities, useful for readers' performances.

The Chef-Auteur and the Chef-Authored Cookbook

The personal narrative performs several functions as a certificate of authenticity. First, the story establishes the geographic specificity of a chef, particularly one whose authenticity as a Southerner could be contested. Chefs like John Currence of New Orleans and Oxford, Mississippi, or Sean Brock of rural Appalachian Virginia and Charleston, South Carolina, are born and raised in uncontested Southern geographies, but chefs like Hugh Acheson, born in Ottawa, or Anne Stiles Quatrano, raised in Connecticut, have to more carefully construct for readers their status as cultural insiders.[18]

Furthermore, the personal narrative establishes the "personal connection" that Johnston and Baumann describe as a badge of authenticity: the "honest intentions" of chefs to innovate with Southern and global cuisines and their qualifications to do so without appropriating or compromising authenticity. As Johnston and Baumann argue, "Food is perceived as good and authentic when it is linked to specific creators with honest intentions — intentions that are not limited to making a quick buck."[19] The personal narrative assures readers that chef-innovators are not outsiders seeking profit from appropriation; rather, they are members of the in-group (even if adopted), disinterestedly giving away a piece of their authentic selves. Johnston and Baumann suggest that in foodie discourse, the "personal connection" strategy for establishing authenticity is largely centered on narrating the credentials of chef-creators: "The personalities used to signal artistry and authenticity were mainly chefs, mostly men, cooking in elite restaurants."[20] The chef is akin to "a sculptor and an *auteur* director" who can "create a piece of culinary art that can be juxtaposed against the art-less world of industrial food and chain restaurants."[21] Narrating the credentials of the chef adds an additional layer of exceptionalism; not only is the chef's creation juxtaposed to inauthentic industrial food, but it is also juxtaposed to anonymous American food, backward Southern food, and cheap bandwagon marketing. The person of the chef is qualified to produce food that is authentic *because* of its deviations from tradition, not in spite of them.

Finally, the personal narrative establishes the recipe as useful for performing an authentic Southern identity that is cosmopolitan, modern, and simultaneously locally, regionally, and globally minded. Because the chef-authors come from a variety of geographies, representing a variety of ethnicities, melding together a variety of influences and cuisines, readers are encouraged to see the boundaries of Southern identity as wide and inclusive enough to hold chefs like Virginia Willis (a white woman raised in Louisiana and Georgia, trained in France) and Edward Lee (a Korean-American man born in Brooklyn, working in Kentucky). Taken together, the personal narratives of New Southern cookbooks suggest that "the American South" might take in almost any body as "an adopted son," as it has "embraced" Lee.[22]

Personal narratives operate on the Burkean principle of identification as a basis for persuasion. The author invites readers to compare their experiences and identities with those of the author, ideally coming to the agreement that, indeed, the readers and the author all belong to the same group.[23] Reading these narratives can support readers' arguments for their own authentic Southern identities. I have argued throughout that authenticity is important because the recipes, when they are performed by a reader (through cooking, eating, imagining, and/or talking) will be in service of a performance of Southern identity. In personal narratives, writers lay out their credentials for authenticity, then ask readers to compare experiences, inviting those readers who might not immediately look like Southerners to imagine themselves as part of a larger, cosmopolitan Southern community. The narrative provides readers with a set of experiences and identity markers that they may use to craft their own personal narrative of Southern identity. I argue in this chapter that chef-authored cookbooks eschew historical narrative as an argument for authenticity, once again, in favor of a shorter and narrower past focused on individuals rather than the greater public experience. This generates a modern and postracial view of the South as a place where any reader might be made "a Southerner for a time," as Nathalie Dupree promised in *New Southern Cooking*.[24]

In this chapter, I turn my attention specifically to contemporary Southern cookbooks authored by professional chefs, which present a unique relationship between history, memory, and identity. Though the recipes and headnotes in chef-authored books are nearly identical in form and convention to those in cookbooks authored by bloggers, home cooks, historians, and other institutions, the restaurant-centric cookbook presents a rhetorical situation different from other kinds of published cookbooks. Bloggers like Stacey Little (see chapter 2) are as invested in the ethos of their network of readers as they are in their own credibility.[25] So, too, writers like Faye Porter in *At My Grandmother's Knee* are almost absent as characters themselves, emphasizing the reception of established knowledge over any kind of originality. In both cases, the product being sold in the book is largely independent of the author's identity.[26] By contrast, chef- and restaurant-centric cookbooks get their market value from the person, the personality, and the personal brand of the chef. Indeed, some of these cookbooks foreground the chef-author or restaurant in the title: *Paula Deen's Southern Cooking Bible*, *Frank Stitt's Southern Table*, *Besh's Big Easy*, *Bill Neal's Southern Cooking*, *The Pat Conroy Cookbook*, *Sweetie Pie's Cookbook*, *B. Smith Cooks Southern-Style*, *Hot and Hot Fish Club Cookbook* (Chris and Idie Hastings), *The Foster's Market Cookbook* (Sarah Foster), and *Poole's* (Ashley Christensen), to name a few.[27] This kind of cookbook functions very differently from a community fund-raiser cookbook, a memoir-style cookbook, or one of *Southern Living*'s many compilation cookbooks in content, rhetorical purpose, and authorial style.

On one level, the chef- and restaurant-centric cookbook functions as a kind of souvenir of a place and experience. As I paid my bill at John Currence's Big Bad Breakfast in Oxford, Mississippi, in the summer of 2014, I took home a souvenir T-shirt (featuring a block of lard with the message "Lard have mercy"), and later that day, in Square Books (not so far from Currence's City Grocery, where I planned to eat my dinner), I bought *Pickles, Pigs, and Whiskey*. The cover announces below Currence's name that he is the owner of City Grocery and "Oxford, Mississippi's Original Big Bad Chef." The inside cover is water-marked with the logos of Currence's Oxford enterprises: Bourè, Snackbar, The Main Event, City Grocery, and Big Bad Breakfast. The book is marketed on the reputation of Currence and his restaurants. On my coffee table, where the cookbook stayed for a few weeks before moving nearer to the kitchen for a different kind of public display, I could hand it to friends and family who had not shared my meals as evidence of the kind of experience I had. Where most souvenirs allow one to call up an abstract memory of a place, a cookbook as souvenir encourages a more concrete reliving of the dining experience through cooking and eating, perhaps preparing again the same meal one ordered at the restaurant. However, just as a snow globe of a city skyline cannot recreate the skyline proper, the recreation of recipes from a restaurant cookbook are almost always (perhaps purposefully) only a near replication. To truly recapture the restaurant experience requires the chef's skill and aura (a la Walter Benjamin), necessitating a return to the restaurant itself.

If there can be such a thing as an aspirational souvenir, the restaurant cook-book may be one. By this I mean that the reader imagines having been to the restaurant through the experience of reading the cookbook without having experienced the restaurant first. While a new hardback edition of any one of the cookbooks described in this chapter goes for thirty-five dollars or more, there is no doubt that a single dinner at Husk or City Grocery or Bacchanalia is likely to cost much more.[28] A restaurant cookbook, then, acts as a kind of fantasy literature, encouraging the reader to imagine experiences they may never have. Or, perhaps, it acts as an advertisement or travel guide, preparing the reader to make the trip to the place as an informed consumer. Similarly, the cookbook may act as a menu guide, introducing readers to the signature dishes, the can't-miss orders, through a more thorough and illustrated guide than the menu itself could ever provide. As a souvenir, the restaurant cookbook assumes and builds on an experience of a singular place (the restaurant) and a singular personality (the chef). Part of what is being marketed and sold in such a cookbook is an authentic personal experience with a one-of-a-kind place and a one-of-a-kind brand.

The collaborative nature of cookbook writing means that even though the narrative elements of the cookbook are written in the voice of the author, it is not always wise to conflate the author of the cookbook with the writer of a par-ticular headnote. In this chapter, I follow with what the rhetoric of the cook-book leads me to believe: that the name on the title page and the first-person voice of the narrative is the source of all the stories. To read in this way means ascribing motives and rhetorical choices to chef personalities even though, in practice, coauthors and ghostwriters might have made the writing choices that I find so significant on analysis. In the article "What It's Like to Be a Cookbook Ghostwriter" for *Bon Appetit,* Katherine Martinelli interviews some of the most well-known cookbook coauthors and ghostwriters, who describe the dramatically different levels of involvement a cowriter might have with a project:

> "In some books I do everything, I mean *everything,*" says [Melissa] Clark. "So the chef will be like, I want a recipe for pasta with anchovies and eggplant and that's all they do and I create the recipe and do everything. And then sometimes the chef will give me the perfect recipe and they are so articulate that they will give me the headnote."[29]

A chef might deliver a "perfect recipe" and an "articulate" headnote that the coauthor must simply take down like dictation. Or the coauthor might have to perform the task of both writer and recipe developer. All of this is to acknowledge that there are limits and caveats to my analysis of personal narrative here. I acknowledge that what appears on the page to be a chef speaking, telling a personal story about him- or herself in the first person, may actually be another writer creating or recreating a narrative about that chef. When I refer to Foster (who openly credits a coauthor) or to Ed Lee (who has some reputation as a writer who has published essays with *Gastronomica* and *Eater,* and who admits to being a "literature major" who "like[s] to see things in metaphors"[30]) as a chef-author, it is with the full knowledge that the same word might describe very different contributions to the text. In this chapter, as throughout the book, I will be using that word *author* as *auteur:* the chef's name is on the book as copyright holder and decision maker. The chef's personality is the product, whether the task of writing the personal narratives belongs to the chef or to a collaborator.

Place and Identity:
The Authentic Local Southerner and the Global South

One of the perceived threats to authenticity in Southern cooking is the potential loss of distinction in an increasingly global society and an increasingly global gourmet foodscape.[31] Much of New Southern cuisine, however, embraces an image of the South as a global community. In the past, these cookbooks argue, the South's diverse cuisine was influenced by slavery and immigration; today, the South is a cosmopolitan community, welcoming migration and taking influences from the best of international haute cuisine. As the academic field of

New Southern studies seeks to examine the US South in the global community, outside of North/South and black/white binaries, there is increasing scholarly attention to the ethnic diversity of the South. A 2008 collection of essays, *Other Souths: Diversity and Difference in the U.S. South*, attempts to recover the history of Southerners who do not fit into the "white stereotypes — bourbon-sipping gentlemen, delicate southern belles, and slow-witted rednecks."[32] These essays explore the understudied influence of groups and individuals in the South marginalized by race, class, or gender. Similarly, a 2013 collection of essays edited by Khyati Joshi and Jigna Desai recovers "the presence and significance of Asian Americans in the South."[33] As the editors explain,

> The figure of the Asian American disrupts popular discourses about the South in multiple ways: the Asian American demonstrates the shifting meaning of Black and White in a region in which this binary is writ large; is associated with foreignness and globalization in a space assumed to be parochial and isolated; and most generally, troubles more simple narratives of America's own amnesia and his/her presence.[34]

The presence of diverse bodies (and the *recognition* of the presence of diverse bodies) in the South changes the narrative of a monolithic and distinct Southern identity and places more emphasis on the person — the body and its ethnic identity. Both of these collections demonstrate that the representation of an authentic Southern identity in contemporary writing about the South must come to terms with the mobility and diversity of twenty-first-century bodies as well as the historic presence of marginalized figures in the region, opening up a more capacious definition of authentic Southern identity. The South is, and always has been, these narratives argue, more diverse than the public imagination would allow.

The field of Southern food studies has also turned its attention to historicizing diversity in the South. Essays in *The Larder: Food Studies Methods from the American South* explore the historic influence of Italian merchants on the New Orleans traditional muffuletta sandwich (Nystrom) and the growing influence of ethnic restaurants in the "salad bowl city" of Charlotte, North Carolina (Hanchett).[35] Similarly, Angela Jill Cooley argues in her essay about segregated public eating spaces that Greek restaurateurs resisted "the designs of the predominantly native-born, middle-class urban authorities" who enforced public segregation. The presence of proprietors who were non-Southern-born and outside of the black/white binary of segregation, Cooley writes, "ensured that public spaces where food was served . . . would represent more diverse venues where people of different backgrounds and life experiences would meet and intermingle."[36] In all three essays, the South of the past and the present is represented as always already diverse, cosmopolitan, and globalized. As John Egerton argues in *Southern Food*, food has proven to be a subject of study where the traditional binaries of Southern identity can be deconstructed, as "Southern food now unlocks the rusty gates of race and class, age and sex."[37] Through those gates may march a variety of persons and bodies that can lay claim to authentic Southern identities through personal experience, supported by historical precedence.

Writers of New Southern cuisine have picked up on some of the same tactics that New Southern studies has created. Rather than representing the migration of outsiders into the South and Southerners out of it as a potential threat to authenticity, the personal narratives agree with the scholars described above that the South is now and has always been a global community, as evidenced by the diversity of bodies and experiences that can now represent the South. Therefore, the embrace of global influences and diverse cuisines is, in fact, more authentic than isolation. The writers of New Southern cuisine recognize that the audience for these cookbooks is made up of people living in the South who were not necessarily born there and who may not have been born in the United States. The chefs themselves are often not born in the South. What attracts readers in and out of the South is the promise that the cookbook will guide them through the performance of authentic Southern identity — no matter where they are or where they are from — through instructions to cook and consume Southern culture.

Cookbooks like Asha Gomez's *My Two Souths*, Edward Lee's *Smoke and Pickles*, and Sandra Gutierrez's *The New Southern Latino Table* all set up arguments of a global South that allows chef authors from outside of the South to merge Southern food with other cuisines.[38] Gomez describes her "two Souths cooking" or "South by South cuisine" as a harmonious blend of cuisines from her birthplace, "the far southern state of Kerala" in India, and her "chosen home in America's southern culinary-savvy city of Atlanta, Georgia." Gomez draws parallels between the two regions in personality as well as geography and climate. In both regions, Gomez argues, "genuine hospitality and meaning are crucial ingredients;" both cuisines are based on "resourcefulness and soulfulness." Both regions also share "a warm, humid climate, abundant produce varieties, expanses of rice acreage, and busy coastal communities along with a spirit of sharing, a gift for entertaining and storytelling, a talent for creating bounty out of an often modest pantry, and a sincere embrace of simplicity."[39] Gomez argues that the two cuisines were already global in nature, even before her creative fusion, since both cuisines are influenced by major global trading hubs like

"Thope and Mumbai in India" and "Savannah, Charleston, New Orleans, and Miami" in the US South. "Port-city cooking" is characterized by easy global exchange, a reliance on seasonal availability, and creativity: "All sorts of ingredients make their way into the larders and pantries of these regions, and certain foodstuffs might only be available for a fleeting period of time. Local cooks learn to work with ingenuity and daring — a sensibility still at play here in the American South."[40] The similarities between these two regions, as presented by Gomez, and their similar global histories allow for a "mingling of cooking styles and flavors" that preserves the authenticity of both cuisines. The cosmopolitan port cities, with their openness to exchange, drive innovation in cuisine and characterize a version of Southern identity that is urban, progressive, and welcoming.

The cosmopolitan New South represented by Gomez and other texts of New Southern cuisine is a strategic reaction against popular representations of the South as "temporally asynchronous with the nation," which is perhaps a polite way of saying "backward." Joshi and Desai argue that the perception of the South as exceptionally violent, racist, and hyperreligious is a strategy to "bolster non-Southern identities and spaces as postracial, secular, and modern in contrast."[41] The authors suggest that the narrative of Southern exceptionalism has caused the South to be "seen as removed from larger national and global processes.... Hence, all Southerners, Black and White, are assumed to be noncosmopolitan and nonmodern, while the region is taken to be disconnected from modern global processes."[42] This narrative, Joshi and Desai argue, does not reflect "any material, cultural, and historical realities" as much as it selects a narrative of American progress and modernity by setting up the South as a contrast.[43] The writers of New Southern cuisine directly combat this representation of the noncosmopolitan and nonmodern South by making arguments that convince readers that Southern identity is and always has been a polyvocal community and not a monolithic, closed society. The evidence is in the food we eat and in the diversity of the people who tell us how to cook. Though the Southern culture industry is invested in Southern exceptionalism (without a distinct South, there is no need for a New Southern cuisine), it is equally invested in creating an exceptional Southern identity that is appealing to a wide audience of diverse readers who might also want membership in that identity group through the representation of exceptionally diverse chef-personalities.

Like Southerners themselves, New Southern cuisine operates in a global gourmet foodscape; therefore, New Southern food is cooked and eaten by non-Southerners, and it is influenced by the ingredients and traditions of other cultures. Chefs who are cooking in Southern restaurants and writing Southern recipes and who may not have been born in the South or even in the United States must account for themselves as cultural insiders. The narrative must confirm the "right" of the nonnative chef to innovate and instruct in authentic Southern foodways. In addition, the recipes of New Southern cuisine regularly use ingredients and techniques combined in global fusion; recipe narratives must distinguish between Southern and global cuisines and explain how the mingling of cuisines can be done with cultural awareness and without losing authenticity.

In addition to making the South always already global, writers have also solved the problem of negotiating distinction and fusion by making this global food personal. As the South participates in the global community, these recipes are made local and personal by focusing the narrative on individual creators, their experiences, and their memories. As it is in art, architecture, and literature, authentic recipes seem to require a recognizable author for authenticity, a single creative mind behind a one-of-a-kind innovation. While the single creative mind is largely a fiction that obscures the collaborative nature of cooking and recipe innovation, for the chef-authored cookbook, the personal narrative is an opportunity to highlight diversity and innovation in Southern haute cuisine without sacrificing the appearance of authenticity.

Citizenship and Belonging: Establishing Authentic Southern Pedigree

Just as recipes are deemed authentically Southern by pinpointing an origin in the geographic South (geographic specificity), so too is a chef's authenticity measured by origin narratives of citizenship and belonging. Certainly, that origin includes birthplace; however, birthplace need not exclude a person from New Southern identity. *Garden & Gun* editor David DiBenedetto states explicitly, "You don't have to be born here to have a passion for real Southern Cooking."[44] This statement is, in part, a nod to the "tribe of young chefs who are redefining — and rediscovering — Southern food," featured in that issue of the magazine (some of whom, like Acheson and Lee, are adopted Southerners); it is also an acknowledgment of the magazine's intended audience of New Southerners who might have been born and raised outside the region. Similarly, in a video from *Garden & Gun's* website connected to the same issue, Acheson claims that a dish need not have an origin in the South to become Southern food:

> You can look at something that is inspired by maybe France, executed in the South from local ingredients, to me that is the New Southern Food.

It's made that leap. It's gone away from being strictly collard greens and shrimp and grits and pulled pork. It's much rounder, much bigger now.[45]

Authentic Southern food, then, does not require an origin story in the South at all. It only needs to be made in the South with local ingredients from the South to bear the name. Southern food lives and works in the South. Canadian-born Acheson, perhaps more than Southern-born chefs, has good reason to make this argument. The first words of the introduction to his cookbook *A New Turn in the South* assure the reader that his birthplace is not a factor against his authenticity: "I AM FROM OTTAWA, CANADA," the first sentence declares in an all-caps, handwritten script, "and I have spent almost a third of my life cooking food inspired by the Southern United States."[46] Rather than focus solely on birthplace as evidence of citizenship, personal narratives allow chef-authors space to draw on childhood experiences, family networks, and ancestry, in addition to birthplace, to establish an origin story that will certify that chef's citizenship and belonging in the US South. These are the formative moments, experiences, and connections that make them always certified — or on their way to becoming certified — as authentic innovators of Southern cuisine, which opens up the possibility for a "much rounder, much bigger" definition of Southern identity.

For Southern-born chefs like Brock, Currence, Willis, and Dupree, birthplace is often foregrounded as evidence of personal authenticity. The cover art for *Heritage* features Brock's outstretched hands cupping two palms full of dried beans in various colors. The tattoos on his forearms announce his birthplace and citizenship: on his right, a crest with Virginia's state bird, the cardinal, and its state flower, the dogwood, overlaid with a banner reading "Virginia." His left forearm is a brightly colored sleeve of local flowers and vegetables, including beets, ramps, radishes, beans, and tomatoes. These images immediately announce Brock's connection to his birthplace and Southern agriculture. The first sentences of the introduction, too, describe Brock's birthplace as an especially vital part of his identity. "That part of Virginia has a unique voice," Brock writes, and "Southwest Virginia has a very distinct way of living." The distinctness of that region is "in my blood; it's part of my DNA."[47] Being born in the South, then, makes Brock Southern on a molecular level. His physical body is presented as the evidence of his Southern authenticity.

In contrast, John Currence writes in *Pickles, Pigs, and Whiskey* that being born in New Orleans (which he announces in the first sentence of the introduction) did not make him automatically a Southerner. "Orleanians do not consider themselves 'Southern,'" Currence writes, because New Orleans seems to be its own place, separate from both the national identity and the regional one. Rather, "Southernness is just not something that New Orleans folks spend a lot of time discussing, cultivating, or considering. Turns out a move north from NOLA to Oxford is what it would take to come to that understanding of my place in the South." A paragraph later, Currence describes finding his Southern identity in a "lightning bolt of understanding" while traveling and cooking in France. Being away from the South reawakened nostalgia and a "craving" for "those Sunday suppers from my grandmother's garden and table" that became "the centerpiece of my food philosophy."[48] This personal narrative acts as a kind of double certificate of authenticity; Currence was born into an exceptionally Southern place, but he also actively chose to cultivate Southern-ness. His journey could also relate to a number of potential readers: those who may have been born in the South without much thought about their Southern identity, those who may have left the South and find their Southern-ness more important to their identities while away, or those who find themselves in the South and now actively choosing to adopt a Southern identity. Currence's narrative journey to Southern identity could serve as a model for readers. While birthplace is a part of Currence's certificate for authenticity, it is not sufficient on its own to certify.

Chris and Idie Hastings's *Hot and Hot Fish Club Cookbook: A Celebration of Food, Family, and Traditions* illustrates a clear contrast between how Southern-born chef-authors use birthplace compared to those born outside of the South.[49] The husband-and-wife team together own and operate the restaurant Hot and Hot Fish Club in Birmingham, Alabama. Chris was born in the South (Pawleys Island, South Carolina), but Idie was not (Cleveland, Ohio). The chapters of the cookbook are divided seasonally by months. The first chapter, "May and June," opens with Chris's memories of growing up on Pawleys Island and spending the summers as a "creek boy," fishing for the family's dinner each day.[50] Throughout the headnotes of that chapter, Chris's childhood experiences are regularly brought up as evidence of authenticity. In the headnote for "Shrimp and Corn Fritters with Chive Aioli," the narrator assures readers that Chris's experiences are representative of the South: "Seafood fritters were always served at the beach when Chris was a child. Fritters have long been an important part of the Southern diet and he grew up eating them for lunch along with sliced tomatoes and succotash."[51] Idie's birthplace and childhood are discussed in the opening of the next chapter, "July and August." The narrative explains that Idie comes from an Italian family, and her childhood was spent in Cleveland, Ohio, and Clymer, Pennsylvania. While Idie's narrative covers three pages, and Chris's only one, the recipe headnotes in that chapter do not make further references to Idie's childhood or birthplace. Instead, "Dad's Grilled Chicken with Summer Vegetables" pays tribute to Chris's father and "one of Chris' favorite meals" as a child.[52] The chapter returns again to Chris's experiences "Crabbing as a Boy on Pawley's Island."[53] The chapter ends with a "Lifestyle Menu" for a "Beach Dinner at the 'Happy House.'" The narrative is written in first person from Idie's point of view, and the "Happy House" of the title refers to a house that Idie's grandmother would rent each summer. The location of that house (whether it is in or out of the South) is not clear in the narrative, but the first words of the narrative situate even Idie's childhood memories in terms of Chris's birthplace: "Always the creek boy, Chris has taught our sons how to catch all of our own seafood for dinner." The black-and-white photograph below the narrative shows five young boys fishing.[54] Though Idie's experience and voice are featured in the narrative, it is Chris's birthplace and experiences that are pulled out as evidence for authenticity.

Being born in the South helps make a case for Southern citizenship, but it does not mean that the chef is done certifying his or her Southern-ness. Southern-born chef-authors have to remind readers of their Southern birth, but birth alone does not seem sufficient evidence. Ancestry and family networks are often employed as secondary supporting evidence for citizenship. Chris and Idie Hastings name their cookbook and restaurant in Birmingham after the Hot and Hot Fish Club, a historic "epicurean gentleman's club" near Murrells Inlet and Pawleys Island, founded "officially" in 1845. The narrative suggests that Chris Hastings's ancestor, his "great-great-great-great-grandfather, Hugh Fraser" may have been a founding member, even before the group had a name and rules. The club rules are printed in the cookbook three times: inside both the front and back covers and on page 19, across from the narrative of the club's founding. This repetition makes clear just how important this historical club (and Chris's ancestral connection to it) is to the story of the restaurant today. The club disbanded with the Civil War, but Chris cites the stories of his ancestor's involvement with the club as "the greatest inspiration behind his career as a chef."[55] The antebellum ancestral claim to Southern citizenship is renewed with each repetition of the name of the restaurant and the cookbook, attaching the certificate of authenticity to recipes through titles like "Hot and Hot Tomato Salad" and "Hot and Hot Spicy 'Tini."[56]

For a chef-author born outside of the South, an antebellum Southern ancestry works to establish personal ethos and a claim to citizenship. Anne Stiles Quatrano, chef and owner of Bacchanalia in Atlanta, makes clear in her introduction to *Summerland* that she and her husband Clifford Harrison (born in Connecticut and Hawaii, respectively) have lived in Georgia since 1992. Quatrano's connection to the South and to Atlanta, however, extends much further back. Her mother's family had owned and farmed land outside of Atlanta "since before the Civil War."[57] Quatrano then narrates her family's relationship to that plot of land beginning with her "great, great, great grandfather, William Henry Stiles" who was born in Savannah, Georgia, in 1809 and bought the land in 1840. According to Quatrano, her ancestor was involved in transactions to "pay the Cherokee Indians for the lands in north Georgia they had deeded to the United States."[58] It was to this ancestral plot, called "Summerland," that Quatrano and Harrison moved in 1992 to open restaurants in Atlanta. Quatrano titled the cookbook *Summerland* as a connection to this most significant certificate of her Southern citizenship (just as the Hastingses name their restaurant and cookbook after their strongest claim to citizenship). Though she was born in Connecticut and trained in San Francisco, Quatrano's nearly unbroken 175–year ancestral connection to "Summerland" establishes her Southern origins and identity. Quatrano reveals later in *Summerland* that the family has another adjoining parcel of land called "Malbone Plantation," "another Stiles family property," occupied by a cousin.[59] These ancestral connections to the South, emphasized in the book's title and in narrative, establish Quatrano's Southern pedigree, allowing her movement to include recipes like "Madeleines" and "Meyer Lemon Gelato" under the name of authentic New Southern cuisine.[60]

Like Quatrano, Barbara Smith argues for her Southern citizenship through ancestral claims. Smith's first sentences of *B. Smith Cooks Southern-Style* set up a contradiction: People think that she is from the South, but she admits that she grew up in southwestern Pennsylvania. Smith explains that her family "ended up in southwestern Pennsylvania by way of North Carolina and Virginia, where the first enslaved Africans arrived." Though as a child she "never differentiated between Northern and Southern cooking," she later discovered that her family's eating habits and recipes were more influenced by their Southern past than their Rust Belt present.[61] Smith highlights the global influences on Southern cuisine, first by acknowledging her family's African origins in connection with Southern-ness. "Southern cuisine," according to Smith, is "a culturally rich and diverse cuisine with history in its ingredients, flavors, and textures. I like to look at it as a cultural artifact of the Old South. What other cuisine has had its journey? New settlers, enslaved Africans, enslavers, and Native Americans all had a stake in it."[62] Smith frames the cuisine as mobile; just as her family migrated out of the South, the cuisine took that "journey" with them. And the cuisine that moved had been equally shaped by many cultures. Though Smith debunks the myth that enslaved Africans brought their favorite foods on slave ships ("Slavery wasn't nice that way"), she does acknowledge that "along with their human cargo, enslavers transported seeds," which enslaved Africans tended. From the French roots of Louisiana Creole cuisine to the British influence on the big Southern breakfast and the Native American origins of vegetables, Smith writes, "When you put all of this history together in a big pot, we call that Southern cuisine."[63] Taken together, Smith's narrative of her own life and of the history of Southern food authorizes a "gal from southwestern Pennsylvania" with ancestral ties to Southern geography and enslaved Africans in the South to be an innovator in Southern cuisine.[64] If her family's ties to the South and Southern traditions were not enough to make her a Southern citizen, then the historical diversity of the South certainly makes space for an outsider to become an integral part of the future of the cuisine.

So far, this discussion of Southern citizenship has been largely abstract. There are no legal procedures by which one becomes a citizen of the South, only arguments that will convince a reader of Southern belonging. But in *My Two Souths*, Asha Gomez must be explicit about her path to legal citizenship in the United States. Gomez explains that her family traveled widely when she was child, and at age thirteen, she visited the United States for the first time. "We arrived as legal immigrants with Green Cards in hand," Gomez explains. Her two brothers enrolled in school and stayed in the United States. Gomez and her parents returned to India, but made frequent trips to the States "to make sure my Green Card didn't expire." Gomez explains that her dual citizenship was a purposeful choice by her father that shaped her life profoundly: "My father's foresight and belief that his children should have a global perspective governed his commitment to our education and broadened our access to the world." Gomez immigrated to the United States permanently after the death of her father, living in Queens, New York, until she moved to Georgia in 2000.[65] The story of Gomez's legal citizenship is presented as evidence of her valid claim to American identity and belonging in a global community. The US South is Gomez's "chosen home," but the narrative makes clear that Gomez is at home in the world as a traveler and culinary professional.[66] As Gomez explains, "Traveling with my family broadened my palate and fed my inquisitive streak as I sampled unaccustomed flavors and ingredients and witnessed new cooking techniques."[67] Gomez's credibility as a citizen of the South is undergirded both by her legal citizenship in the United States and by her cosmopolitan childhood, which prepared her to be a willing student of Southern cuisine, able to

mix cuisines through a culturally aware "global perspective." Regardless of her
birthplace, Gomez demonstrates a personal ability to belong everywhere, suggesting that membership in the Southern family is open.

Stories of childhood experiences overlap with narratives that identify birthplace and/or ancestry as evidence of personal Southern identity. Chef-authors
born in the South, like Chris Hastings, also recall formative childhood experiences there, as his chapter full of "creek boy" stories suggests. Those born outside of the South often share narrative memories of experiencing the South as
children — usually through visiting family networks and ancestral lands. Hugh
Acheson recalls living in Atlanta with family for the first time as an eleven-year-
old. The "Southern things" he remembers most are not exclusively food related:
"my step-grandmother's fried okra, my stepfather's collards, the teenage mur-
murs around the local pool about a great band from Athens (R.E.M.), the dogwood trees on my walk to school, the neighbors' calming drawl, Apalachicola
oysters from the Gulf, and the Varsity, Atlanta's favorite drive-in."[68] A few years
later, Acheson's "education in Southern food and culture continued" with a
move to Clemson, where Acheson had his first job in food service, met his
future wife, Mary, and was introduced to dishes that would become staples in
his future Athens, Georgia, restaurant, Five and Ten.[69] These childhood experiences living in the South, totaling four formative preteen and teen years, add
up in Acheson's calculation of spending "almost a third of [his] life cooking
food inspired by the Southern United States," and they serve as evidence of his
authenticity through an "education in Southern food and culture."[70]

Chef-authors without specific childhood experiences in the geographic
South rely instead on narratives of childhood encounters with foods (sometimes explicitly Southern) outside of the South that seem to set them on a path
toward a love for Southern food. In Cooking in the Moment, Andrea Reusing
describes falling in love with food as a child in New York. In the introduction,
Reusing reports that one of her earliest memories is of eating chicken pot pie
from the floor; her grandmother Marie's homemade pie had fallen into the floor
accidentally, and Reusing and her cousin ate it anyway, "the desire to comfort
Marie nearly as great as our hunger for her pot pie." This incident teaches the
future chef that "food is love."[71]

Similarly, Edward Lee describes in detail in Smoke and Pickles his formative
food experiences. The introduction is subtitled with two foods that seem to
capture the two influences on Lee's cuisine, "Rice and Remoulade." The plain
white rice served daily in his family's kitchen represents "the fundamental Zen
of the Asian table."[72] Remoulade comes to represent Lee's introduction to fine
dining. Remoulade, a sauce served at his first "fancy pants dinner" in a fine

dining restaurant, is a symbol of everything that his culture is not. Lee jokes, "What in Buddha's name is this tongue-coating goodness?"[73] Though remoulade is French in origin, it is best known as a condiment for Louisiana seafood dishes. Lee emphasizes the Southern origin of remoulade by recommending Duke's brand mayonnaise in his recipe and photographing the finished product with a jar of Duke's scraped nearly clean. An old-fashioned whisk circles the lid off to one side like a halo, highlighting the print on the lid: "Duke's: The Secret of Great Southern Cooking."[74] Because of that remoulade experience, Lee decides to become a chef: "Life would become a struggle to find that magical intersection between rice and remoulade, between two disparate cultures that overlapped inside me, somewhere neither here nor there, at once flawed and yet desirable. A place like a kitchen."[75] Even before Lee had ever been to the South or seen a restaurant kitchen, the childhood moment that made him want to become a chef happened over a Southern sauce, putting him always on a path to his most authentic identity: a New Southern chef.

Training and Mentorship: Establishing Authentic Chef Credentials

While Southern citizenship through birth, ancestry, or childhood experience is important to establish through a connection with the geographic South, another important credential is the Southern chef's authenticity as chef, even if that formal training is not undertaken in the geographic South. The chef's training abroad (whether "abroad" means California or Calabria) does not seem to undercut that chef's authenticity as Southerner. Rather, narratives about training seem to be about certifying the chef as a skilled and knowledgeable professional who can innovate thoughtfully and skillfully with received classics. These stories convince the readers that the chef's recipes can be trusted not only for performing Southern-ness but also for being tasty, accurate, and professional.

These narratives are similar to citation narratives in structure and purpose. They connect the chef-author to a network of authorized sources of culinary and cultural knowledge to demonstrate authenticity. But instead of giving those sources credit for any particular text (or to preempt any claims of copyright infringement), narratives that acknowledge training and mentorship are solely focused on authorizing the chef as an authentic source of knowledge and responsible innovation. Culinary school is not always indicated in introductions, but employers and mentors are often "name dropped" in the first few pages. These mentors may be great lights in Southern cuisine (Currence cites his first job at Crook's Corner under the tutelage of Bill Neal; Willis reports that her first job was with the legendary Nathalie Dupree) or master chefs in other cuisines (the Hastingses cite Bradley Ogden of Lark Creek Inn; Acheson, Robert Bourassa of Café Henry Burger and Rob MacDonald of Maplelawn Café, both of Ottawa).[76]

Mentors need not be Southern in order to certify the chef. Virginia Willis's claim to Southern citizenship is unimpeachable. In the introduction to *Basic to Brilliant, Y'all*, Willis details her childhood and ancestry in the South, declaring, "My deep roots in the South and family history continually help me define my journey, what I will be, and where I will go."[77] The part of Willis's identity that calls for authentication in the introduction is her ability to faithfully fuse French and Southern cooking through proof of her identity as French-trained chef. Unlike the other chef-authors examined in this chapter, Willis is not connected to a brick-and-mortar restaurant, and her recipes are intended for home cooking. Willis explains in the introduction that her career has been on television and in food writing rather than fine dining restaurants. Therefore, Willis emphasizes her training in classical French cooking at "L'Academie de Cuisine in Bethesda" and her time spent living in France, working for Anne Willan at La Varenne. Readers would recognize the TV personalities that she worked for and with: Nathalie Dupree, Bobby Flay, and Martha Stewart.[78] These are the credentials that will assure readers that Willis can provide both "Basic recipes," which Willis "might teach in a cooking class," and "Brilliant versions," which are "chef inspired, something to prepare for dinner guests on the weekend." Even the "chef inspired" recipes remain very personal: "something I might prepare for you if you were a guest in my home." They also remain very Southern: "the culinary version of the fine Southern tradition of dressing up for company."[79] Willis's explanation of her training, travel, and mentorship offer evidence for her ability to blend "Brilliant" French haute cuisine with "Basic" Southern recipes.

Similarly, John Currence describes his time spent working for Bill Neal in Chapel Hill and his training in New Orleans kitchens as formative experiences. Through narrative, Currence humbly connects himself to "the man who was fast becoming a giant in Southern cooking and is credited with legitimizing the food of the Southern family table." Currence writes of his time at Crook's Corner:

It was in those years that I received my first glimpse of the actual beauty of the food of my grandmother's table and the dishes from my mom's kitchen. Stewed Okra and Tomatoes (page 55) and Chicken Skin Cornbread (page 225) were foods we could be proud of, foods that told a story about our lives, our history, our families. It was not food that needed to be relegated to those home tables, it was food to be explored, examined, and celebrated.[80]

Currence's description of the lessons he learned from Neal serve as an argument authenticity in two ways. First, he has been trained by a chef acknowledged to be a major force in convincing consumers that Southern food could be fine dining. Therefore, Currence, too, knows how to make Southern food appropriate for fine dining. But implicit in the narrative is another acknowledged mentor — Currence's grandmother. Not only does Currence know Southern food as haute cuisine, but he also knows it as home cooking, and Bill Neal has helped to teach him the difference. Readers can expect to learn this from Currence, too.

As I argued in chapter 2, the grandmother as mentor is a common convention in personal narratives. Currence credits his grandmother in the passage cited above, but he also cites summers spent with grandparents in North Carolina and Georgia as formative experiences. Spending time in his North Carolina grandparents' gardens "provided me with an understanding of and appreciation for those individual vegetables and fundamental building blocks for a variety of preservation techniques" that he employs directly in his restaurants and the pages of his cookbook.[81] In fact, Currence cites the grandparents first, suggesting that not only did those experiences occur first chronologically, but they are also the more important influences. Later in "My Manifesto," Currence explains that he relies on and "dearly" loves his great-grandmother's copy of *Joy of Cooking* for the "three generations of handwriting on the pages" that has taught him "that recipes, no matter how simple, are just a guideline for the cook."[82] The mentorship that means most to him is from his Southern grandmother. This, too, is implied in Brock's title, *Heritage,* and made explicit through references to his grandparents and their garden in the opening pages. And Virginia Willis credits her grandparents and her mother before giving her CV.

Like Willis, Dora Charles credits her grandmother, Hattie Smith, for teaching her to cook. Charles also acknowledges a long tradition of cooks in the family "going right back to slavery."[83] Charles describes in detail the labors of her parents' and grandparents' generations as African American sharecroppers who endured both privation (hauling water from a spring) and plenty (canning "a thousand quart jars" from the garden).[84] At six years old, in 1903, Charles' grandmother went to work as a cook and learned on the job.[85] When Charles was six years old, she asked her grandmother to teach her to cook, too. Charles explains that she wanted to learn to cook like her grandmother, whose meals the family loved: "I was always fascinated by cooking and by food itself, how it could be magical in the hands of someone who knew what they were doing and kind of hopeless in the hands of someone else."[86] Charles details the six years of her apprenticeship, which ended with her grandmother's unexpected death, never writing down recipes but learning to "eyeball" measurements and to test temperatures and textures by touch and sound.[87] Charles describes her training as formal, even though it takes place in her home; she never finishes her public high school education, but her grandmother's training sets her up for a career: "I didn't know how you went about becoming a professional cook," Charles admits, "but I decided to just go for it."[88] In addition to her grandmother's training, Charles herself becomes an educator, which serves as another marker of her authority as a "real Southern cook." Charles reports training "more than sixty people to cook,"[89] mostly employees working under Charles in Paula Deen's Savannah restaurants. As a teacher, Charles relied on her grandmother's methods: "Build the flavor and cook it slow so it can bloom. Put love into it and pay attention — that care you take with it is what will make it delicious."[90] Charles is an authority on Southern food because she has inherited culinary knowledge through her grandmother and because she has been a trustworthy teacher. Readers can be assured that the recipes provided in the book come from a qualified instructor who has been authorized by a recognized authority.

Notably absent in Charles's narrative of training is Paula Deen. Though Deen seems to serve as a kind of sponsor who recognizes and capitalizes on Charles's knowledge and skills, Deen has little to teach Charles, according to the narrative. Charles is hired by Deen because of her already established reputation and the similarity of their cooking backgrounds. In their first meeting, Deen interviews Charles: "She'd ask me how I'd cook something in particular, and I'd tell her how my grandmother cooked it, and she'd say that's almost exactly how *her* grandmother cooked it."[91] What unites Deen and Charles as a team is the coincidence of the knowledge they received from their grandmothers; as Charles remarks, they'd have the most fun in the kitchen when they would "talk about our grandmothers and their cooking while we were working, tell stories and laugh."[92] By highlighting both her grandmother as a source of authentic knowledge and the similarity of their inherited knowledge, Charles suggests that Deen doesn't have much specialized knowledge to teach Charles that Charles didn't already receive from her grandmother. Charles also passed her grandmother's knowledge to Deen's other employees, suggesting that Deen herself was not an instrumental link in that transmission, either. However, Deen asks Charles to teach her some things, including how to be calm in the kitchen under stress, and asks, "How do y'all black people know how to clap and snap your fingers and stomp your feet all at the same time?" Charles is a gracious narrator, claiming that "Paula's way of letting it all out and then getting over it was actually better" than her serenity in the "big pressure cookers" of restaurant kitchens and laughing good-naturedly at Deen's attempts at dancing in the kitchen.[93] While some of the chef-authors in this sample use their employers and mentors as evidence of authority and authenticity, Charles mostly bypasses her employer. Her grandmother taught her to cook, and it was Charles's cooking that made Deen's restaurants famous. This same bypassing of Deen is summarized pithily in a quotation from a *New York Times* article from June 2013 responding to Deen's removal from the Food Network in the midst of a discrimination law suit: "Many chefs who look at Southern food through this lens [of "the pre-processed, agrarian South"] see Ms. Deen as neither an embarrassment nor an influence — in fact, they barely see her at all." In context, the author, Julia Moskin, separates Deen from a globally inflected historical approach to Southern cooking that acknowledges "the culinary contributions of all the region's early inhabitants: American Indian hunters, African slave cooks, Italian rice barons and French pastry chefs." Moskin quotes Atlanta chef Todd Richards, who is more explicit in his condemnation of Deen's ahistorical — and by implication, inauthentic — approach to Southern food: "I don't see her smoking ducks and hams, studying the preservation techniques that the ancestors used and that made Southern cooking what it is . . . I don't look to how she cooks."[94] In Charles's narrative, her white employer is a threat to her perceived authenticity, and Charles responds to that threat by explicitly focusing on her own African American grandmother as the source of her authority, knowledge, and skills.

The grandmother figure is so powerful as evidence for arguments of authenticity that non-Southern grandmothers are equally useful for personal narratives. Idie Hastings's grandmother Rosina Marie Scerbo immigrated from Calabria, Italy, to Clymer, Pennsylvania, and it was from her grandmother that Idie learned to eat and to cook as "a labor of love," and that "trips to the market were an adventure, not a chore."[95] This emotional mentorship from family is what makes Idie's cooking personal in the way that Johnson and Baumann describe it — connected to "honest intentions," and separated from the marketplace. The narrator makes a direct connection between how this mentorship looks at home and how it affects Idie's work in the restaurant:

On Sundays, as Idie stirs a pot of homemade soup on the stove at home or rolls out handmade pasta for her boys, she feels the presence of her dad Jim who was so often found in their kitchen doing the exact same thing. And at the restaurant when the lights are dimmed and the dining room hums with activity, it is almost as if her dad, aunts, and uncles are right there, sitting at their favorite spot, table 14, discussing the menu and reminiscing about meals they shared back home. These warm memories of family and food nurture Idie's soul.[96]

While Idie's family cannot mentor her in authentic recipes from the US South, they can — and have — mentored her soul, so that Idie's creations come from an overflow of emotion rather than in the less authentic pursuit of profits or mass production. Idie's personal authenticity is certified.

Andrew Ticer and Michael Hudman combine both kinds of mentors — professional and familial — in *Collards & Carbonara: Southern Cooking, Italian Roots*. Their restaurants, Italian Kitchen and Hog & Hominy, combine Southern and Italian cuisines. The chef-authors were born in the South to "big Italian families" and traveled abroad to be trained in Italian cuisine.[97] The combination of training in Italy and connection to family heritage (dually Southern and Italian) is what qualifies them to innovate with Southern food through fusion with a global cuisine. They are able to do this authentically, they argue, because of their personal heritage and experiences.

The chef-authors are upfront in the introduction with their rhetorical aim in the cookbook:

> We have tried — and hopefully succeeded — to make a convincing argument about how the food of the South and the food of Italy can be mixed to make beautiful music together.... As you make your way through the pages, we hope that you come to appreciate what fuels us and helps us create menus that marry our Italian philosophy with our southern heritage.[98]

Throughout the text, Ticer and Hudman trickle out the story of their fusion cuisine, foregrounding their travel and study in Italy. Ticer reports in the headnote to "Crostini with Truffled Chicken Livers" that they learned the recipe from Fabio Bertoni "when we were students at the Italian Institute for Advanced Culinary Arts in Calabria."[99] The full narrative of their connection to Italy appears in the middle of the second chapter, "On Italy and Its Power to Inspire." Speaking in the first-person plural, "we," Ticer and Hudman explain that they take from Italy and Italian cuisine their "philosophy." In "the motherland," they found:

a food culture that respected ingredients, that took pride in tomatoes grown in a neighbor's garden, eggs from a farm down the road, and garlic from a backyard plot. . . . We now cook with a wholehearted respect for raw ingredients by using them when they grow and where they grow, by manipulating them as little as possible, and by allowing them to shine on the plate.[100]

In the headnotes, the authors make clear that they learned many techniques and recipes in Italy, as well, but they are able to innovate with this cuisine authentically because they understand and respect it, both on a personal level and through personal relationships with their host family in Calabria and their coworkers and teachers.

This respectful education in Italy, combined with their Italian family heritage and birthplace in the South, lets them combine "Collards and Carbonara" with authenticity. In both locations and cuisines, they take technical training and emotional mentorship from personal relationships. In "On Family and Food" from the third chapter, Ticer and Hudman describe their childhoods in Italian families in the South. This combination is best represented in the photo collage in the center of the narrative. The four pages of photos show Ticer and Hudman cooking with their families. The first full-page photo shows two older men (not identified by name or relationship) rolling pasta with tools for making ravioli in front of them. The man on the left wears a University of Memphis sweatshirt. The image emphasizes that though the recipes are Italian, they are being executed in the South by people who identify themselves with as Southerners; they are in a conversation between the local and the global. The narrative "On Family and Food" is divided into two parts, with each chef narrating in turn. The first is narrated by Hudman and focuses on the training and mentorship he received from his grandmother, called Maw Maw, whom he credits for inspiring him to become a chef: "Whenever someone asks me to name the moment that I realized I wanted to be a chef, I answer that there was no single moment. A whole childhood of memories of Maw Maw, cooking with her, was her gift to me."[101] Hudman learned from her both technical and emotional lessons, both the recipe for her signature ravioli and the lesson that "you can never be satisfied. You must always push yourself to be the best."[102] In this personal narrative, the reader learns about the chef-authors' family networks, especially mentorship from their grandmothers, who identify as both Italian and Southern, without conflict. Not only do the chef-authors learn Southern dishes and techniques from their grandmothers, but they also learn to create holistic identities from two cultures and cuisines. The narrative serves as evidence that both cuisines are personal to the chefs, through formal and family mentorship, supporting the personal authenticity of their fusion cuisine.

Living and Working in Place:
Establishing Authentic Connection to Community

Wherever the chefs of New Southern cuisine were born and trained, they are in the South now. As Acheson claims, the key marker of "the New Southern Food" is to be "executed in the South from local ingredients."[103] This definition of Southern food and Southern identity appears wide open to almost anyone who identifies their location as the South and who can buy or grown an heirloom tomato. Of course, where the South begins and ends is up for some scholarly debate, and we know that access to heirloom tomatoes is bound up in complex issues of class and race. This claim is not as democratic as it first appears. However, it is a claim that prioritizes the concept of originality over authenticity, making space for innovation and a cosmopolitan New Southern food that is globally inflected and locally executed. The concept of authentic Southern identity in these narratives extends from an investment in the geographic place and the social space of the South through local living and working: farming, sourcing, researching, and networking in the local South.

Most of the chef-authors examined in this chapter live and work in places generally recognized to be in the South: Memphis and Nashville, Tennessee; Charleston, South Carolina; Oxford, Mississippi; Birmingham, Alabama; Atlanta, Georgia; Louisville, Kentucky; Chapel Hill, North Carolina. The narratives make clear that the chef-authors physically inhabit the geographic space of the South. The act of repeatedly naming cities and restaurants in narratives, headnotes, and titles is one way that chef-authors can emphasize their personal authenticity as dwellers in the South. For example, in *Heritage*, Brock mentions his two restaurants, Husk and McCrady's, sixty-five times. Nashville is mentioned twelve times. Charleston is mentioned 134 times, including variations like "Charleston's warm waters" and "Charlestonians." The region around Charleston, the Low Country, has thirty-eight mentions. In the six pages of introduction alone, Brock references ninety-three place names. In a 325–page text, with many full-page photographs, much of the textual space is devoted to naming and describing locations and Brock's connection to place. The naming and renaming of the specific geographic places notes Brock's engagement with the local.

This reliance on local naming does not necessarily suggest compensation for contested Southern-ness. Brock's Southern citizenship is well established by pedigree. By contrast, one might expect Acheson to remind readers that he lives and works in the South more often. However, Brock far outstretches Acheson in geographic specificity. Acheson names his cities — Athens and Atlanta, Georgia — forty-seven times (to Brock's 146), and his restaurants Empire State South and Five and Ten thirty-five times (to Brock's sixty-five). Both writers name the South generally (in its many, many variations) as a location where they belong, but again, Brock exceeds Acheson by a large margin: 107 to Acheson's eighty. I will come back to this data and geographic naming as a rhetorical strategy in the final chapter, but in these personal narratives, repetition of places and place names remind readers of the chef-author's personal authenticity as "a local," one who lives and works in the geographic South.

In addition to living and working in Southern cities, many of these chef-authors describe in detail local sourcing and networking as evidence of their authentic Southern-ness as an extension of local and geographic investment. Local farmers and artisans demonstrate authenticity, proving that the chefs are connected to their locations as ethical and benevolent consumers and producers, and that they are connected to the rural South, not just urban cities. Brock, Lee, Acheson, and Hastings and Hastings all include multipage narratives about their relationships with local farmers, ranchers, suppliers, and other producers through their cookbooks. These stories illustrate the chefs' commitment to Southern-based artisans, businesses, heritage ingredients, and native plants and animals. Lee's supplier narratives take a few different forms. Some are folded into narratives about ingredients like the page-long "Southern-Bred Oysters" essay that introduces readers to Travis and Ryan Croxton, oyster farmers "along the Rappahannock River in eastern Virginia."[104] Others are half-page marginal notes like "The Craftsman," a story of Robert Clifft, "master turkey caller and maker of handmade turkey calls aptly named The Last Call" or "The Ham Lady," a profile of Nancy Newsom of Col. Bill Newsom's Kentucky Country Hams.[105] Other farmer profiles are blended into the chapter introductions with other memories and reflections. For example, in the introduction to "Lamb and Whistles," Lee describes three lamb-centric memories, the third of which is his introduction to Craig Rogers of Patrick Springs, Virginia, who provides lamb to his restaurants.[106] Though Lee has not spent a lifetime building these local networks, the narratives suggest that he has worked diligently to cultivate them, investing deeply in his place. If the New Southern food is anything cooked in the South with local ingredients, then these narratives serve as evidence of both.

In *Hot and Hot Fish Club Cookbook*, Hastings and Hastings devote full-page sections at regular intervals to their local Birmingham suppliers, many of whom they come into contact with through Birmingham Farmers Market. These narratives describe a mutually beneficial partnership between the restaurant and the supplier. For instance, "Farmer Chris Bennett" is identified as a former employee at Hot and Hot Fish Club. According to the narrator, "Chris approached us several years ago to share his dream of creating an organic farm on his family's land with the ultimate goal of becoming one of our suppliers." Bennett not only cultivates organic produce, but he also "makes it a point to comb the property in order to forage for us a number of things — sassafras, wild ginger, tiny strawberries, elderberries, huckleberries, persimmons, earthy mushrooms, and honeysuckle blossoms so sweet they bring tears to your eyes."[107] The chef-authors emphasize seasonality and locality in their recipes. The signature dish of the restaurant, "Hot and Hot Tomato Salad," depends entirely upon the appearance of heirloom tomatoes in the farmer's market, and their tomato supplier, "Mike." In the narrative of the "Origin of the Hot and Hot Tomato Salad," the narrator demonstrates the chefs' deep connection to the Southern agricultural seasons and the suppliers, and the narrative describes the local community's investment in the restaurant. Though the restaurant waits until the perfect timing of the seasonal supply of local heirloom tomatoes to serve this dish, patrons begin calling in April, the narrator says, to find out when they will be able to order the Tomato Salad. "The Hot and Hot Tomato Salad," the narrator writes, "is memory cuisine for many of our patrons now."[108] These two narratives demonstrate the mutually beneficial and deeply connected relationship between the chefs and their locations. The restaurant serves as a predictable market for farmers like Bennett, but the authors declare that their success is dependent upon local ingredients and suppliers:

> We never stop saying that our purveyors are the real heroes of our restaurant. Certainly the bounty Chris Bennett harvests enables us to take our cooking to new heights. . . . Talent and skill can take a cook just so far before one moves beyond good common sense when it comes to cooking. The only other vehicle for true creativity is access to phenomenal products.[109]

In other words, their originality extends from their ingredients, which are authentic in two senses — both one-of-a-kind and directly pulled from the Southern landscape. Narratives like these serve as evidence of the chef's ethics and their investment in local Southern networks.

New Southern chef-authors encourage readers, whether they are in the South or not, to engage with their own local markets, or better yet, to engage with Southern suppliers that deliver by mail. Sections at the end of the cookbooks titled "Sources" or "Resources" direct readers to suppliers that have been vetted by the chef-authors as approved and authentic suppliers. In the body of the recipes and in headnotes, the authors will often introduce brand names or the names of specific varieties of vegetables or animals that are offered as evidence of local investment. Duke's mayonnaise, for example, is regularly suggested as a preferred brand. Vidalia onions (from Vidalia, Georgia) may also serve as a Southern identifier. Perhaps the most common supplier among this set of chef-authored cookbooks is Anson Mills of Columbia, South Carolina. Brock identifies Anson Mills in recipes or narratives more often than he names his own restaurants: sixty-three times. Anson Mills is identified as a source for Carolina Gold rice, grits, cornmeal, wheat flours, and benne seeds. Brock mentions Anson Mills by name both because their products are available for purchase online and because their mission, "to repatriate the Carolina Rice Kitchen, so chefs and everyone else can sample these heirloom ingredients," is so closely aligned with Brock's: "to help bring the small local farmer back to prominence by respecting the work of local growers, and to encourage farmers to reach back beyond the hybrid varieties, wasteful practices, and chemical inputs that have transformed agriculture (and the taste of food) over the last century."[110] By buying from Anson Mills, readers can be assured of a product that is local, ethical, and historically accurate. And Brock, through his personal relationship to that authentic supplier, is further identified with Southern authenticity.

Memory and Feeling:
Establishing Authentic Southern Homes

The narrative strategies described above connect chef-authors to Southern geography, marketplaces, and individuals. But, as Johnson and Baumann define "personal" authenticity, what is most required is "honest intentions," a feeling of personal attachment. What all the chef-authors express, regardless of their birthplace or experiences, is a deep and abiding love for the South: the landscape, the weather, the people, the traditions, and, of course, the food. Perhaps the most important authenticating factor in personal narratives is the testimony of love for the South.

The opening lines of Donald Link's *Down South* profess his lifelong love of the South and his deep connection to the region as home. In one long sentence, Link describes both the major accomplishments and cultural contributions of the South, "the birthplace of Elvis, the blues, jazz, rock and roll, and country music" and his personal experience with those accomplishments throughout his life. His love for the South is ineffable: "This region is a part of my DNA in a way that you can't explain to someone who wasn't raised here, but every Southerner knows exactly what I'm talking about."[111] Link offers a tour of the South, cataloging each microregion and state's food traditions, claiming, "It's impossible for me to say which part of the South has the *best* food, because each place has its own soul." Link concludes by describing the powerful feelings of longing for home and love of place that drive him: "I've eaten some amazing food and seen some incredible places, but eventually I long to get *back down South*. I yearn for my people and my home, and especially for its food. It's me. *It's a Southern thing*."[112] As an introduction, it is perhaps less informative than many of the others examined here. It does not name Link's restaurants. It does not detail his birth or ancestry. It does not name any of his chef-mentors or even a Southern grandmother (briefly, he notes the "local ingredients" from "my grandfather's garden" as something lost in the modern South).[113] Instead, Link's introduction makes clear that he is intimately familiar with the South's cities and food traditions. And while he has also traveled and eaten and cooked all over the world, this travel has only reaffirmed his Southern identity and his love for that place. This love is *"a Southern thing,"* accessible only to other authentic Southerners, that cannot be explained. If the reader can relate and imagine this inexplicable yearning for the South, then they, too, may identify with Link and share in his authentic identity.

Virginia Willis also describes her abiding connection to Southern identity, despite years of living away from the South. In the introduction to *Basic to Brilliant, Y'all*, Willis reports that when people ask where she's from, she answers, "My family is from Evans, Georgia," even though "I haven't lived there since I was three years old and I've lived a dozen places since."[114] Willis could have chosen any other location to define her identity, but she has chosen to construct her identity around that specific place. Evans is the location where her maternal grandparents "made a family, helped start a community, built a church, and most importantly, left a long-lasting legacy of what home really is." That town becomes a touchstone for Willis's Southern identity and her understanding of belonging: "Home is far more complex than a mailing address," Willis writes. "My deep roots in the South and family history continually help me define my journey, what I will be, and where I will go."[115] Willis explains that in the aftermath of 9/11, after living in France and New York for nearly a decade, she wanted to go home.[116] The idea of *home* permeates *Basic to Brilliant* more intensely than the other cookbooks examined here because it is purposefully directed toward home cooks as a representation of Willis's own home cooking. Therefore, when Willis describes home as "talking for hours with my mother, fresh garden vegetables, pulling the wishbone with my sister just like we did when we were young, and sharing sweet kitchen memories," she is inviting readers to imagine themselves similarly at home, wherever they are.[117] Willis purposefully and intentionally chose which place in her experience she would like to be from, and readers are encouraged to do likewise. The feeling of security at home that Willis describes is not specifically located in a Southern city or landscape, so it is accessible to almost any reader. If an authentic Southern feeling is a longing for home and nostalgia for childhood comforts, then readers may easily share in that feeling from where they are.

Link and Willis are both self-identified native Southerners, but the feeling of being adopted into the Southern family and community is similarly expressed as an appreciation and love for a place that is reciprocal; the South loves you back. Lee describes his move to Louisville, Kentucky, in 2003 as transformative: "I had to reinvent my identity, both culinary and personal, through the lens of tobacco and bourbon and sourghum and horse racing and country ham. . . . Over time, Louisville, and, by extension, the American South, embraced me as an adopted son. I was not surprised by that. It was effortless."[118] As a chef not born in the South, not conforming to the black/white racial binary that dominates conversations of Southern identity, Lee might have expected resistance. Instead, he found more similarities than differences between his Korean American identity and cuisine and Southern identity and cuisine. The similarities drew him back to memories of his own childhood experiences:

> What I didn't expect was how I'd come full circle and rediscover myself as a child of Korean immigrants. That all the lovely and resourceful traditions of the Southern landscape would propel me back to the kitchen of my grandmother's spicy, garlicky foods: Soft grits reminded me of congee; jerky of cuttlefish; chowchow of kimchi. My Korean forefathers' love of pickling is rivaled only by Southerners' love of pickling. BBQ, with its intricate techniques of marinades and rubs, is the backbone of both cuisines. Buttermilk has become my miso.[119]

Lee suggests that cuisines will mingle in organic ways when people of different origins and backgrounds work together in a common home. He criticizes the hypocrisy of restaurants whose menus are strictly bracketed into single cultures, "hampered by traditions and limitations," while their kitchens are diverse and their staff meals are wild experiments in cultural cross-pollination.[120] Keeping traditions separate is artificial and stifles creativity, Lee argues. As a result, Lee describes his not-fusion of Southern and Asian foods as the result of natural similarities between the cultures discovered through his own personal experiences: "From the sizzling Korean grills of my childhood to the barbeque culture that permeates the South, I have always lived in an environment where food was wrapped in a comforting blanket of smokiness . . . smoke is the intersection that connects my two worlds."[121] The South has become his home because it is so similar to the home he always knew, and while he did have to "reinvent [his] identity, both culinary and personal," he did not have to abandon his ethnic identity to be accepted into a community that would adopt him and vouchsafe his authenticity as a Southerner, too. Lee's narrative allows him to maintain two kinds of authenticity: he remains his authentic self that is true to his heritage and childhood experiences, and he is adopted easily and organically into local Southern identity.

Like Lee, Sandra A. Gutierrez writes about choosing a home in the South and feeling welcome to create innovative cuisines that blend her Latina identity with her Southern identity. In the introduction to *The New Southern-Latino Table*, Gutierrez describes her childhood of shared citizenship between the United States, where she was born, and Guatemala, where her parents were born and where she lived as a child. Gutierrez described these two identities as harmoniously blending in her memory, summarizing, "I embraced my American home and at the same time nurtured my ethnic roots."[122] This harmonious blend extended to food and food traditions; her family "celebrated the Day of the Dead with fiambre, a salad composed of pickled vegetables, deli meats, pig's feet, sausages, cheese, and olives, and Thanksgiving with a turkey dinner that included all the trimmings."[123] Gutierrez and her husband (who was also from Guatemala) moved to Durham, North Carolina, in the 1980s, and Gutierrez sought out foods that would satisfy her nostalgia but make use of ingredients that were available in her new home. Gutierrez writes that "combining flavors came naturally to me," and the "family's motto" became "Hola, Y'all!"—an open-hearted adoption of the South in line with Gutierrez's upbringing.[124] Though Gutierrez remained nostalgic for Guatemalan foods, she writes that "Southern food found my soul. . . . As my two worlds melded, so did the food in those worlds. The Latina discovered her Southern belle within, and it was magic for me."[125] This personal embrace of Southern-ness is both modeled and reciprocated on a larger scale. According to Gutierrez, "Latin and Southern cuisines are blending into new combinations that complement and build on existing dishes of both cultures" as a result of "the merging of peoples over time, naturally." Gutierrez emphasizes equal exchange and easy recipro-cation: "Latinos are finding it easy to become passionate about Southern food. Likewise, Southerners are embracing all types of Latin cuisine."[126] In her nar-rative, the merging of traditions is joyful and based on feelings of pride of place in both the South and in the country of origin. She claims, "These Latinos have brought forth their own traditional ingredients, cooking techniques, and gastronomic history and are having a great time with them in the culinary context of their new homes."[127] Gutierrez's arguments for her authority to blend these cuisines is based on nostalgia for childhood place and feelings of acceptance in the South. The final words of the introduction draw together these feelings of belonging in two cultures, seamlessly connected: "With gratitude, respect, and pride, I wish to serve up a taste of how the culinary heritages of the Americas, in the widest sense, meet at the New Southern-Latino table, and prove, deliciously, that food brings people together. Here, there is something for everyone."[128]

Implications: Toward a Conclusion

Arguments for authenticity in contemporary cookbooks — especially chef-centric ones — depend heavily on the person and personality of the chef-author. The impulse to look carefully at the ethos and character of the chef-author is connected to the central problem of New Southern cuisine: How can this cuisine be new and authentic at the same time? If a chef is going to innovate with a cultural tradition, that chef may be asked by critics to prove insider status or risk charges of appropriation. How does the chef's person (body, ethnicity, memory, feeling) and personal network (birthplace, ancestry, training, experience) certify that person to be an authentic source of knowledge? I argue that writers anticipate objections to their authenticity and use narrative as a strategy to excuse or mitigate those objections. Still, the need to narrate personal authenticity suggests that some body of cultural arbiters must decide when a person is Southern *enough* to take ownership of Southern cuisine. Who makes this judgment? Who owns Southern food?

This very question has been the subject of a recent conversation, carried out online and in social media, about what it means to cook and sell Southern food. Though questions about the ethics of eating and cooking the cuisine of a culture to which one does not belong by birth are by no means new or specific to Southern foodways, the conversation was refreshed in March 2016 when an article by Hillary Dixler on *Eater* challenged Charleston's fine-dining restaurants (led by white chefs) for profiting unfairly from the influence of Gullah cuisine. Dixler's article quoted Michael Twitty, a well-respected historian of African and African American foodways, as well as Gullah chef B. J. Dennis, who expressed disappointment that Gullah culture and cuisine were being appropriated by cultural outsiders. Twitty criticizes Charleston chefs for "**projecting ownership and making it about them**, not even considering the people who have been marginalized and exploited" by their appropriation (emphasis in original). Dennis, too, suggests that a cultural outsider cannot faithfully rec-reate the cuisine of another culture. Dixler explains, "As for non-Gullah cooks approaching Gullah recipes, Dennis likens it to if he went to Italy or China to study cooking. 'I may think I got it, but I'll never be good as that mother who has that soul. That's the same here. You may be able to do it, but somebody who's born into it has the soul for it. I think that goes for any cuisine.'"[129] Twitty's and Dennis's arguments revolve around the authenticity of the person doing the cooking, not the ingredients or recipes themselves. Twitty and Dennis both object to cultural outsiders innovating with a cuisine because authenticity, in their formulation, is established primarily through birthright and ancestry.

The controversy (and tweet storm) that followed focused on that claim, which, over time, was grossly oversimplified into its broadest strokes: white chefs should not profit from the food of black slaves. In his summary of the conflict in *Oxford American*, titled "Who Owns Southern Food," John T. Edge calls out critics who further questioned the personal authenticity of those involved. Dixler was criticized for "asking questions from a perch in New York City." Twitty's right to speak for Gullah culture was similarly critiqued; though he is indeed "a Gullah descendant," he "is also from, as they say, off." For both, the credibility of their claims is being questioned because of their personal authenticity, compromised by their geographic location outside of Charleston. Edge distances himself from these critiques, saying that the conversation con-nects to issues too important and too deeply rooted to only be about where we live or where we were born: "At a moment when conversations about food have become central to the American dialogue about identity, the issues Dixler and Twitty raised about authenticity and ownership and appropriation will fester if they're not further explored."[130]

In the column, which Edge shares with Nigerian-born chef Tunde Wey, Wey suggests that the wrong voices were speaking for others. Dixler should not have used the article to defend a culture not her own: "The story should have been written in a Gullah voice, full stop — as my mother would say in verbalized punctuation." Unexamined privilege led white chefs to criticize beyond their bounds: "That Sean Brock or Jeff Allen would openly quarrel with Michael Twitty — and question his perspective on white folks who unabashedly cook black food — is the epitome and a caricature of this prerogative." To his credit, Wey questions the appropriateness of his own voice in the conversation. "I am not a Southerner," Wey claims. "I have lived in the South for only about a year — in New Orleans, 'the most African city in America' . . . I am African, neither a Southerner nor a chef." Though Wey admits he is often called upon to offer opinions on "the 'black' experience," he wonders why he has been given the microphone "instead of any of the many more qualified Southern African-American commentators."[131] Again, the conversation and critique, as Wey outlines it, is centered on personal identity and authenticity: What gives you or me the right to speak? What about your character gives you the ethos to make such arguments?

Twitty addressed the social media response in an open letter to Sean Brock on his blog, *Afroculinaria*, calling for more serious conversation. In the essay, which was later given *Saveur*'s Food and Culture Essay Award, Twitty affirms the "right" of chefs "to 'do you,' however you please. You can cook whatever you want, call it whatever you want, stand tall in your convictions and communicate the message you want on your own terms and charge what you will for the experience." However, Twitty notes that white chefs like Brock often receive attention for researching and promoting African American foodways while "culinarians of color" who do the same are not recognized, amounting to what Twitty equates with "gentrification."[132] For Twitty, the conversation cannot be separated from identity and personal authenticity. I claimed throughout this chapter that personal narrative arguments for authenticity seemed intended to broaden membership in a more spacious Southern identity; however, in light of Twitty's criticism, these narratives that make space for more members may only serve to push marginal voices farther to the margins, centering once again the most capitalized and privileged voices — chiefly the white, male chef.

Twitty's response is shaped around arguments about his own personal authenticity in response to ad hominem tweets like the one from Charleston farmer and food writer Jeff Allen, questioning Twitty's own origins in "suburban NOVA." In the essay, Twitty affirms his ancestral connections to Africa: "I am proud to tell you I am an Akan many times over and I am a Mende — a son of rice growers through Sierra Leone leading backward to the grandeur of Old Mali and beyond that to West African prehistory on the river Niger." He also affirms his ancestral connections to African slaves in the US South, narrating his experience of visiting Sullivan's Island, where "roughly 40 percent" of slaves brought to America passed into Charleston, South Carolina, and onto Southern plantations. Twitty's emotional and physical response to this site is a narrative of his own personal origins: "This is why I insist on my right of return as the descendant of Charleston's enslaved and of the rice growers that gave the Lowcountry a story to sell." Twitty further affirms his right to speak for enslaved people by emphasizing his personal investment in recreating the historical, physical labor of antebellum foodways:

The research, recreation and interpretation of enslaved people's food is not personally or communally easy — and it goes beyond creativity and taste — it is in many ways a willed descent into hell. I assure you it is taxing, painful and revelatory — but I have no choice — as you have no choice but to be who I was created to be.

His final signature of the essay is one last claim of personal authenticity, identifying himself as, "Your friend in skillet — your cousin in mind — The Antebellum Chef, Michael W. Twitty, grandson of a great living South Carolinian — Gonze Lee Twitty, founding member, Federation of Southern Cooperatives." Twitty argues for his honest intentions, to be "friend" and "cousin" to his rhetorical adversary. He marks his historical and traditional knowledge as "The Antebellum Chef," and he reaffirms his ancestry and geographic connection to the South as "grandson of a great living South Carolinian."[133] From first to last, the argument depends on origin narratives and the evidence of personal authenticity.

The argument took place over a few months of tweets, blog posts, and newspaper editorials, bringing up significant issues about race, class, and privilege. The conversation about appropriation goes on. I'm using the last moments of this chapter to outline this conflict in order to highlight the high stakes and the many stakeholders in this conversation about personal authenticity. The personal narrative is not just a cute story or a conventional trope in some cookbooks. It is a discourse in the public sphere, and the comments and commentary demonstrate how fragile — and yet how vitally important — are these claims to Southern authenticity. The moves that writers make in their introductions and recipe headnotes have consequences that extend far beyond the pages of those books. In September 2016, Twitty reiterated in his blog the need to continue to "assess and consider the authenticity of the connection between authors, chefs, jornalists [sic] and their matter of subject." Honest intentions would no longer be sufficient for claiming authentic membership:

Expertise, proficiency, connection to the communities we cook in and cook with, amplification of those without access to the same forums, and a spirit of selfless desire to empower our neighbors who struggle with issues of access, income equality, representation, and cultural and economic self-determination are the new commandments that accompany us into the kitchen.[134]

Calls like Twitty's ensure that personal narratives like the ones examined in this chapter will not be going away. It will not be enough for a chef to merely be born in the South or to spend summers with grandparents in vegetable gardens or to call for the patronage of local farms and farmers markets to prove authentic identity in personal narrative. Those tactics described in this chapter may demonstrate "expertise, proficiency, and connections to the communities we cook in and with," but we may see a call in the future for more cookbook writers to use personal narratives to clearly outline their political identities, community engagement, and commitment to social justice. This does not mean necessarily that the Southern umbrella will become smaller, only that the claims and arguments that writers will need to make to claim coverage may have to engage more directly with issues of race, class, gender, and sexuality, and their intersections with privilege, power, and what it means to be Southern. The easy claims of a cosmopolitan, postracial New South will become harder to make convincing as the readers, writers, and arbiters of Southern food culture become both more critical of claims of authenticity and further entrenched in authenticity as a real quantity that one can measure with confidence.

—CHAPTER FOUR—

BEYOND NARRATIVE

❧

Using Certificates of Authenticity

The connection between a food and a specific place is central
to determining a food's authenticity. . . . Foodies value foods
prepared and consumed in specific locations (e.g., Chinese food
from Shenzhen, or pulled pork from Charlotte, North Carolina),
and confer less status on placeless foods that are found
everywhere and come from nowhere special or specific.
—Josee Johnston and Shyon Baumann,
Foodies: Democracy and Distinction in the Gourmet Foodscape[1]

You can't get much more Southern than sweet tea. Well, maybe
kudzu is more Southern than sweet tea, but you can't drink kudzu.
—Virginia Willis, *Basic to Brilliant, Y'all*[2]

IN THIS BOOK, I have looked fairly narrowly at small parts of cookbooks.
Headnotes may be ubiquitous and conventional across the genre, but they take
up relatively little real estate on the actual pages of most cookbooks in comparison to recipes and photographs. While this study at times has looked to narrative elements of introductions and chapter interludes for additional support,
the analysis has still been limited to a very specific pattern of text around the
recipes.

I've further narrowed my scope by looking specifically at headnotes that
describe origins. Quite often, headnotes do other things besides describe origins of traditions or texts or chefs. Headnotes may be procedural or instructional, describing techniques or equipment needed to execute the recipe, giving
instructions for sourcing ingredients or suggestions for serving the dish. The

headnote may be devoted to a sensory description of the finished dish or offer evidence of prior success. Bryant Terry's headnote for "Sugared Pecans" in *Afro-Vegan* is an example of a headnote without an origin narrative: "Simple and sweet, these nuts can be enjoyed as a snack or as a sugary bite after a meal. I also use them to add texture to other desserts. I really like pecans prepared this way, but I encourage you to experiment with other nuts to see what moves you."[3] This headnote does not invoke history, describe a recipe contributor, or call on the writer's personal memories, experiences, or identity. It is unconcerned with the origin of pecans or sugar or the practice of candying pecans. Instead, the headnote is aimed at convincing the reader to cook by leading the reader to imagine a future when the pecans have already been prepared, describing the many possibilities for serving sugared pecans. It cannot be said to tell a story about origins. It follows, then, that there is much more to say about how cookbook writers use headnotes to convince than I have been able to address in this volume through an investigation of origin narratives.

Indeed, my focus on authenticity as an argument is similarly limiting. Dianne Jacob, author of *Will Write for Food* and host of a blog by the same name, writes in a 2010 blog post about being convinced by two recipe headnotes to bake unfamiliar recipes for an important event. Jacob asks in the title, "What Makes a Recipe Headnote So Good You Want to Rush into the Kitchen?" Spoiler alert: it's not an origin narrative with claims of authenticity. Instead, Jacob provides this answer: "I like headnotes by trusted writers with strong voices." Jacob points out the specific sentences in the headnotes that convinced her to cook. The first one could be called an origin narrative:

> This orange-olive oil cake was, without a doubt, the hardest recipe to develop in *The New Portuguese Table*. Cindi Kruth, one of my recipe testers, and I made 13 versions of it until I knew it was as good as the recipe I got at Papas, the tiny restaurant up the hill from my apartment in Lisbon.[4]

The paragraph describes how the recipe was developed and gives credit to a collaborator like a citation narrative. It also makes an appeal to authenticity, claiming that the recipe on offer is "as good as" a *real* Portuguese restaurant's cake. The speaker's authority to speak on authenticity is supported by the personal experience of living in Lisbon. However, according to Jacob, the part of the narrative that convinced her was not the claim to authenticity but the appeal to authority. She was convinced by the claim of thorough testing and the authoritative voice of the narrator: "their reassurance, their strong voices, and their no-fail offers." The second headnote that convinced Jacob to rush into the kitchen was not an origin narrative at all: "When I asked readers for their favorite dishes from the *Times*, this apple cake recipe one was near the top, with thirty-seven votes."[5] Perhaps this is a citation that relies on the authority and authenticity of the *New York Times* as a source, but, again, Jacob is convinced by the approval of other readers, proof that the recipe would work. Jacob was convinced that the untried recipes were trustworthy because the writers of the headnotes pointed out that the recipes were thoroughly tested and developed, and that the recipes were popular, reader-approved. These most convincing appeals do not depend on the kind of narratives I've described in this book so far. There is much to be gained from reading recipe headnotes for something other than origin narratives as arguments of authenticity. It is my great hope that this study may lead other scholars to examine these conventional cookbook features as literary, rhetorical, and meaningful.

The central argument of this book has one very specific, concrete limitation. The unspoken assumption of this book is that rhetorical headnotes have an audience. As I have suggested as a caveat in other chapters, headnotes have to be read to be convincing and meaningful. To be perfectly frank, the headnote and the introduction may be parts of the text that appeal to a minority of cookbook readers. Commenters in online communities express differing opinions about what to do with that paragraph of text. While Jacob, as a writer and mentor of writers, is clearly invested in reading recipe headnotes and admits to finding them convincing, this is not a universal practice. A September 2011 post on TheKitchn.com asked boldly, "Recipe Headnotes: Do We Really Need Them?" The author, Emma Christensen, expresses ambivalence about the headnote, remarking that she preferred narrative elements to be separated from recipes in introductions: "I often skip over the headnotes. Even when I'm reading a cookbook for pleasure instead of in a need to get dinner on the table, I'm usually more interested in the recipe itself than, say, the writer's trip to Spain."[6] This suggests that origin narratives, especially personal narratives about the writer's experience, may be the least appealing to a reader like Christensen. Still, Christensen admitted, a headnote could be "engaging" and "enhance the recipe and give it context." Comments from users on the post ranged from "I almost always skip them"[7] to "Um, I think I would toss a cookbook out the window if it had no headnotes."[8] The conversation on the post does not offer a consensus on how readers actually approach the headnote.

However, the comments did seem to draw a distinction between recipe *readers* and recipe *users*. Commenters marked the paragraph-length headnote as a distinguishing feature of the cookbook as a genre. As commenter Jg09 put it, effective and relevant headnotes "are one of the reasons I still buy cookbooks rather [than] just find a recipe online." According to the commenter, "Folks like to read about the dish/its inspiration/creation/how-it-went/etc. Otherwise, Allrecipes would dominate the world."[9] While cookbooks with origin narratives seem to appeal to *readers*, recipe-database sites like Allrecipes.com — presumably a collection of impersonal recipes detached from story or context — are strictly for recipe *users*. Commenters expressed a lack of interest in the headnote writer's personal life (details one might find in an origin narrative), but most agreed that an instructional, descriptive, obviously relevant, not-too-personal headnote was the most desirable. As a user with the handle thinkingwoman writes:

> I find them helpful if they truly introduce the recipe — like if they offer a good summary of the cooking process, or suggestions for multitasking, especially for a long or complex recipe (i.e. 'do X while Y is simmering.'). If it's an ethnic recipe, something about the culture is nice, or if the recipe has some historical significance. I find I am rarely interested in the inspiration unless it's a really good story.[10]

Again, an origin narrative is identified as the least desirable or interesting kind of headnote, though historical narratives might be "nice."

Other commenters pointed out that while writing a headnote seemed an inescapable reality of the cookbook's generic conventions, reading them was optional. Users LacyBones and Josh B. both dismissed headnotes as attempts at textual ownership. "I hate headnotes," LacyBones writes on Christensen's post, "but a recipe can't be copyrighted. Headnotes can. Thus they exist. Sometimes to the point of nausea."[11] If the story attached to a recipe in a headnote is good enough to be repeated, then perhaps the author's name and credit will remain attached to the recipe. On Christensen's post, the commenters seem to note claims of textual ownership as a reason to skip the headnote entirely. To the contrary, Penni Wisner, a blogger and "kitchen coach," commented on Jacob's post that good headnotes were a gift to a cook and hostess who could bake the cake, serve it to guests, and then "tell the original story and embellish it — I heard about it from [someone] and oranges are in season and this olive oil was a present from Jane. Etc. Etc."[12] While Wisner does intend to retell the story she read in the headnote and give credit to the source of the recipe, the headnote serves merely as a starting point for her own performance; she is already thinking ahead to how she will make it her own, using it in her own pursuit of culinary capital. This thread of the conversation suggests that cookbook writers feel pressure to write good headnotes, but readers' reactions to those headnotes are hard to predict and often diametrically opposed.

While the sampling of commenters discussed above is by no means a carefully constructed survey, it does represent some of the most active readers of cookbooks, recipes, and food writing. The two blog posts illustrate opposite camps, and readers interested enough to comment have some vested interest in cooking and recipe reading. Jacob's commenters are mostly self-identified bloggers and food professionals, while Christensen's commenters appear to be readers and consumers of blogs and cookbooks. These writers and commenters are in the best position to describe how real writers, readers, and recipe users approach headnotes. The evidence shows that it's a mixed bag; a headnote writer cannot be assured that any given reader — even one like me who writes critically about headnotes as a practice — will actually read and process the headnote, using the narrative or information there to make the decision to cook or not cook.

Because a cookbook writer and designer can be assured neither that the headnote will be read nor that the headnote alone will be convincing, I argue that the narrative headnote is only one of many textual, paratextual, and visual strategies that work in concert in order to convince readers of the authenticity of a dish, a recipe, a writer, or a cuisine. By way of conclusion, this chapter briefly describes the many other nonnarrative devices that cookbook writers, designers, and publishers use in addition to headnotes to establish authenticity, including nonnarrative headnotes, titles, place names, ingredients and brand names, cover art and design, photography, blurbs and forewords, keywords, and other marketing strategies. I describe these as *certificates of authenticity*.

Unlike the narrative arguments of authenticity examined in previous chapters, certificates of authenticity have more in common with badges, a visual shorthand that may or may not be read in the word-by-word, left-to-right, line-by-line method of reading typical of English language. While narratives often *state* their objectives in clear language, certificates like photography and design typically *suggest*. In addition, certificates and badges are usually awarded or assigned by outside authentication agencies and governing bodies. So, too, the certificates like jacket blurbs and forewords come from individuals at a distance from the work itself, as agents qualified to issue such evaluations. All the elements of design and marketing, together with the headnotes and narrative introductions, suggest that cookbooks are written and designed with arguments of authenticity foremost in mind. Cookbooks do not rely on headnotes alone to make this argument.

As in other chapters, here I treat the cookbook's named author as auteur. The particular elements described in this chapter are the elements most likely to be chosen or influenced by editors, designers, and other representatives of the publishing industry, not the chef persona at the center of the cookbook's story. The person whose name is on the cover very likely did not design that cover and may not have had any input on its final appearance. Therefore, whenever possible, I will name the photographer, artist, coauthor, or other decision-maker, if credited. This is often difficult to ascertain, since the cookbook itself—like many other collaborative artistic endeavors—often obscures the many other players involved in publishing it. While it is not likely that chef-authors are also responsible for the layout, design, photography, or marketing of their books (they may not even be responsible for writing the narratives), I maintain that the named author—as copyright holder and authorial personality—remains at the center as the author, the auteur.

Southern Varieties: Naming the South as Certificate

The next section of this chapter focuses on uses of terms within and around narratives that function as certificates of authenticity. This includes uses of variations on *South* and *Southern* in phrases that assert authenticity through geographic specificity, as defined by Johnston and Baumann.[13] The accumulation of these variations, deployed strategically in titles and narratives, connect the cookbook as a whole to a regional cuisine that is distinct and defined.

Within the text, whether narrative or not, perhaps the most direct kind of certificate a writer can provide of authentic Southern-ness is to state explicitly that a thing is Southern—that is, unique and essential to Southern identity. This includes using *South* and its many linguistic varieties as modifiers (Southern culture, the Southerner's DNA, the Southern kitchen) and as nouns (the South, Southerners, Southernization). Declarations of what is Southern are implicitly, if not explicitly, claims of authenticity. The repetition of *South* and *Southern* in titles, narratives, and generalizations creates a catalog of recipes, ingredients, behaviors, and characteristics that define a distinct Southern identity. In these instances, the word *South* is used as a brand, and the sentences and uses of the word describe what is and is not in line with the South as brand. These claims may appear in origin narrative–style headnotes, but they often appear in introductions, callout boxes, sidebars, and titles. Individually, varieties of *South* make direct claims in sentences and phrases, but the repeated use of such phrases throughout a text can have an accumulating effect, authenticating not just a specific recipe but an entire book, author, persona, or cuisine.

To begin to understand how cookbooks build a Southern brand, I draw on some methods of data mining and digital humanities to count and account for various uses of keywords in a sample of cookbooks in order to measure how often authors name the South or how often they identify specific traits, traditions, or ingredients as distinctly Southern. With the help of research assistants, we recorded mentions of specific locations (cities, businesses, farms, restaurants) and general ones (states, countries, ethnic groups) into a database. Each place name was assigned a description to categorize the usage of particular words in a text in order to track trends in how place names were used. For example, a place name might be coded "ingredient" and "variety" if it was used to describe an ingredient's biological variety, like "Vidalia onions" or "Charleston Hot Peppers." It might be a coded "region" and "title" if the place name were part of a recipe title like "Lowcountry Shrimp Boil." Or it might be coded "restaurant" and "influence" if the place name referred to a restaurant where a chef received training that influenced the recipe on offer. The goal of this ongoing project is to track the places or people that are identified as a part of the South, an influence on Southern cuisine, or otherwise an origin that makes a recipe authentically Southern.

Southern Titling

Contemporary cookbooks are an especially apt site for an investigation of intentional Southern branding through cookbook titles. According to data collected by Lily Kelting, the last two decades have seen a marked increase in the use of the words *South* and *Southern* as branding in titles, increasing from 2 percent of cookbooks published in the United States in 1990–2000 to 7.5 percent in 2010–2015.[14] The statistic seems to suggest that the label or brand of *Southern* acts as a certificate, communicating to readers or potential buyers a set of expectations, and that titling a book *Southern* indicates that the contents intend to represent a distinct cuisine of a distinct region. Of the fifty cookbooks consulted in this project, thirty use a variety of *South* in the title. Matt and Ted Lee's title contains the most: *The Lee Bros. Southern Cookbook: Stories and Recipes for Southerners and Would-Be Southerners*.[15] Four more refer to specific cities, states, or regions within the South in their titles (Charleston, New Orleans, Virginia, Southern Appalachia). Dora Charles's cookbook contains both the general region and a specific city: *A Real Southern Cook: In Her Savannah Kitchen*.[16] With that word *Real* as code for authenticity, Charles also makes a claim to being the definitive source of authentic recipes, as do titles like Paula Deen's *Southern Cooking Bible* or Nathalie Dupree's *Mastering the Art of Southern Cooking*.[17] The titles also indicate a difference between *South*, *Old South*, and *New South*. Books like Damon Fowler's *Classical Southern Cooking* and Virginia Willis's *Bon Appetit, Y'all: Recipes and Stories from Three Generations of Southern Cooking* are contrasted with *New Southern Cooking* (Dupree), *A New Turn in the South* (Acheson), *The New Southern-Latino Table* (Gutierrez), *Smoke and Pickles: Recipes and Stories from a New Southern Kitchen* (Ed Lee), and *A Southern Gentleman's Kitchen: Adventures in Cooking, Eating, and Living in the New South* (Moore).[18] The branding of the *New South* in these titles suggests that innovations within these cookbooks will still be recognizable as authentically Southern even as they represent modern cuisine and global trends.

The remaining cookbooks that do not refer to the South in their titles instead hint at other kinds of authenticity (as outlined by Johnston and Baumann) rather than geographic specificity. Three refer to specific restaurants (*Foster's Market Favorites* and *Hot and Hot Fish Club Cookbook*) or author's names (*The Pat Conroy Cookbook*) for branding, highlighting a personal connection between a specific producer and the contents of the book.[19] Brock's title *Heritage* suggests both personal connection and historical tradition.[20] *Come Home to Supper* (Jordan) and *Cooking in the Moment* (Reusing) suggest simplicity, honest, local, and natural offerings.[21] Kevin Gillespie's *Fire in My Belly: Real Cooking* does not identify a specific region in its title but does promise personal connection through an author who will be "true" to himself.[22] Even though these titles do not imply that their contents are representative of Southern regional cuisine, they still make appeals to arguments of authenticity. The non-narrative branding of titles points to an overarching interest in authenticity that communicates to readers even if they fail to read the narrative elements.

Titling Recipes

Just as the titles of books make claims to representing the whole of Southern cuisine, recipe titles similarly use *South* or *Southern* as branding. By titling a recipe with the adjective *Southern*, authors are claiming that this dish is canonical to Southern cuisine and the recipe provided is an authentic version appropriate for performing Southern identity. For example, Stacey Little (*The Southern Bite Cookbook*) uses *Southern* in titling for "Southern Chocolate Gravy" and "Southern Fried Corn" in a section titled "Heirloom Bites" along with "Southern Cornbread Dressing" and "Southern Layered Salad."[23] The headnotes associated with these titles do not clarify what exclusive connection these recipes have to the South as a region, even though chocolate gravy is often cited in other texts as a uniquely Appalachian tradition. The titles imply that these dishes are traditional fare in the South, even though the narratives do not attempt to support that implication. Even the section title, "Heirloom Bites," communicates historical authenticity. Together, these linguistic certificates accumulate into an overarching argument for authenticity carried out in narrative and nonnarrative elements of the cookbook.

Another usage of the *Southern* title is to take a dish not typically associated with the South and include an ingredient that is intended to represent Southern cuisine. Acheson's "Southern Carbonara" uses this technique. As Acheson explains in the headnote: "The Southernization of this Italian classic comes in the form of country ham replacing the usual pancetta and a green component in the form of collards."[24] In other instances, the Southern connection is implied: Acheson's "Southern Pimm's Cup" (a cocktail usually associated with the United Kingdom) is recommended with ginger ale made in South Carolina, which "gives this version a Southern kick."[25] It isn't clear which ingredient makes Little's "Southern Layered Salad" unique to the region (iceberg lettuce, canned peas, cooked bacon, red onion, mayonnaise, cheddar cheese), but the title still makes the claim to regional authenticity, even without a narrative providing corroborating evidence.

This kind of Southern branding in titles is not uniformly applicable across the sample. Martha Hall Foose's *A Southerly Course: Recipes and Stories from Close to Home* does not use "Southern" in any recipe titles.[26] Neither does Anne Stiles Quatrano's *Summerland*.[27] Though Brock often mentions the South in his narratives, he does not do so in titles except for his cocktail "Southern Screwdriver."[28] He is more likely to use cities, regions, or restaurant names in the titles to suggest geographic specificity: "The Charleston Bamboo," "Lowcountry Hoppin' John," or "Husk Hot Sauce."[29] In addition to "Southern" titling, other recipe title strategies suggest authenticity through personal connections. "Hugh's Lobster Pie," subtitled "an homage to Bill Neal" from Acheson's *A New Turn in the South*, not only promises the chef-author's personal recipe but also connects the recipe to the late legendary chef, Bill Neal of Crook's Corner in Chapel Hill, North Carolina.[30] Similar techniques often appear along with citation narratives, marking the recipe as authentic because of its connection to capitalized matriarchs: "Mama's Mashed Potatoes" in Ronni Lundy's *Victuals* or "Nanny's Cranberry Mold" in Quatrano's *Summerland*.[31] Others stake their claim to authenticity by suggesting age, history, or uniquely Southern traditions: "Heirloom Bloody Marys," "Deer Stand Old-Fashioned," "The Charleston Light Dragoon Punch 1792."[32] All of these titling strategies make implicit claims that the recipes that follow are authentic representations of a defined regional cuisine, while the headnotes may or may not articulate those claims explicitly.

Accumulation of Souths

In addition to the titles of books and recipes, the prose elements of cookbooks also make claims about what defines Southern authenticity. The number of repetitions of these variations of *South* throughout the text varies dramatically among the sample.[33] For instance, in *Basic to Brilliant, Y'all*, Virginia Willis uses variations on *South* 103 times. Fifty-one of those are various uses of *Southern* as a modifier ("Southern tradition," "southern cuisine," "a very traditional Southern nibble," "a Southern-kissed hors d'oeuvres platter," "Southern ears," "a Southern classic," "down-home Southern cooking," etc.).[34] By contrast, Andrea Reusing only uses thirteen variations on *the South* in *Cooking in the Moment*. While most of Willis's uses are adjectives, Reusing uses the noun form, referring to a specific location, usually in historical narratives, as in this note about Ossabaw hogs: "Brought to the American South in the sixteenth century by Spanish explorers, these hogs were stranded on Ossabaw [island]."[35] The accumulation of *Souths* marks the rhetorical purposes of these texts very differently. While Willis is invested in making claims about Southern culture and cuisine at large, Reusing appears to be more invested in seasonal and local arguments, as evidenced by the title (*Cooking in the Moment: A Year of Seasonal Recipes*), the arrangement of the chapters (spring, summer, fall, and winter), and the repetition of specific farmers and suppliers, which she cites 133 times throughout the book, more than any other naming strategy. The count suggests that Willis is invested in geographic specificity as an argument for authenticity, but Reusing builds her case for authenticity on simplicity, seasonality, and locality. Clearly both authors are invested in giving the impression of authenticity, even though they use different strategies to communicate it.

Varieties, Breeds, Brands, and Suppliers

In the recipes themselves, cookbook authors use the ingredient lists and instructions as another opportunity for displaying certificates of authenticity. In the recipe text and headnotes, authors may call for specific varieties of produce, breeds of animal, brand-name products, and farms or other suppliers that serve as certificates of authentic Southern cuisine. These may be popular names for biological varieties associated with Southern geography, like Vidalia onions, of Vidalia, Georgia, or Ossabaw hogs from Ossabaw Island, or the recipes may call for ingredients sourced from the South, like Gulf Coast shrimp. While any sweet onion would probably serve the purpose of a recipe, authors specify Vidalia onions as a signifier of geographic specificity. Sean Brock, in particular, builds recipes around a variety of pepper called "Charleston Hots," and even though he suggests in his "Resources" appendix that readers order them from a company based in Chico, California, the name links directly to Charleston, South Carolina, and the Low Country — the region and cuisine Brock represents.[36] Brock notes that the more widely available cayenne is a sufficient substitute, but "Charleston Hots" is a specifically named ingredient in three recipes and featured in the title "Boiled Peanuts with Smoky Pig's Tails and Charleston Hots" to suggest geographic specificity.[37]

Southern-made brands like Duke's mayonnaise, Tabasco sauce, Benton's bacon, and Anson Mills grains appear often as certificates of Southern authenticity. The brand-name supplier that Brock relies on most is Anson Mills in Columbia, South Carolina, purveyor of heritage ingredients like Carolina Gold rice and benne seeds, as well as varieties of grits, flour, and cornmeal. Brock mentions Anson Mills in narrative and recipes sixty-seven times, even more than his own restaurants, Husk (forty-eight) and McCrady's (nineteen). Baking recipes, especially, may call for multiple varieties of Anson Mills products: "My Sister's Chocolate Éclair Cake" calls for "Anson Mills Antebellum-Style Rustic Coarse Graham Flour" and "Anson Mills Pizza Maker's Flour."[38] The "Antebellum Benne-Blackberry Tart with Brown Butter Ice Cream" calls for "Anson Mills New Crop Antebellum Bennecake Flour" and "Anson Mills Antebellum Benne Seeds."[39] In both recipes, the Anson Mills products are intended to link the recipe to the geographic South and the antebellum past as signals of Southern authenticity. Brock is clear in his headnotes that substituting another brand-name product will not be authentic and is not advised: "if you want the real thing, you'll have to order benne from Anson Mills."[40] Moreover, the Anson Mills products elevate the dish to a higher cuisine. Brock contrasts his chocolate éclair recipe with "the version I grew up on," made with mass-produced supermarket ingredients like "store-bought graham crackers, Jell-O pudding, and Cool Whip." Brock admits that these convenience ingredients were part of the reason he loved the cake to begin with, but his version is made with "Anson Mills Graham Flour and homemade vanilla pudding and whipped cream."[41] This elevated recipe is distanced from the lowbrow and inauthentic convenience ingredients; it is simultaneously updated to current cuisine and connected to antebellum past promised by Anson Mills products for historical authenticity. Ironically, although the Anson Mills product is available for purchase online, it is not considered store-bought like the much-maligned Jell-O pudding. Instead, the Southern-made, antebellum-linked, and widely available brand name of Anson Mills makes authenticity accessible to any reader.

Taken together, these geographically based certificates of varieties, breeds, brand names, and suppliers are intended to point to three kinds of authenticity: 1) geographically specific, Southern-made products, 2) "honest" and "personal" products contrasted with the anonymous mass-production of mechanized agribusiness, and 3) exact replicas of the chef's cooking, as the chef does it and intends for it to be done, true to the chef's intentions. These ingredients with place names are connected to terroir — the notion that flavor is connected physically to geography and place. For authentic Southern food, authentic Southern soil is needed. Whether recipes are calling for Kentucky bourbon generally or Buffalo Trace specifically, Vidalia onions or tomatoes from "your local farmer's market," the branding of ingredients by location in titles and recipe text is another certificate of authenticity that compounds the narratives of authenticity.

Photography and Design

For cookbook browsers and those utilitarian types who skip the headnotes, photography can be a certificate of authenticity that is difficult to miss. Reading text, even skimming titles and ingredients lists, requires a certain amount of attention and intention. But the photography and design are almost absorbed. A picture may be the hook that convinces a browser to read the text. Photographs serve as certificates of authenticity by suggesting age and tradition through the vague oldness present in antique spoons or rustic wooden tables, or through recognizably Southern-made goods like Mason jars. Vintage, antique, or retro-looking dishes suggest age, and the time origin of the recipe may be marked visually in the photography. Inside the front cover of Virginia Willis's *Basic to Brilliant, Y'all* is a two-page spread, sepia-toned photo of antique-looking kitchenware, including an antique glass butter churner, a Mason jar with okra, a Ball jar with a dark liquid, cast-iron cookware in various sizes, a pair of knives with silver filigree and white handles, a white ceramic serving dish with a pattern of grapes and leaves, and a stack of table linens. The same image is in full color in the introduction.[42] The dishes are dated and vaguely old looking, and the text around the full-color image describes Willis's family and their long connection to the South. Taken together, the image and the text suggest a link between inherited knowledge and inherited goods. The photographer, Hélène Dujardin, has staged many of the full-page, full-color photos of plated dishes with antique-looking silverware in the front of the frame with more flatware and dishes out of focus just beyond the plated food. The object nearest to the viewer is the silver. This pattern can be seen in the photos of "Southern Salad Macédoine,"

"Arugula with Country Ham and Pecans," "Kale Omelet," and "Grandmother's Chicken."[43] Another common prop for suggesting Southern authenticity is the glass canning jar, commonly Mason or Ball brand jars. Willis's inside cover includes eight glass jars of various sizes and brands. In *A New Turn in the South*, Acheson not only offers images of canning jars but includes Mason jars in the recipe instructions. The image, paired with the opening of the first chapter, "Libations," is of Acheson (whose identifying forearm tattoo of a radish is prominently featured) pouring tea from a large glass canning jar into a smaller Ball-brand jar.[44] The first recipe of the chapter is for "Lemonade with Vanilla, Mint, and Rosemary," and the instructions explicitly note that the lemonade should be stored in Mason jars.[45] On the following page is a full-page, full-color photo of "Watermelon Limeade" served in a glass jar.[46] The next recipe is for "A-team Waiter Sweet Tea." The headnote calls for "two nice clean quart jars," and the accompanying image is a different angle on the first: Acheson with visible tattoo pouring tea between Ball-brand jars.[47] The repetition of canning jars as images and instructions links Acheson's recipes not only to traditions of canning and preserving but also to the overall aesthetic of the book—a very casual, do-it-yourself craftiness that prefers drinking jars to fine china and white tablecloths. Cast iron serves a similar purpose as Mason jars, and John Currence features one on the cover of *Pickles, Pigs, and Whiskey*. The visual rhetoric of the cast iron is similar to the canning jar, suggesting down-home humility and timelessness. Currence's instructions for making roux features four photographs of roux in four shades of brown, repeating the same cast-iron skillet on the same rustic wooden surface. The instructions insist "Cast iron is not the *only* choice for cooking roux," but other kinds of pans "can more easily lend a hand to a failed roux."[48]

Images and design may also certify authenticity through a personal connection, a glimpse into the chef-author's singular world. This might include images of the chef at work or with family; the presence of a body in the image (especially close-ups of hands or unique tattoos as in Acheson above and the cover of Brock's *Heritage*) suggests an intimate, personal connection with the chef. Just as authenticity communicated the opposite of mass production, authenticity may also be suggested with images that appear to be candid, captured in the moment and unstaged, indicating not only Southern authenticity but also a more general sense of a personal, handcrafted, unscripted look into the chef's real world.

Acheson's *A New Turn in the South* demonstrates an overall design aesthetic that suggests this kind of personal authenticity. The layout is evocative of a scrapbook or journal. The inside cover looks like lined notebook paper with handwritten lists of pairings and procedures for proteins. For example, under the heading "Trout" on the top left corner, is this list: "bacon, mustard, capers, frisee, butter beans, campfire tomatoes, thyme." The lists seem to be notes from the chef to himself. The handwritten script continues as a design element throughout the book, appearing in titles, headings, lists, pull quotes, and sidebars. The introduction opens with this handwriting, in Acheson's first-person narrative voice, suggesting that the handwriting is his own. The handwritten titles appear on three kinds of squares of note paper: yellow legal pad, blue or green graph paper, and a cream-colored lined paper with a perforation at the top. The titles are sometimes accompanied by a hand-drawn illustration, like the cartoon doodle of crab under "She-Crab Soup" or a shrimp under "Shrimp with andouille and hominy grits."[49] Even type-set text appears to be cut from plain paper and pasted into the scrapbook. Text boxes have white backgrounds and may be placed over photographs or graph paper. These design touches, while not specifically suggestive of Southern-ness, point to an intimacy with the chef-author who is personally invested in each page of the cookbook. The design implies that Acheson has literally written the cookbook by hand. And that may actually be the case. Acheson is given credit for illustrations on the Library of Congress publication information page.[50] The scrapbook aesthetic also connects to the time-honored tradition of manuscript recipe collections like the ones studied by Janet Theophano in *Eat My Words: Reading Women's Lives through the Cookbooks They Wrote*.[51] Given this connection, Acheson seems to be presenting a cookbook that is handcrafted — the work of a singular author who is cook, writer, and designer — as cookbooks have been historically crafted for generations. This personally annotated and handwritten collection is equated with the annotated and handwritten collection one might inherit from a grandmother.

Forewords and Blurbs

In some ways, forewords and book jacket blurbs are the most obvious certificates of authenticity. Regardless of genre, conventional book jacket blurbs are meant to entice browsers to become buyers, just as all arguments of authenticity in cookbooks are meant to make readers into cooks and storytellers. The voices on book jackets and forewords act as guarantors who lend their credibility to vouch for the authenticity of the contents of the book and its author. These are certificates in the most common sense of the word: awards issued by authorities outside of the text that certify the book as a whole and its author.

As in all genres, the cookbook jacket blurb recreates the author's network of connections to other authorities. The reader assumes a personal connection between the blurbist and the book's author, a relationship of mutual respect that signifies the communities the author might belong to or be welcomed by. For example, Virginia Willis's 2008 cookbook *Bon Appetit, Y'all* has four blurbs from entities that suggest this book is welcomed and admired by experts in scientific home cooking (Alton Brown of *Good Eats* and Shirley O. Corriher of *CookWise*), classic French cooking (Anne Willan of École de Cuisine La Varenne), and Southern foodways (John T. Edge of the Southern Foodways Alliance).[52] Each endorsing agent represents a particular audience of this book, which mixes classic French technique with traditional Southern dishes, intended to be replicated in the home. The particular challenge to authenticity posed by Willis's book is this unorthodox mixing of traditions that threatens distinct identity. Though it is unrealistic to expect that all four of these names would be familiar to every interested reader, each voice represents a single community that could be legible to a reader within the overlapping target audiences of this book. The combination of voices places Willis in a network of individuals in overlapping communities with authority to approve the experiment of fusing cuisines.

The foreword of the book, written by Nathalie Dupree (author of *New Southern Cooking*, legendary food TV personality, and cofounder of the Southern Foodways Alliance), similarly places Willis in an authorized network. Dupree highlights Willis's professional network, noting that she has "worked with some of the top names in the food world, from Anne Willan to Martha Stewart" and "allow[ed] herself to be influenced by many brilliant cooks, both French and American." Again, the combination of cuisines is an outcropping of personal experience, a chef being true to herself. Because Dupree's reputation is as teacher of Southern cuisine, she endorses Willis as a student and as an authentic Southerner: "This book reflects Virginia's quintessential Southernness. In the South, the first thing one is asked is, 'Who are your people?' She has always claimed her people, her mother and grandmother among them, through her food."[53] Forewords and blurbs are a way of identifying an author's people, placing the author into a community as an authority among and approved by other recognized authorities.

Notably, in this sample, Nathalie Dupree and John T. Edge write a significant number of blurbs and forewords: eleven and seven, respectively. Dupree and Edge are each authors and public figures in their own right, as seen above, but as representatives of the Southern Foodways Alliance, they have an

additional institutionalized power as voices for Southern food in both popular and academic circles. Edge is called upon to write blubs for Chris and
Idie Hastings's *Hot and Hot Fish Club Cookbook*, Andrew Ticer and Michael
Hudman's *Collards & Carbonara*, Ed Lee's *Smoke and Pickles*, Sean Brock's
Heritage, Virginia Willis's *Bon Appetit, Y'all*, and Jean Anderson's *A Love Affair
with Southern Cooking*. In these blurbs Edge is alternately identified as editor
of the series *Cornbread Nation: The Best of Southern Food Writing*,[54] author
of *Southern Belly: The Ultimate Food Lover's Companion to the South*,[55] and
coeditor of *The Southern Foodways Alliance Community Cookbook*.[56] These
appellations all identify Edge as an expert witness on Southern food and good
writing. However, Currence, Lee, and Brock specifically identify Edge in connection with the Southern Foodways Alliance, an important signal of cultural
awareness, historical scholarship, and institutional approval. All three also note
their collaborations with the Southern Foodways Alliance symposium within
their cookbooks' narratives, emphasizing their experiential connection to this
authenticating agency.[57] Being associated with the SFA through Edge's endorsement and their own narratives of direct experience connect those authors with
a powerful authenticating agency.

This discussion of Edge and the SFA as certificates of authenticity is not in
itself a criticism of the SFA. All organizations that issue membership badges
are engaged in authentication practices; card-carrying members of any organization use that membership as building materials for their personal and public
identities. As a member of the SFA myself, I count on that organization's reputation to build my own professional and personal legibility, right alongside my
membership in the MLA and my local public radio station. The alliance is not
unduly wielding its influence or engaging in anything subversive by authenticating its members through book jacket blurbs, but it is relevant to note that
within the community of New Southern food, Edge's name and affiliation with
the SFA on the back cover are significant and sought-after certificates that communicate membership in an authoritative network.

The power of a blurb or foreword to authenticate seems dependent upon a
reader knowing how that certifier fits in the network of Southern cookbooks.
The most authority and authenticity is granted by the figures who are the most
connected and recognizable. However, knowing that book jacket blurbs must
appeal to readers outside the community as well, we cannot ignore the content
of blurbs and forewords in this analysis. The combination of blurbists and their
claims can be a good indicator of the cookbook's intentions and aspirations.
The rhetorical appeals in these paratextual elements communicate authenticity

with strategies that mirror those found in headnotes, especially geographic specificity, personal connection, and "honesty."

Not only does being associated with Edge and the Southern Foodways Alliance suggest the approval of an authority, but the content of Edge's blurbs also point to some of the same kinds of authenticity that have been employed by headnote writers. Edge writes for the *Hot and Hot Fish Club Cookbook*, "If you're looking for evidence of the ongoing evolution of Southern restaurant culture, thumb the Hot and Hot tome. From bobwhite quail to clam pirlou to fig-infused bourbon, Chris Hastings serves up modern riffs on pan-regional culinary traditions."[58] Edge grants the book geographic specificity by identifying its Southern location, but more importantly, he describes the book's organic relationship between historical "culinary traditions" and the restaurant's "modern riffs" through the ever-upward natural process of "evolution." The book can be trusted to provide a cuisine for a New South. Edge's blurb for Ticer and Hudman's *Collards & Carbonara* also emphasizes the chef-authors' organic blending of culinary traditions:

> Full of righteous devotion to their hometown of Memphis, inspired by the cookery of their Italian grandmothers, Andy and Michael have staked out a compelling geography where Tennessee abuts Parma, *sformato* gets swaddled in neck bone gravy, and collards come perfumed with *nduja*. To get a handle on what the best American food looks, smells, and tastes like in this postprovincial moment, cook your way through this book.[59]

The blurb immediately places the chef-authors in the geographic South while claiming that their fusing of cuisines extends naturally from an authentic source in the form of "their Italian grandmothers." The authors are true to their experiences, and the results are simple, harmonious combinations that do not exploit this "postprovincial moment" but represent the best that national and regional border crossing can create.

Of all the authenticating strategies discussed in this chapter, blurbs and forewords are perhaps the most ubiquitous across all literary genres, and while their purposes vary little across genre and region, they are significant to this study as further evidence of the cookbook's investment in authenticity as a rhetorical concept. When taken together, from the title on the front cover to the blurb on the back, all of these textual and visual cues point to an agreement between writers, designers, publishers, and auteurs that audiences care about authenticity. Arguments of authenticity turn browsers into buyers, readers into performers.

Implications: Toward a Conclusion

This rapid reading of the nonnarrative persuasive elements of cookbooks is by no means a complete analysis of the methods that cookbook writers, designers, and editors use to make arguments of authenticity. This book has been moving "Toward a Conclusion" without ever arriving. Even now, this concluding chapter is not aimed at closing this study; rather, I hope I have opened up new possibilities for further analysis and demonstrated some methods of reading that might offer fruitful paths forward for other writers. In the final pages here, I will continue to resist foreclosing interpretations or making definitive claims. Instead, I'll lay out a case for why the important work of critically reading cookbooks — especially from the US South — is an unfinished and worthy project.

Perhaps this book has widened the divide between scholars who question authenticity and the popular writers who gain power from using the language of authenticity. It was this gap that inspired this study in the first place. On one hand, I heard the scholarly voices of John Egerton, predicting the end of Southern distinction.[60] Scott Romine understood the "real South" to be "a set of anxious, transient, even artificial intersections, sources, or common surfaces between that are themselves remarkably fluid," bound up in "its fraught and anxious relation . . . with authenticity."[61] Michael Kreyling's *The South That Wasn't There* critiqued the Southerner's revision of history and the great lengths they would go to offer "reassurance that the present is indeed continuous with a past in which their origins were unambiguously established fact and that history is nothing less than the story of their (our) foreordained triumph. The-way-we-were is the way-we-are."[62] Jennifer Rae Greeson wrote of the South as a "geographic fantasy."[63] But on the other hand, every issue of *Garden & Gun* claims to know what products and traits and recipes make the South unique.[64] Chef-authors claim to hold Southern distinction in their DNA, like Donald Link, who knows "Southern hospitality is not a myth — it's real."[65] Scholars may argue that such claims of authenticity emerge from an existential dread of global homogenization, but the pages of Ed Lee's *Smoke and Pickles* don't seem too anxious about the end of a distinct Southern identity. Southern-ness is alive and well, capitalized and ready for the market.

Thinking about authenticity as *invented* does not undermine either of these camps. Romine, Kreyling, Greeson, and others are still right: Southern-ness is unstable, mutable, a constructed binary. But it does not follow that contemporary Southern food writers are naïve, uncritical thinkers, or unskilled writers because they support a distinct Southern identity. Instead, they prove to be quite savvy readers of the market and manipulators of conventions, taking those unstable boundaries of Southern-ness and firming them up in text, making them fit their own agendas, using the conventions of the cookbook to reinforce their roles as cultural arbiters, taste makers, celebrities, and authors. If authenticity is invented, then those who claim it are inventors and their texts are inventions worth studying.

Despite the scholarly questions about whether the South ever really existed outside of the popular imagination, cookbooks are still in the business of imagining and defining a distinct Southern identity. Even if "the South" does not exist, it matters a great deal that individuals and groups believe that it does, and, to this study in particular, it matters a great deal that those beliefs are written down in the form of narrative arguments about the authenticity of recipes. This belief in a coherent and distinct South is central to the success of New Southern cuisine, which means that authenticity is central to their success, as well. As these cookbooks define authentic food and foodways through narratives about the origins of Southern distinctiveness, they argue that authenticity can be consumed as well as performed. In other words, buying Southern products and collecting essential Southern experiences are effective methods of communicating an authentic Southern identity.

At the end of this project, I have come to think of authenticity as a language, a set of signs that a community informally agrees upon and constantly revises. Clearly, it matters who speaks for Southern food, who profits from it and who does not, who pays for it and how much, who shares credit for it and who does not, who teaches it and who learns it, who claims membership in its community and who feels excluded from it. Authenticity is a language between a listener and a speaker that sets scripts for the interaction between people, shaping how the speaker speaks and how the listener listens.

In terms of coins or art or action figures, for example, the language of authenticity is fairly easy to assess. The signs are few. Is the coin made of the material of which it is said to be made? Is the painting actually painted by the person by whom it is reported to have been painted? Was the action figure made when it was said to have been made? Are the claims to authenticity supported by measurable, physical evidence and documented provenance? Then authenticity of objects is certified. Further, the language of authenticity in coins and art and action figures is spoken only by a select and powerful few in each field. Their certificates are meaningful because they are rare. While the dollar amount invested in such signs of authenticity may be great, the stakes for personal identity making are low. A certificate of authenticity for a coin will make it instantly valuable for market, potentially making its owner rich, but not necessarily changing how the owner imagines being imbricated in the world of overlapping identities. Coins and art and action figures are not people.

To speak of the authenticity of *people* and their identities, of bodies and of cultures and of selves, is to muddy the waters significantly. Instead of a single language with a discreet set of agreed-upon signs practiced by only a few, we have instead a cacophony of competing languages; everyone seems to speak some dialect of *authentic* when it comes to cuisine. Certainly, certificates of personal authenticity carry market value, but the stakes are exponentially higher than can be measured in mere dollars and cents. To speak of a person as authentic is to ascribe to them an identity, to circumscribe a set of qualities as definitive, to proscribe any other qualities as inauthentic, invalid, unwelcome. Just as Meredith Abarca argued that the label of *authenticity* may stymie innovation in cuisine, so, too, authenticity can essentialize, obscure, and deny intersectional identity, suggesting that the borders of identity are rigid and narrow.[66]

To say, from the position of scholar and critic of language, that *authenticity* as a language is arbitrarily made and may therefore be unmade is to deny and diminish the very real pain and anger of very real people. As the controversy over the appropriation of Gullah cuisine in Charleston described in the last chapter can attest, the passion and burning outrage in the articles and open letters of the ongoing conversation are palpable. The fragile categories of identity, made and unmade with mere words, feel ironclad to those invited in or left out of a group to which they wish to belong. Especially when the economic success of their ventures as entrepreneurs, restaurateurs, chefs, and authors depends on a legible and convincing group membership.

True enough, authenticity is made by narrative, but an end to narrative is not what is called for. This examination of narrative strategies of authenticity is not intended to say that nothing is authentic, or even that everything *could be* authentic. To the contrary, amplifying the multiplicity of narratives above — the variety of signs being employed, the diversity of bodies and selves speaking, all making claims to authenticity — is one way forward into an intersectional Southern identity. Acknowledging historical roots, citing the contributions of innovators, embedding in a local network and working for its good: these may be the ethical prerequisites for claiming some original turf on the foodscape of New Southern cuisine. Through identification, the variety of voices and bodies that lay claim to a piece of Southern identity and cuisine in cookbooks may lead to a greater variety of readers and diners who will use their similarities with diverse chef-authors as a basis for making their own identities.

I have always thought it idealistic, maybe even naïve, to suggest that food is the key that unlocks "the rusty gate" of divisions of race, class, gender, regionalism, ethnicity. Claims like these give far too much agency to caloric mixtures and solutions subjected to heat and cold in chemical reactions, erasing the divisions of power and labor before and after the meal by imagining that the magic only happens in the eating, after the table is set. But perhaps the narratives of authenticity here can undo that erasure by revealing the actors and agents in the exchange of story for certificate. *Storytelling* is the key to that rusty gate, and *readers*, if convinced by the story, have the agency to twist that key in the lock. The gatekeepers of cuisine are the readers, diners, performers, consumers. They vote for authenticity with their dollars and their forks. As Ed Lee wrote for *Eater* in 2013, in response to "the Paula Deen Scandal," a community is made and defined by its members (emphasis in original):

> The South that I live and travel in is one that is buoyed by **diversity, acceptance, generosity and love** –; the people and kitchens of the American South have enriched my life with culture and respect. Does the antediluvian stains [*sic*] of racism exist here too? Of course it does. Just like any place where Old World values collide with progressive change, where tradition is asked to bend to modern society. So bascially [*sic*] any place in America. But the South that I choose to live in does not happen by chance, or by wishful thinking. It happens because **people choose to participate**. They choose to gather and question and communicate and include and shake hands. It takes work to build a community.[67]

Lee's statement places the agency and the power for defining authentic community in the choices of the community itself. The voices represented by the chef-authors in this chapter — born in New Orleans and New York, trained in San Francisco and Italy, mentored by Southern legends and Korean grandmothers — defy categorization in a box as small as *authentic*. But by narrating themselves into that box anyway, by convincing readers that they are citizens of the South through their choices to live, work, grow, buy, help, and dig in there, they make the box bigger.

I hope that what emerges from this conversation of authenticity is more gathering, questioning, communicating, and hand shaking, as Lee says. And perhaps some version of what Twitty wrote in his open letter to Sean Brock for "hummus summit"–style peace talks:

> It doesn't matter who made the hummus first or who made it better, or whose hummus is more authentic; the point is we both make hummus,

we both love hummus and we want people to appreciate what hummus means to us and we want people to keep making hummus, secure in the knowledge that hummus is a part of everyone's story and that hummus will endure.[68]

If we can continue to have richer conversations in the public sphere about authenticity, we may be able to create more inclusive definitions of Southernness and the South.

These conversations about authenticity and their ultimate goals of fostering reconciliation will necessitate frank conversations about the South's past. Though I applaud the myriad ways in which writers have narrated themselves into positions of power by defining Southern authenticity broadly, I still find the relationship to history in these cookbooks to be problematic, especially the refusal to describe white slaveholders as active agents in slavery. Certainly, writers do not deny that slavery shaped Southern cuisine; as we saw in chapter 1, a claim of antebellum origins is a strong indicator of authenticity. But writers refuse to write sentences with humans as subjects of sentences. Sean Brock writes in *Heritage*:

> The Lowcountry is where rice was born in America, and the plantation agriculture that it brought along profoundly shaped the people and their way of life. It also shaped my cooking. It took me some time in Charleston to fully appreciate the significance of rice, how it contributed to the city's wealth, created winners and losers, and wove itself into the fabric of Charleston's history.[69]

Though these sentences are clearly about an agricultural product produced by a slave economy, those words never appear. People are neither subjects of sentences nor agents of actions. Rice was born in America. Rice brought along the euphemistic "plantation agriculture." That euphemism vaguely yet "profoundly" shaped unknown people and their "way of life." While Brock hints at the darker side of this economy, it is still rice that contributed to wealth and picked the winners and losers in these sentences. Further in the essay, Brock again does grammatical gymnastics to remove human actors from slavery: "Antebellum plantations were where grain was grown, be it rice, corn, or wheat."[70] The crops were grown without the aid of bodies or laborers.

Even Bryant Terry, author of *Afro-Vegan* and representative of the foodways of the African diaspora in the Caribbean and the US South, uses passive constructions to soften references to the history of slavery. Terry writes about rice:

A number of starchy mashed dishes seen throughout Central and West Africa made their way to the Caribbean and Brazil by way of the trans-atlantic slave trade and were adapted to local ingredients. Moreover, enslaved Africans from the western part of the continent brought rice to the New World, and it became an important crop in the slave economy of the United States. In fact, the rice economy of the southeastern United States thrived because of the expertise that enslaved Africans brought with them from the rice-growing regions of coastal West Africa.[71]

Terry names the slave trade directly, but notice those passive verbs without human actors: dishes "made their way" and "were adapted." Though "enslaved Africans" are named as subjects of sentences, bringing rice and knowledge of rice to the United States, the entities who "brought" them are absent from this narrative. Terry's narrative "celebrates" African contributions to Southern food-ways, but it erases white guilt. Only Barbara Smith calls out enslavers as sub-jects of sentences, stating directly that "along with their human cargo, enslavers transported seeds" and "enslaved Africans" planted and cultivated them.[72]

How can reconciliation be enacted over food without a frank recognition of the agents who created the fracture? As Timothy Tyson famously wrote in *Blood Done Sign My Name*, "In any case, if there is to be reconciliation, first there must be truth."[73] This book has been about the machinery of authentic-ity that is necessitated by the refusal to engage with history, by the failure of history to be convincing. In some ways, the celebratory tone of the cookbook, centered on the pleasures of the kitchen and the family and the body, may not be "the right place" to engage with such issues. In rhetoric, this is called kairos: the appropriateness of the time, place, genre, audience, and occasion for making an argument— "the circumstances that open moments of opportunity."[74] Do Southerners want to be reminded of the "burden of Southern history" as they are making dinner? Will adopted Southerners *want* to be "made Southern for a time," as Dupree promises, if it means being the inheritor of a history of slavery? If they perform Southern identity in their kitchens by cooking a recipe with an origin in "plantation agriculture," to use Brock's euphemism, are they perform-ing as slaves or masters?[75] Is either role desirable or pleasurable?

And yet the discourse of Southern food tells us that the kitchen and the table are exactly the right places to enact reconciliation and social justice. As Wendy Atkins-Sayre and Ashli Quesinberry Stokes argue in "Crafting the Cornbread Nation," the discourse of the Southern Foodways Alliance "serve[s] a consti-tutive, or identity-building, function by helping to craft a Southern identity based on diverse, humble, and hospitable roots. This identity offers a hopeful alternative to those identities based on race and class divisions and regional stereotypes." Atkins-Sayre and Stokes argue that "this constitutive work has the potential to open up dialogues in the South and to create communities by allowing for a 'safe nostalgia' through the celebration of the food." While the authors acknowledge "troubling memories of the segregated and poverty-ridden South," they also suggest that those memories must be "temporarily [set] aside" for celebration to occur.[76] This interpretation is at odds somewhat with the SFA's stated mission, which emphasizes both history and reconciliation: "The Southern Foodways Alliance documents, studies, and explores the diverse food cultures of the changing American South. Our work sets a welcome table where all may consider our history and our future in a spirit of respect and reconciliation." The SFA "Values" center on historical recovery, as well: "We tell honest and sometimes difficult stories about our region. We embrace Southern history, the realities of the Southern present, and the opportunities for Southern futures. In other words, we don't flinch from talking about race, class, religion, gender, and all the other biggies."[77] There is a gap between the SFA that is willing to unflinchingly "tell honest and sometimes difficult stories" and cookbooks (written by friends of the SFA like Brock, Currence, and Lee) that are not willing to name human actors in the slave trade. How might cookbooks follow the model of the SFA? "Rather than waxing nostalgic," Atkins-Sayre and Stokes write, the SFA "is humble in its approach to Southern history, relying on simple Southern foods to help recognize past mistakes and to move forward with those mistakes in mind."[78] How could the writers, editors, designers, and auteurs of New Southern cookbooks join in this effort?

What if, instead of setting aside history as an invalid argument for authenticity, we set aside authenticity as an invalid argument for performance? Historical narratives might then be employed to truly inform, to "recognize past mistakes," or to "tell honest and sometimes difficult stories about our region" rather than make spurious claims to "firstness." Citation narratives might be used honestly to "recognize men and women whose hard work enriches the landscape of Southern food and culture" rather than borrow capital from those contributors without a fair exchange. Personal narratives — which readers of "Recipe Headnotes: Do We Really Need Them?" kind of hated anyway — might not need to rely on tropes of grandmothers and vegetable gardens to prove the chef's authority to speak. They might instead be used to make real connections between writers and their audiences. Notice my modifiers: "truly," "honestly," "real." I'm still calling for authenticity in the form of earnestness. Meredith Abarca calls for a move from a discourse of authenticity that freezes and essentializes cuisine to a discourse of originality that allows individuals to stand for their own creativity instead of their entire culture or ethnicity.[79] But even originality is dependent on the authenticity of being true to oneself. Maybe there is truly no setting authenticity aside in food discourse. Maybe there are only better and worse ways to deploy arguments of authenticity for better and worse rhetorical ends.

This critique of the machinery of authenticity may provide marginalized cookbook writers (those with less capital than white, male celebrity chefs) a playbook for using authenticity strategically to take a larger share of Southern identity. I have pointed out ways that the narrative strategies already in play can be employed for subverting metanarratives, breaking stereotypes, empowering voices at the margins, encouraging reconciliation and social justice. When Bryant Terry invokes the history of slavery, however obliquely, he moves the experience of African Americans in the South to the center of the narrative of Southern identity. When Edward Lee claims his authority as an innovator and an adopted son of the South, he makes space for other colonized writers to become colonizers. Love her or hate her, Paula Deen takes as much ownership of the public history of the South and professional kitchen as she does of her own private network and home. The push toward hyperregionality, toward the cuisines of microregions and ever-smaller local footprints, will lead chef-authors to make fewer and fewer sweeping generalizations about the South as a monolithic imagined space, but more and more claims about the authentic origins of their narrower cuisines.

NOTES

Introduction. Recipe Origin Narratives

1. Sarah Camp Arnold, "Editor's Note," *Gravy* 46 (Dec 2012): 1.

2. Candice Goucher, *Congotay! Congotay! A Global History of Caribbean Food* (New York: Routledge, 2013), xv.

3. Sean Brock, *Heritage* (New York: Artisan, 2015), 22–23.

4. John Currence, *Pickles, Pigs, and Whiskey* (Kansas City, MO: Andrews McMeel, 2013), xix.

5. Susan J. Leonardi, "Recipes for Reading: Pasta Salad, Lobster a la Riseholme, and Key Lime Pie," *PMLA* 104, no. 1 (1989): 340–47, JSTOR.

6. Anne Bower, ed., *Recipes for Reading: Community Cookbooks, Stories, Histories,* (Amherst: University of Massachusetts Press, 1997).

7. Leonardi, "Recipes for Reading," 344.

8. Arjun Appadurai, "How to Make a National Cuisine: Cookbooks in Contemporary India," *Comparative Studies in Society and History* 30, no. 1 (Jan 1988): 3, JSTOR.

9. Ibid., 22.

10. Donna Gabaccia, *We Are What We Eat: Ethnic Food and the Making of Americans* (Cambridge, MA: Harvard University Press, 1998), 176.

11. John Egerton, *The Americanization of Dixie: The Southernization of America* (New York: Harper's Magazine Press, 1974), xxi.

12. John Egerton, *Southern Food: At Home, on the Road, and in History* (New York: Knopf, 1987), 3.

13. Ibid.; Joe Gray Taylor, *Eating, Drinking, and Visiting in the South* (Baton Rouge: Louisiana State University Press, 1982).

14. Martha Washington, *Martha Washington's Booke of Cookery and Booke of Sweetmeats*, ed. Karen Hess (New York: Columbia University Press, 1996); Mary Randolph, *The Virginia Housewife*, ed. Karen Hess (Columbia: University of South Carolina Press, 1996); Abby Fisher, *What Mrs. Fisher Knows about Old Southern Cooking*, ed. Karen Hess (Bedford, MA: Applewood Books, 1995).

15. Elizabeth S. D. Engelhardt, *A Mess of Greens: Southern Gender & Southern Food* (Athens: University of Georgia Press, 2011). Allison Carruth's *Global Appetites: American Power and the Literature of Food* (New York: Cambridge University Press, 2013) does the same for American texts and food, broadly defined.

16. Doris Witt, *Black Hunger: Food and the Politics of U.S. Identity* (New York: Oxford University Press, 1999); Andrew Warnes, *Hunger Overcome? Food and Resistance in Twentieth-Century African American Literature* (Athens: University of Georgia Press, 2004); Psyche A. Williams-Forson, *Building Houses out of Chicken Legs: Black Women, Food & Power* (Chapel Hill: University of North Carolina Press, 2006). Rebecca Sharpless,

Cooking in Other Women's Kitchens: Domestic Workers in the South, 1865–1960 (Chapel Hill: University of North Carolina Press, 2010); and Jessica Harris, *High on the Hog: A Culinary Journey from Africa to America* (New York: Bloomsbury, 2011).

17. Marcie Cohen Ferris, *The Edible South: The Power of Food and the Making of an American Region* (Chapel Hill: University of North Carolina Press, 2014); Ashli Quesinberry Stokes and Wendy Atkins-Sayre, *Consuming Identity: The Role of Food in Redefining the South* (Jackson: University Press of Mississippi, 2016).

18. Frederick Douglass Opie, *Southern Food and Civil Rights: Feeding the Revolution* (Charleston, SC: American Palate, 2017).

19. Angela Jill Cooley, *To Live and Dine in Dixie: The Evolution of Urban Food Culture in the Jim Crow South* (Athens: University of Georgia Press, 2015).

20. John T. Edge, *The Potlikker Papers: A Food History of the Modern South* (New York: Penguin Press, 2017).

21. John T. Edge, Elizabeth S. D. Engelhardt, and Ted Ownby, eds., *The Larder: Food Studies Methods from the American South* (Athens: University of Georgia Press, 2013).

22. Tara Powell and David Davis, *Writing in the Kitchen: Essays on Southern Literature and Foodways* (Oxford: University Press of Mississippi, 2014).

23. See also Carrie Helms Tippen, "'Acting It Out Like a Play': Flipping the Script of Kitchen Spaces in Faulkner's *Light in August*," *Southern Quarterly* 53, no. 2 (Winter 2017): 58–73, https://doi.org/10.1353/soq.2016.0017.

24. Jennifer Cognard-Black and Melissa Goldthwaite, "Books That Cook: Teaching Food and Food Literature in the English Classroom," *College English* 70, no. 4 (March 2008): 423–24, JSTOR.

25. Ibid., 422.

26. The panelists were Allison Carruth, University of California, Los Angeles (English and "a faculty member in the Institute for Society and Genetics and the Institute of the Environment and Sustainability"); Anne Cheng, Princeton University (English and the Center for African American Studies, "Director for Program in American Studies and affiliated with Program in Gender and Sexuality Studies and the Committee on Film Studies"); J. Michelle Coghlan, University of Manchester (English and American Studies); and Kyla Wazana Tompkins, Pomona College (English and Gender and Women's Studies). Only Amy Tigner, University of Texas, Arlington, has a single affiliation in English.

27. Barbara Kirshenblatt-Gimblett, "Playing to the Senses: Food as Performance Medium," *Performance Research* 4, no. 1 (1999): 1–30, JSTOR.

28. Margaret Atwood, *The CanLit Foodbook: From Pen to Palate, a Collection of Tasty Literary Fare* (Toronto, Ontario: Totem Books, 1987): 1.

29. I examine the use of descriptive language in recipes in contemporary lifestyle magazines in "'Squirrel, if You're So Inclined': Recipes, Narrative, and the Rhetoric of Southern Identity." *Food, Culture, and Society* 17, no. 4 (Dec 2014): 555–70.

30. Atwood, *CanLit Foodbook*, 1.

31. Kevin Gillespie and David Joachim, *Fire in My Belly: Real Cooking* (Kansas City, MO: Andrews McMeel, 2012): 1–14.

32. Michel Foucault, "Nietzsche, Genealogy, and History," in *The Foucault Reader*, ed. Paul Rabinow (New York: Pantheon Books, 1984), 76.

33. Ibid., 77.

34. Ibid., 80.

35. Ibid., 76.

36. Ibid., 351.

37. Lisa Heldke, *Exotic Appetites: Ruminations of a Food Adventurer* (New York: Routledge, 2003), 7.

38. Ibid., 21.

39. Ibid., 33.

40. Josee Johnston and Shyon Baumann, *Foodies: Democracy and Distinction in the Gourmet Foodscape* (New York: Routledge, 2010), 69.

41. Ibid., 70.

42. Ibid., 76.

43. Ibid., 77.

44. Andrew Warnes, "Edgeland *Terroir*: Authenticity and Invention in New Southern Foodways Strategy," in Edge, Engelhardt, and Ownby, *Larder*, 345–62.

45. Nathalie Dupree, *New Southern Cooking* (New York: Knopf, 1990), xi.

46. Ibid., xii.

47. Diana Taylor, *The Archive and the Repertoire: Performing Cultural Memory in the Americas* (Durham, NC: Duke University Press, 2003), 2–3.

48. Faye Porter, *At My Grandmother's Knee: Recipes & Memories Handed Down by Women of the South* (Nashville, TN: Thomas Nelson, 2011).

49. Sara Foster and Emily Wallace, *Foster's Market Favorites: 25th Anniversary Collection* (Dallas, TX: Brown Books, 2015); Sara Foster and Tema Larter, *Sara Foster's Southern Kitchen* (New York: Random House, 2011); Sara Foster and Carolyn Carreno, *Sara Foster's Casual Cooking: More Fresh Simple Recipes from Foster's Market* (New York: Clarkson Potter, 2007); *Fresh Every Day: More Great Recipes from Foster's Market* (New York: Clarkson Potter, 2005); Sara Foster and Sarah Belk King, *The Foster's Market Cookbook: Favorite Recipes for Morning, Noon, and Night* (New York: Random House, 2002).

50. Foster and Larter, *Sara Foster's Southern Kitchen*, 381.

51. Pat Conroy and Suzanne Williamson Pollack, *The Pat Conroy Cookbook: Recipes and Stories of My Life* (New York: Nan A. Talese, 2009), 5.

52. Julia Moskin, "I Was a Cookbook Ghostwriter," *New York Times*, March 13, 2012, http://nyti.ms/20eXkjZ.

53. Marilyn Fabe, *Closely Watched Films: An Introduction to the Art of Narrative Film Technique* (Oakland: University of California Press, 2014), 121.

54. Stephen Best and Sharon Marcus, "Surface Reading: An Introduction," *Representations* 108, no. 1 (Fall 2009): 1, JSTOR.

55. Ibid., 2.

56. Ibid., 7.

57. Ibid., 8–9.

58. Ibid., 9.

59. Ibid., 11.

60. Leonardi, "Recipes for Reading," 340.

61. Lily Kelting, "The Entanglement of Nostalgia and Utopia in Contemporary Southern Food Cookbooks," *Food, Culture and Society* 19, no. 2 (2016): 381, https://doi.org/10.1080/15528014.2016.1178549.

62. Egerton, *Southern Food*; Dupree, *New Southern Cooking*; Ronni Lundy, *Victuals: An Appalachian Journey, with Recipes* (New York: Clarkson Potter, 2016); Asha Gomez with Martha Hall Foose, *My Two Souths: Blending the Flavors of India into a Southern Kitchen* (Philadelphia: Running Press, 2016).

63. Lloyd Bitzer, "The Rhetorical Situation," *Rhetoric and Philosophy* 1, no. 1 (1968): 1–14, http://www.jstor.org/stable/40236733.

64. Editors of *Southern Living, The Southern Cookie Book* (Birmingham, AL: Oxmoor House, 2016); and *The Southern Baker Book* (Birmingham, AL: Oxmoor House, 2015).

65. Sheri Castle, *The Southern Living Community Cookbook* (Birmingham, AL: Oxmoor House, 2014); Morgan Murphy, *Bourbon and Bacon* (Birmingham, AL: Oxmoor House, 2014); Matt Moore, *A Southern Gentleman's Kitchen: Adventures in Cooking, Eating, and Living in the New South* (Birmingham, AL: Oxmoor House, 2015); and Tasia Malakasis, *Southern Made Fresh* (Birmingham, AL: Oxmoor House, 2015).

66. Kelly Alexander, *No Taste Like Home: A Celebration of Regional Southern Cooking and Hometown Flavor* (Birmingham, AL: Oxmoor House, 2013), 7.

67. Hugh Acheson, *A New Turn in the South* (New York: Clarkson Potter, 2011). It also occurred to me that even though these *Southern Living* branded texts had named authors, I still wanted to exclude them for some of the same reasons food adventurers skip the national chains: *Southern Living* was just too big and too commercial to be "authentic." This puts into conflict some of the shifting definitions of authenticity identified by Johnston and Baumann. Under the aegis of *Southern Living*, a certain amount of authenticity is assumed because of the power of that brand, giving it a kind of authenticity associated with timeless, traditional integrity. On the other hand, having that powerful brand on the cover automatically disqualifies the book from another kind of authenticity: personal, handcrafted, artisan, noncommercial. There is much more to be said and explored about this special category of cookbooks (and those similar publications being released by *Southern Living*'s rival, *Garden & Gun*, to say nothing of both magazines themselves and their delivery of cooking, serving, and eating instructions) than can be addressed in this present volume—both for their complex relationships with authenticity and Southern identity and for their sophisticated rhetoric of authenticity and food.

68. Brock, *Heritage*.

69. Ashely Christensen and Kaitlyn Goalen, *Poole's: Recipes and Stories from a Modern Diner* (Berkeley: Ten Speed Press, 2016), 13.

70. Ibid., 59, 62, 29. In fact, Christensen undercuts the Southern origin of pimento cheese by claiming "it has roots in the industrial food revolution in New York. Sometime around the 1950s, Southerners claimed it" (59).

71. James C. Cobb, *Away Down South: A History of Southern Identity* (New York: Oxford University Press, 2007), 9.

72. Ashley B. Thompson and Melissa M. Sloan, "Race as Region, Region as Race: How Black and White Southerners Understand Their Regional Identities," *Southern Cultures* 18, no. 4 (Winter 2012): 73, http://bit.ly/2fz2DdF.

73. Patricia G. Davis, *Laying Claim: African American Cultural Memory and Southern Identity* (Tuscaloosa: University of Alabama Press, 2016), 3.

74. Cobb, *Away Down South*, 9.

75. Thompson and Sloan, "Race as Region," 74.

76. Davis, *Laying Claim*.

77. Gretchen Hoffman, "What's the Difference between Soul Food and Southern Cooking? The Classification of Cookbooks in American Libraries," in *Dethroning the Deceitful Pork Chop: Rethinking African American Foodways from Slavery to Obama*, ed. Jennifer Jensen Wallach (Fayetteville: University of Arkansas Press, 2015), 64.

78. Ibid., 67–68.

79. Ibid., 69.

80. Ibid., 71.

81. Adrian Miller, *Soul Food: The Surprising Story of an American Cuisine, One Plate at a Time* (Chapel Hill: University of North Carolina Press, 2013), 4.

82. Frederick Douglass Opie, *Hog and Hominy: Soul Food from Africa to America* (New York: Columbia University Press, 2010), xiii.

83. Ibid., xii.

84. Miller, *Soul Food*, 29.

85. Ibid., 40.

86. Ibid., 31.

87. Ibid., 44.

88. Ibid., 45.

89. Ibid., 45.

90. Bryant Terry, *Afro-Vegan: Farm-Fresh African, Caribbean, and Southern Flavors Remixed* (Berkeley, CA: Ten Speed Press, 2014); and *Vegan Soul Kitchen: Fresh, Healthy, and Creative African American Cuisine* (Cambridge, MA: De Capo Press, 2009).

91. Alice Randall and Caroline Randall Williams, *Soul Food Love: Healthy Recipes Inspired by 100 Years of Cooking in a Black Family* (New York, Clarkson Potter, 2015), 9.

92. Ibid., 10.

93. Francis Lam, "Edna Lewis and the Black Roots of Southern Cooking," *New York Times Magazine*, October 28, 2015, http://nyti.ms/2wC3bn8.

94. Edna Lewis and Scott Peacock with David Nussbaum, *The Gift of Southern Cooking: Recipes and Revelations from Two Great Southern Cooks* (New York: Alfred A. Knopf, 2003), xii.

95. Ibid., xii–xiii. It is interesting to note that the white writer of this introduction claims that his black coauthor is most influenced by white European cuisines, while he is most influenced by cuisines of people of color, connecting this reversal of expectations to the historical influences of Southern microregions rather than experiences of race or class.

96. Ibid., xiii.

97. Ibid., xiv.

98. Nicole A. Taylor, *The Up South Cookbook: Chasing Dixie in a Brooklyn Kitchen* (New York: Countryman Press, 2015); Robbie Montgomery with Ramin Ganeshram, *Sweetie Pie's Cookbook: Soulful Southern Recipes from My Family to Yours* (New York: Amistad, 2015); Barbara Smith, *B. Smith Cooks Southern-Style* (New York: Scribner, 2009); and Delilah Winder, *Delilah's Everyday Soul: Southern Cooking with Style* (Philadelphia: Running Press, 2006).

99. Taylor, *Up South*, 12.

100. Ibid., 13.

101. B. Smith, *B. Smith Cooks Southern-Style*, 1.

102. Ibid., 2.

103. Ibid., 3.

104. Dora Charles with Fran McCullough, *A Real Southern Cook: In Her Savannah Kitchen* (New York: Houghton Mifflin Harcourt, 2015), 27, 30.

105. Ibid., 30.

106. John Guillory, *Cultural Capital: The Problem of Literary Canon Formation* (Chicago: University of Chicago Press, 1995), vii.

107. Ibid., ix.

108. Cognard-Black and Goldthwaite, "Books That Cook," 422.

1. Historical Narrative

1. Lisa Heldke, *Exotic Appetites: Ruminations of a Food Adventurer* (New York: Routledge, 2003), 24.

2. Robert F. Moss, *The Fried Green Tomato Swindle and Other Southern Culinary Adventures* (Mt. Pleasant, SC: Palmetto New Media, 2011), 60.

3. "First Pot of Brunswick Stew Made on St Simon's Isle," *Way Marking*, last modified July 11, 2009, http://bit.ly/2p3kN7B.

4. "Welcome to the 2014 Brunswick Rockin' Stewbilee," Brunswick Rockin' Stewbilee, accessed November 2014, http://www.stewbilee.com/.

5. "Brunswick County, Virginia–'The Original Home of Brunswick Stew' Marker, U-91," *Marker History*, accessed November 2014, http://bit.ly/2p3kklL.

6. Josee Johnston and Shyon Baumann, *Foodies: Democracy and Distinction in the Gourmet Foodscape* (New York: Routledge, 2010), 88.

7. Raymond Sokolov, *Fading Feast: A Compendium of Disappearing American Regional Foods* (New York: Farrar Strause Giroux, 1979); John Egerton, *Southern Food: At Home, on the Road, and in History* (New York: Knopf, 1987); Matt Lee and Ted Lee, *The Lee Bros. Southern Cookbook: Stories and Recipes for Southerners and Would-Be Southerners* (New York: W. W. Norton, 2006); Matt Moore, *A Southern Gentleman's Kitchen: Adventures in Cooking, Eating, and Living in the New South* (Birmingham, AL: Oxmoor House, 2015).

8. Nathalie Dupree, *New Southern Cooking* (New York: Knopf, 1990); Dora Charles and Fran McCullough, *A Real Southern Cook: In Her Savannah Kitchen* (New York: Houghton Mifflin Harcourt, 2015).

9. Dupree, *New Southern Cooking*; Paula Deen and Melissa Clark, *Paula Deen's Southern Cooking Bible* (New York: Simon and Schuster, 2011); Faye Porter, *At My Grandmother's Knee: Recipes & Memories Handed Down by Women of the South* (Nashville, TN: Thomas Nelson, 2011); Christy Jordan, *Come Home to Supper: Over 200 Casseroles, Skillets, and Sides (Desserts, Too) to Feed Your Family with Love* (New York: Workman Publishing, 2013); Charles and McCullough, *Real Southern Cook*, 2015.

10. Allison Glock, "Southern Women: A New Generation of Women Who Are Redefining the Southern Belle," *Garden & Gun*, August/September 2011.

11. William Faulkner, *Requiem for a Nun* (New York: Vintage, 1994), 73.

12. Eudora Welty, "From Where I Live," in *Occasions: Selected Writings*, ed. Pearl Amelia McHaney (Jackson: University of Mississippi Press, 2009), 244–45.

13. Lily Kelting, "The Entanglement of Nostalgia and Utopia in Contemporary Southern Food Cookbooks," *Food, Culture and Society* 19, no. 2 (2016): 363–64, https://doi.org/10.1080/15528014.2016.1178549.

14. Ibid., 365.

15. Ibid., 363.

16. Ibid., 365.

17. Tracy Thompson, *The New Mind of the South* (New York: Simon and Schuster, 2013), 81.

18. Egerton, *Southern Food*, 4 and 35.

19. Thompson, *New Mind of the South*, 11.

20. Damon Lee Fowler, *Classical Southern Cooking*, rev. ed. (Salt Lake City, UT: Gibbs Smith, 2008), 11–12.

21. James Villas, *The Glory of Southern Cooking* (New York: John Wiley & Sons, 2007), viii.

22. Ibid., ix–x.

23. Ibid., xi.

24. Welty, "From Where I Live," 245.

25. Hayden White, *Metahistory: The Historical Imagination in Nineteenth-Century Europe* (Baltimore, MD: Johns Hopkins University Press, 1973), 2.

26. Ibid., 5.

27. Ibid., 6.

28. Ibid., 22.

29. Kenneth Burke, "Terministic Screens," in *Language as Symbolic Action: Essays on Life, Literature, and Method* (Berkeley: University of California Press, 1966), 45.

30. Ibid., 46.

31. Ibid., 45. Emphasis in original.

32. Edmund E. Jacobitti, introduction to *Composing Useful Pasts*, ed. Edmund E. Jacobitti (Albany: State University of New York Press, 2000), ix.

33. Ibid., x.

34. Edmund E. Jacobitti, "Role of the Past in Contemporary Political Life," in *Composing Useful Pasts*, ed. Edmund E. Jacobitti (Albany: State University of New York Press, 2000), 24.

35. Ibid., 20.

36. Ibid., 21.

37. Ibid., 23.

38. Ibid., 27.

39. Andrew F. Smith, "False Memories: The Invention of Culinary Fakelore and Food Fallacies," in *Food and the Memory: Proceedings of the Oxford Colloquium on Food and Cookery 2000*, ed. Harlan Walker (London: Prospect Books, 2001), 255.

40. Ibid., 255.

41. Ibid., 257.

42. Michael Kreyling, *The South That Wasn't There: Postsouthern Memory and History* (Baton Rouge: Louisiana State University Press, 2010), 2.

43. Saddler Taylor, "Brunswick Stew," in *Foodways*, vol. 7 of *The New Encyclopedia of Southern Culture*, ed. John T. Edge (Chapel Hill: University of North Carolina Press, 2007), 131.

44. Smith, "False Memories," 255.

45. Ibid., 255.

46. Ibid., 257.

47. Sokolov, *Fading Feast*, 8.

48. Ibid., 10.

49. Ibid., 84.

50. Ibid., 92.

51. Ibid., 75.

52. Ibid., 76.

53. Ibid., 75.

54. Anthony Stanonis, "Just Like Mammy Used to Make: Foodways in the Jim Crow

South," in *Dixie Emporium: Tourism, Foodways, and Consumer Culture in the American South*, ed. Anthony Stanonis (Athens: University of Georgia Press, 2008), 209, 213.

55. Sokolov, *Fading Feast*, 76.

56. Ibid., 76–77.

57. Ibid., 77.

58. Ibid., 77.

59. Lee and Lee, *Lee Bros.*, 1.

60. Ibid., 252.

61. Ibid., 252.

62. Ibid., 252.

63. Ibid., 252.

64. Egerton, *Southern Food*, 7.

65. Ibid., 7.

66. Ibid., 275.

67. Ibid., 13.

68. Ibid., 15.

69. Ibid., 15.

70. Ibid., 275.

71. Ibid., 16.

72. Ibid., 16.

73. Taylor, "Brunswick Stew," 132.

74. Wiley Prewitt, "Game Cookery," in Edge, *Foodways*, 56.

75. Marilyn Moore, *The Wooden Spoon Book of Home-Style Soups, Stews, Chowders, Chilis and Gumbos: Favorite Recipes from The Wooden Spoon Kitchen* (New York: Atlantic Monthly Press, 1994), 97.

76. Villas, *Glory*; *Pig: King of the Southern Table* (New York: John Wiley & Sons, 2010).

77. Villas, *Glory*, ix.

78. Ibid., 110.

79. Ibid., 110.

80. Ibid., 110.

81. Ibid., ix.

82. Villas, *Pig*, 74–75.

83. Ibid., 74.

84. Moore, *Southern Gentleman's Kitchen*, 93.

85. Deen and Clark, *Paula Deen's Southern Cooking Bible*, xviii.

86. Ibid., 73.

87. Charles and McCullough, *Real Southern Cook*, 19.

88. Ibid., 20.

89. Ibid., 24.

90. Ibid., 26.

91. Ibid., 25–26.

92. Ibid., 12.

93. Ibid., 58.

94. Ibid., 126.

95. Ibid., 126, 79.

96. Ibid., 57.

97. Jordan, *Come Home to Supper*, 90–91. Emphasis in original.

98. Ibid., 91.

99. Rebecca Lang, *Quick-Fix Southern: Homemade Hospitality in 30 Minutes or Less* (Kansas City, MO: Andrews McMeel, 2011): 80.

100. "Nathalie Dupree," interview by April Grayson, *Southern Foodways Alliance*, October 7, 2004, http://bit.ly/2ppYkRq.

101. Dupree, *New Southern Cooking*, 59.

102. Porter, *At My Grandmother's Knee*, 149.

2. Citation Narratives

1. Barbara Gibbs Ostmann and Jane L. Baker, *The Recipe Writer's Handbook: Revised and Expanded* (Hoboken, NJ: John Wiley & Sons, 2001), 11.

2. Karen Hess, "Recipe for a Cookbook: Scissors and Paste," *Harper's Magazine* 269, no. 10 (October 1975): 85, Academic Search Complete.

3. Toni Tipton-Martin uses this phrase "knowledge, skills, and abilities" in her book, *The Jemima Code* (Austin: University of Texas Press, 2015): 2, and sometimes abbreviates it as "KSA's" on her blog by the same name. She specifically contrasts KSAs with the assumption that black female cooks "by virtue of their race and gender—are simply born with good kitchen instincts," highlighting that the "creative culinary artistry" of black cooks is learned and deserving of hard-won respect.

4. Faye Porter, *At My Grandmother's Knee: Recipes & Memories Handed Down by Women of the South* (Nashville, TN: Thomas Nelson, 2011), 149; Nathalie Dupree, *New Southern Cooking* (New York: Knopf, 1990), 59.

5. Alex Danchev, "Provenance," *Journal for Cultural Research* 10, no. 1 (2006): 24, Academic Search Complete.

6. Ibid., 28.

7. Ibid., 31.

8. Susan Scafidi, *Who Owns Culture? Appropriation and Authenticity in American Law* (New Brunswick, NJ: Rutgers University Press, 2005), 35.

9. Susan J. Leonardi, "Recipes for Reading: Pasta Salad, Lobster a la Riseholme, and Key Lime Pie," *PMLA* 104, no. 1 (1989): 340, JSTOR.

10. Pierre Bourdieu, *The Field of Cultural Production*, ed. Randal Johnson (New York: Columbia University Press, 1993), 76.

11. Ibid., 76.

12. Ibid., 77.

13. Ibid., 86.

14. Ibid., 81.

15. Jason Mazzone, *Copyfraud and Other Abuses of Intellectual Property Law* (Stanford, CA: Stanford Law Books, 2011), ix.

16. Though there is a body called the International Association of Culinary Professionals that does offer suggested guidelines for ethical treatment of sources, there is no uniform citation style or governing body equivalent to the MLA or APA. Standards for citation appear to be dictated by the house style of the press or publisher.

17. Quoted in Edward Samuels, *The Illustrated Story of Copyright* (New York: Thomas Dunne Books; St. Martin's Press, 2002), 127.

18. Ibid., 128.

19. Quoted in Ibid., 128.

20. John Whiting, "Authentic? Or Just Expensive?" in *Authenticity in the Kitchen: Proceedings of the Oxford Symposium on Food and Cookery 2005*, ed. Richard Hosking (London: Prospect Books, 2006), 435.

21. Samuels, *Illustrated Story of Copyright*, 185.

22. Ibid., 129.

23. Martha Woodmansee and Peter Jaszi, eds., *The Construction of Authorship: Textual Appropriation in Law and Literature* (Durham, NC: Duke University Press, 1994), 11.

24. Peter Jaszi, "On the Author Effect: Contemporary Copyright and Collective Creativity," in Woodmansee and Jaszi, *Construction of Authorship*, 29–31.

25. Joan Whitman and Dolores Simon, *Recipes into Type: A Handbook for Cookbook Writers and Editors* (New York: HarperCollins Publishers, 1993), 9.

26. Ostmann and Baker, *Recipe Writer's Handbook*; Dianne Jacob, *Will Write for Food: The Complete Guide to Writing Cookbooks, Blogs, Reviews, Memoirs, and More*, 2nd ed. (Cambridge, MA: Lifelong Books, 2010).

27. Whitman and Simon, *Recipes into Type*, 161.

28. Ostmann and Baker, *Recipe Writer's Handbook*, 212.

29. Ibid., 213.

30. Ibid., 212.

31. Jacob, *Will Write for Food*, 82.

32. Ibid., 206.

33. Ibid., 210.

34. Ibid., 82.

35. Ibid., 210–11.

36. Ostmann and Baker, *Recipe Writer's Handbook*, 212.

37. Ibid., 212.

38. Jacob, *Will Write for Food*, 187.

39. Ostmann and Baker, *Recipe Writer's Handbook*, 212.

40. Ibid., 11.

41. Whitman and Simon, *Recipes into Type*, 9–10.

42. Ibid., 9.

43. Virginia Willis, *Bon Appetit, Y'all: Recipes and Stories from Three Generations of Southern Cooking* (Berkeley, CA: Ten Speed Press, 2008), 1.

44. Ibid., 2.

45. Edward Lee, *Smoke and Pickles: Recipes and Stories from a New Southern Kitchen* (New York: Artisan, 2013), vii.

46. Sean Brock, *Heritage* (New York: Artisan, 2015), 13.

47. John Currence, Pickles, Pigs, and Whiskey (Kansas City, MO: Andrews McMeel, 2013), xiii.

48. Josee Johnston and Shyon Baumann, *Foodies: Democracy and Distinction in the Gourmet Foodscape* (New York: Routledge, 2010), 62.

49. Michael Pollan, "Six Rules for Eating Wisely," *Time*, June 11, 2006, http://ti.me /2nPoaSL.

50. Ibid.

51. Porter, *At My Grandmother's Knee*, 277–78.

52. Ibid., 119.

53. In this section, I use the capitalized *Grandmother* and *Granddaughter* to describe

the archetypal characters who represent the idealized versions of these individuals. The Grandmother, in this case, is the character who represents authentic culinary knowledge of the past, concentrated in one figure.

54. Porter, *At My Grandmother's Knee*, 101, 134.

55. Ibid., 154.

56. Ibid., 24.

57. Ibid., iv–v.

58. Ibid., 79.

59. Ibid., 86.

60. Bryant Terry, *Afro-Vegan: Farm-Fresh African, Caribbean, and Southern Flavors Remixed* (Berkeley, CA: Ten Speed Press, 2014), 152.

61. Ibid., 139.

62. Ibid., 175.

63. Ibid., 3–4.

64. Damon Lee Fowler, *Classical Southern Cooking*, rev. ed. (Salt Lake City, UT: Gibbs Smith, 2008); Nancy Carter Crump, *Hearthside Cooking: Early American Southern Cuisine Updated for Today's Hearth and Cookstove*, 2nd ed. (Chapel Hill: University of North Carolina Press, 2008). See also John T. Edge, ed., *A Gracious Plenty: Recipes and Recollections from the American South* (New York: G. P. Putnam's Sons, 1999); Sarah Roahen and John T. Edge, eds., *The Southern Foodways Alliance Community Cookbook* (Athens: University of Georgia Press, 2010); Sheri Castle, *The Southern Living Community Cookbook* (Birmingham, AL: Oxmoor House, 2014.

65. Fowler, *Classical Southern Cooking*, cover.

66. Ibid., 13.

67. Ibid., 37.

68. Crump, *Hearthside Cooking*, ix.

69. Ibid., xi–xii.

70. Joan E. Aller, *Cider Beans, Wild Greens, and Dandelion Jelly: Recipes from Southern Appalachia* (Kansas City, MO: Andrews McMeel, 2010), ix, dust jacket.

71. Ibid., ix–x.

72. Ibid., xi.

73. Ibid., vi–vii.

74. Ibid., 2.

75. Ibid., 17.

76. Ibid., 64.

77. Ibid., 140, ellipses in original.

78. Ibid., 141.

79. Ibid., 141.

80. Ibid., 141.

81. Ibid., 106.

82. Estelle Woods Wilcox, *Buckeye Cookery* (Minneapolis, MN, Buckeye Publishing, 1877), PDF, *Feeding America: The Historic American Cookbook Project,* Michigan State University, http://bit.ly/2wUWwUm; and Estelle Woods Wilcox, *Dixie Cook-Book* (Atlanta, GA: L. A. Clarkson, 1883), PDF, http://bit.ly/2uAFDSe.

83. Kelly Alexander, *No Taste Like Home: A Celebration of Regional Southern Cooking and Hometown Flavor* (Birmingham, AL: Oxmoor House, 2013), 32.

84. Ibid., 37.

85. Jacob, *Will Write for Food*, xv.

86. Ibid., 60.

87. Ibid., 60.

88. Ibid., 61.

89. Stacey Little, *The Southern Bite* (blog), http://southernbite.com/about/.

90. Ibid.

91. Stacey Little, *The Southern Bite Cookbook* (Nashville, TN: Thomas Nelson, 2014), xiii.

92. Ibid., xiv.

93. Ibid., 9.

94. Ibid., 64.

95. Ibid., 77.

96. Ibid., 76.

97. Patsy Caldwell and Amy Lyles Wilson, *Y'all Come Over: A Celebration of Southern Hospitality, Food, and Memories* (Nashville, TN: Thomas Nelson, 2013); *Bless Your Heart: Saving the World One Covered Dish at a Time* (Nashville, TN: Thomas Nelson, 2010); *You Be Sweet: Sharing Your Heart One Down-Home Dessert at a Time* (Nashville, TN: Thomas Nelson, 2012).

98. Caldwell and Lyles, *Y'all Come Over*, 85.

99. Ibid., ix.

100. Ibid., 2.

101. Ibid., 3.

102. Ibid., 5.

103. Ibid., 22.

104. Ibid., 7.

105. Ibid., 25.

106. Ibid., 29.

107. Ibid., 35.

108. Ibid., 31.

109. ibid., 127, 246.

110. Ibid., 176.

111. Maya Angelou, *Hallelujah! The Welcome Table* (New York: Random House, 2004), 51.

112. Ibid., 52.

113. Ibid., 53.

114. Ibid., 52.

115. Ibid., 50.

116. Ibid., 52.

117. Sidney Mintz, "Cuisine: High, Low, and Not at All," in *Tasting Food, Tasting Freedom: Excursions into Eating, Culture, and the Past* (Boston, MA: Beacon Press, 1996), 96.

118. Ibid., 97.

119. Scafidi, *Who Owns Culture?*, 53.

120. Whitman and Simon, *Recipes into Type*, 9.

121. Martha Woodmansee, "On the Author Effect: Recovering Collectivity," in Woodmansee and Jaszi, *Construction of Authorship*, 15.

122. Mario Biagioli, Peter Jaszi, and Martha Woodmansee, eds., *Making and Unmaking Intellectual Property: Creative Production in Legal and Cultural Perspective* (Chicago: University of Chicago Press, 2011), 9.

3. Personal Narratives

1. Donald Link and Paula Disbrowe, *Down South: Bourbon, Pork, Gulf Shrimp & Second Helpings of Everything* (New York: Clarkson Potter, 2014), 11.

2. Edward Lee, *Smoke and Pickles: Recipes and Stories from a New Southern Kitchen* (New York: Artisan, 2013), 22–23.

3. Eudora Welty, *One Writer's Beginnings* (Cambridge, MA: Harvard University Press, 2003), 3.

4. Quoted in Don Lee Keith, "Eudora Welty: 'I Worry Over My Stories,'" in *Conversations with Eudora Welty*, edited by Peggy Whitman Prenshaw (Jackson: University Press of Mississippi, 1998), 95.

5. Colleen Cotter offers a very convincing contradiction to this statement in her 1997 essay "Claiming a Piece of the Pie: How the Language of Recipes Defines Community," in *Recipes for Reading: Community Cookbooks, Stories, Histories*, ed. Anne Bower (Amherst: University of Massachusetts Press, 1997), 51–71. While I agree with Cotter that the word choices in recipes are meaningful and show editorial and rhetorical choices of an authorial persona, the headnote and other narrative elements not only offer more freedom for creative expression than the recipe instructions, but they also have become a generic convention and expectation, specifically designed for the purpose of constructing an authorial identity and voice.

6. John Egerton, *Southern Food: At Home, on the Road, and in History* (New York: Knopf, 1987); Damon Lee Fowler, *Classical Southern Cooking*, rev. ed. (Salt Lake City, UT: Gibbs Smith, 2008).

7. Meredith Abarca, "Authentic or Not, It's Original," *Food and Foodways* 12, no. 1 (January 2004): 18, JSTOR, https://doi.org/10.1080/07409710490467589.

8. Ibid., 2.

9. Ibid., 18.

10. Ibid., 19.

11. Lee, *Smoke and Pickles*, 4, 8, ix.

12. Ibid., xii–1.

13. Sean Brock, *Heritage* (New York: Artisan, 2015), 22–23; John Currence, *Pickles, Pigs, and Whiskey* (Kansas City, MO: Andrews McMeel, 2013), xix–xxv.

14. Brock, *Heritage,* 22–23.

15. Ibid., 19.

16. Ibid., 265. Currence includes a Mississippi equivalent: "University Grays Punch" in *Pickles, Pigs, and Whiskey*, 21.

17. Currence, *Pickles, Pigs, and Whiskey*, 226.

18. Currence, *Pickles, Pigs and Whiskey*; Brock, *Heritage*; Hugh Acheson, *A New Turn in the South* (New York: Clarkson Potter, 2011); Anne Stiles Quatrano, *Summerland: Recipes for Celebrating with Southern Hospitality* (New York: Rizzoli, 2013).

19. Josee Johnston and Shyon Baumann, *Foodies: Democracy and Distinction in the Gourmet Foodscape* (New York: Routledge, 2010), 85.

20. Thus, this chapter examines cookbooks authored by chefs, mostly men, cooking in

elite restaurants. I have, quite purposefully, sought out and included the voices of women cooking in elite restaurants, too. While white men still outnumber women and people of color in the restaurant and gourmet cookbook industries, there are many excellent examples to be included in this chapter.

21. Johnston and Baumann, *Foodies*, 86.

22. Lee, *Smoke and Pickles*, viv.

23. Kenneth Burke, *A Rhetoric of Motives* (Berkley: University of California Press, 1969), 19–23.

24. Nathalie Dupree, *New Southern Cooking* (New York: Knopf, 1990), xii.

25. Stacey Little, *The Southern Bite Cookbook* (Nashville, TN: Thomas Nelson, 2014).

26. Faye Porter, *At My Grandmother's Knee: Recipes & Memories Handed Down by Women of the South* (Nashville, TN: Thomas Nelson, 2011).

27. Paula Deen and Melissa Clark, *Paula Deen's Southern Cooking Bible* (New York: Simon and Schuster, 2011); Frank Stitt, *Frank Stitt's Southern Table: Recipes and Gracious Traditions from Highlands Bar and Grill* (New York: Artisan, 2004); John Besh, *Besh's Big Easy: 101 Home Cooked New Orleans Recipes* (Kansas City, MO: Andrews McMeel, 2015); Bill Neal, *Bill Neal's Southern Cooking* (Chapel Hill: University of North Carolina Press, 1989); Pat Conroy and Suzanne Williamson Pollack, *The Pat Conroy Cookbook: Recipes and Stories of My Life* (New York: Nan A. Talese, 2009); Robbie Montgomery with Ramin Ganeshram, *Sweetie Pie's Cookbook: Soulful Southern Recipes from My Family to Yours* (New York: Amistad, 2015); Barbara Smith, *B. Smith Cooks Southern-Style* (New York: Scribner, 2009); Chris Hastings, Idie Hastings, and Katherine Cobbs, *Hot and Hot Fish Club Cookbook: A Celebration of Food, Family, and Traditions* (Philadelphia: Running Press, 2009); Sara Foster and Sarah Belk King, *The Foster's Market Cookbook: Favorite Recipes for Morning, Noon, and Night* (New York: Random House, 2002); Ashley Christensen and Kaitlyn Goalen, *Poole's: Recipes and Stories from a Modern Diner* (Berkeley, CA: Ten Speed Press, 2016).

28. The restaurants of Brock, Currence, and Quatrano, respectively.

29. Katherine Martinelli, "What It's Like to Be a Cookbook Ghostwriter," *Bon Appetit*, January 10, 2017, http://www.bonappetit.com/story/cookbook-ghostwriters.

30. Lee, *Smoke and Pickles*, 45.

31. See John Egerton, *The Americanization of Dixie: The Southernization of America* (New York: Harper's Magazine Press, 1974), for one example.

32. Pippa Holloway, Introduction to *Other Souths: Diversity and Difference in the U.S. South, Reconstruction to Present*, ed. Pippa Holloway (Athens: University of Georgia Press, 2008), 1.

33. Khyati Joshi and Jigna Desai, Introduction to *Asian Americans in Dixie: Race and Migration in the South,* ed. Khyati Joshi and Jigna Desai (Chicago: University of Illinois Press, 2013), 1.

34. Ibid., 2.

35. Justin A. Nystrom, "Italian New Orleans and the Business of Food in the Crescent City: There's More to the Muffuletta Than Meets the Eye," in *The Larder: Food Studies Methods from the American South*, ed. John T. Edge, Elizabeth S. D. Engelhardt, and Ted Ownby (Athens: University of Georgia Press, 2013), 128–54; and Tom Hanchett, "A Salad Bowl City: The Food Geography of Charlotte, North Carolina," in Edge, Engelhardt, and Ownby, *Larder*, 166–83.

36. Angela Jill Cooley, "The Customer Is Always White: Food, Race and Contested Eating Space in the South," in Edge, Engelhardt, and Ownby, *Larder*, 249.

37. Egerton, *Southern Food*, 4.

38. Asha Gomez with Martha Hall Foose, *My Two Souths: Blending the Flavors of India into a Southern Kitchen* (Philadelphia: Running Press, 2016); Lee, *Smoke and Pickles*; Sandra Gutierrez, *The New Southern-Latino Table* (Chapel Hill: University of North Carolina Press, 2011).

39. Gomez and Foose, *My Two Souths*, 9.

40. Ibid., 13.

41. Joshi and Desai, introduction to *Asian Americans in Dixie*, 4.

42. Ibid., 5.

43. Ibid., 6. C. Van Woodward made much the same argument in *The Burden of Southern History* in 1953.

44. David DiBenedetto, "Editor's Letter," *Garden & Gun,* Oct/Nov 2011, 8.

45. "G&G and Le Creuset's Chefs' Roundtable," *Garden & Gun,* May 2, 2011, http://bit.ly/20mzItN.

46. Acheson, *New Turn in the South*, 13.

47. Brock, *Heritage*, 13.

48. Currence, *Pickles, Pigs, and Whiskey*, xv.

49. *Hot and Hot Fish Club Cookbook* is coauthored with Katherine Cobbs. Most of the narratives are a mixture of first- and third-person pronouns, using "we" and "our restaurant" but also identifying Chris and Idie both by name. The Hastingses write in one first-person voice in the acknowledgments: "Katherine Cobbs effortlessly compiled our writing and our thoughts into a seamless manuscript. . . . Her careful eye and thoughtful conversations with our purveyors were invaluable" (9). A few narrative interludes between chapters and recipes are in first person, such as "Chris' Memories from the Strawberry Patch" (49).

50. Hastings, Hastings, and Cobbs, *Hot and Hot Fish Club Cookbook*, 17.

51. Ibid., 27.

52. Ibid., 103.

53. Ibid., 115.

54. Ibid., 118.

55. Ibid., 18.

56. Ibid., 83–87, 277.

57. Quatrano, *Summerland*, 7.

58. Ibid., 8.

59. Ibid., 33.

60. Ibid., 44, 47.

61. B. Smith, *B. Smith Cooks Southern-Style*, 1.

62. Ibid., 2.

63. Ibid., 2.

64. Ibid., 3.

65. Gomez and Foose, *My Two Souths*, 10.

66. Ibid., 9.

67. Ibid., 10.

68. Acheson, *New Turn in the South*, 13.

69. Ibid., 14.

70. Ibid., 13–14.

71. Andrea Reusing, *Cooking in the Moment: A Year of Seasonal Recipes* (New York: Clarkson Potter, 2011), 8.

72. Lee, *Smoke and Pickles*, 3.

73. Ibid., 5, 8.

74. Ibid., 7.

75. Ibid., 8.

76. Currence, *Pickles, Pigs, and Whiskey*, xiii; Virginia Willis, *Basic to Brilliant, Y'all: 150 Refined Southern Recipes and Ways to Dress Them Up for Company* (Berkeley, CA: Ten Speed Press, 2011), 3; Hastings, Hastings, and Cobbs, *Hot and Hot Fish Club Cookbook*, 11; Acheson, *New Turn in the South*, 14.

77. Willis, *Basic to Brilliant, Y'all*, 2.

78. Ibid., 3–4.

79. Ibid., 5.

80. Currence, *Pickles, Pigs, and Whiskey*, xiii.

81. Ibid., xii.

82. Ibid., xix.

83. Dora Charles with Fran McCullough, *A Real Southern Cook: In Her Savannah Kitchen* (New York: Houghton Mifflin Harcourt, 2015), 12.

84. Ibid., 13.

85. Ibid., 14.

86. Ibid., 16.

87. Ibid., 17.

88. Ibid., 19.

89. Ibid., 17.

90. Ibid., 25.

91. Ibid., 19.

92. Ibid., 23.

93. Ibid., 23, 22.

94. Julia Moskin, "A Culinary Birthright in Dispute," *New York Times*, June 25, 2013, http://www.nytimes.com/2013/06/26/dining/paula-deens-words-ripple-among-southern-chefs.html.

95. Hastings, Hastings, and Cobbs, *Hot and Hot Fish Club Cookbook*, 71–72.

96. Ibid., 73.

97. Andrew Ticer and Michael Hudman, *Collards & Carbonara: Southern Cooking, Italian Roots* (San Francisco: Olive Press, 2013), 78.

98. Ibid., 2.

99. Ibid., 33.

100. Ibid., 48.

101. Ibid., 78.

102. Ibid., 83.

103. "G&G and Le Creuset's Chefs' Roundtable."

104. Lee, *Smoke and Pickles*, 52.

105. Ibid., 97, 129.

106. Ibid., 13.

107. Hastings, Hastings, and Cobbs, *Hot and Hot Fish Club Cookbook*, 23.

108. Ibid., 83.

109. Ibid., 32.

110. Brock, *Heritage*, 15, 27.

111. Link and Disbrowe, *Down South*, 9.

112. Ibid., 11.

113. Ibid., 11.

114. Willis, *Basic to Brilliant, Y'all*, 2.

115. Ibid., 2.

116. Ibid., 3.

117. Ibid., 5.

118. Lee, *Smoke and Pickles*, viv.

119. Ibid., viv.

120. Ibid., 9.

121. Ibid., xi.

122. Gutierrez, *New Southern-Latino Table*, 2.

123. Ibid., 1.

124. Ibid., 3.

125. Ibid., 3–4.

126. Ibid., 4.

127. Ibid., 5.

128. Ibid., 8.

129. Hillary Dixler, "How Gullah Cuisine Has Transformed Charleston Dining," *Eater*, March 22, 2016, http://www.eater.com/2016/3/22/11264104/gullah-food-charleston.

130. John T. Edge and Tunde Wey, "Who Owns Southern Food?," *Oxford American*, June 3, 2016, http://www.oxfordamerican.org/magazine/item/870–who-owns-southern -food.

131. Ibid.

132. Michael Twitty, "Dear Sean, We Need to Talk," *Afroculinaria* (blog), March 23, 2016, https://afroculinaria.com/2016/03/23/dear-sean-we-need-to-talk/.

133. Ibid.

134. Michael Twitty, "Saveur Blog Awards Was a Blast!" *Afroculinaria* (blog), September 30, 2016, https://afroculinaria.com/2016/09/30/saveur-blog-awards-was-a-blast/.

4. Beyond Narrative

1. Josee Johnston and Shyon Baumann, *Foodies: Democracy and Distinction in the Gourmet Foodscape* (New York: Routledge, 2010), 74.

2. Virginia Willis, *Basic to Brilliant, Y'all: 150 Refined Southern Recipes and Ways to Dress Them Up for Company* (Berkeley, CA: Ten Speed Press, 2011), 145.

3. Bryant Terry, *Afro-Vegan: Farm-Fresh African, Caribbean, and Southern Flavors Remixed* (Berkeley, CA: Ten Speed Press, 2014), 119.

4. Dianne Jacob, "What Makes a Recipe Headnote So Good You Want to Rush into the Kitchen?," *Will Write for Food* (blog), November 29, 2010, http://bit.ly/20Jwh1Z.

5. Ibid.

6. Emma Christensen, "Recipe Headnotes: Do We Really Need Them?," *Kitchn*, September 19, 2011, http://bit.ly/2pyJPeZ.

7. Brian Mac, September 2011, comment on Christensen, "Recipe Headnotes."

8. Julia's Bookbag, September 2011, comment on Christensen, "Recipe Headnotes."

9. Jg09, September 2011, comment on Christensen, "Recipe Headnotes."

10. Thinkingwoman, September 2011, comment on Christensen, "Recipe Headnotes."

11. LacyBones, September 2011, comment on Christensen, "Recipe Headnotes."

12. Penni Wisner, November 30, 2010, comment on Jacob, "What Makes a Recipe Headnote So Good You Want to Rush into the Kitchen?," https://diannej.com/2010/what-makes-a-recipe-headnote-so-good-you-want-to-rush-into-the-kitchen/#comment-5149.

13. Johnston and Baumann, *Foodies*, 74–76.

14. Lily Kelting, "The Entanglement of Nostalgia and Utopia in Contemporary Southern Food Cookbooks," *Food, Culture and Society* 19, no. 2 (2016): 381, https://doi.org/10.1080/15528014.2016.1178549.

15. Matt Lee and Ted Lee, *The Lee Bros. Southern Cookbook: Stories and Recipes for Southerners and Would-Be Southerners* (New York: W. W. Norton, 2006).

16. Dora Charles with Fran McCullough, *A Real Southern Cook: In Her Savannah Kitchen* (New York: Houghton Mifflin Harcourt, 2015).

17. Paula Deen and Melissa Clark, *Paula Deen's Southern Cooking Bible* (New York: Simon and Schuster, 2011); Nathalie Dupree and Cynthia Graubart, *Mastering the Art of Southern Cooking* (Salt Lake City, UT: Gibbs Smith, 2012).

18. Damon Lee Fowler, *Classical Southern Cooking*, rev. ed. (Salt Lake City, UT: Gibbs Smith, 2008); Virginia Willis, *Bon Appetit, Y'all: Recipes and Stories from Three Generations of Southern Cooking* (Berkeley, CA: Ten Speed Press, 2008); Nathalie Dupree, *New Southern Cooking* (New York: Knopf, 1990); Hugh Acheson, *A New Turn in the South* (New York: Clarkson Potter, 2011); Sandra Gutierrez, *The New Southern-Latino Table* (Chapel Hill: University of North Carolina Press, 2011); Edward Lee, *Smoke and Pickles: Recipes and Stories from a New Southern Kitchen* (New York: Artisan, 2013); Matt Moore, *A Southern Gentleman's Kitchen: Adventures in Cooking, Eating, and Living in the New South* (Birmingham, AL: Oxmoor House, 2015).

19. Sara Foster and Emily Wallace, *Foster's Market Favorites: 25th Anniversary Collection* (Dallas, TX: Brown Books, 2015); Chris Hastings, Idie Hastings, and Katherine Cobbs, *Hot and Hot Fish Club Cookbook: A Celebration of Food, Family, and Traditions* (Philadelphia: Running Press, 2009); Pat Conroy and Suzanne Williamson Pollack, *The Pat Conroy Cookbook: Recipes and Stories of My Life* (New York: Nan A. Talese, 2009).

20. Sean Brock, *Heritage* (New York: Artisan, 2015).

21. Christy Jordan, *Come Home to Supper: Over 200 Casseroles, Skillets, and Sides (Desserts, Too) to Feed Your Family with Love* (New York: Workman Publishing, 2013); Andrea Reusing, *Cooking in the Moment: A Year of Seasonal Recipes* (New York: Clarkson Potter, 2011).

22. Kevin Gillespie and David Joachim, *Fire in My Belly: Real Cooking* (Kansas City, MO: Andrews McMeel, 2012).

23. Stacey Little, *The Southern Bite Cookbook* (Nashville, TN: Thomas Nelson, 2014), 183, 174, 148, 127.

24. Acheson, *New Turn in the South*, 86.

25. Ibid., 37.

26. Martha Hall Foose, *A Southerly Course: Recipes and Stories from Close to Home* (New York: Clarkson Potter, 2011).

27. Anne Stiles Quatrano, *Summerland: Recipes for Celebrating with Southern Hospitality* (New York: Rizzoli, 2013).

28. Brock, *Heritage*, 264.

29. Ibid., 261, 15–17, 238.

30. Acheson, *New Turn in the South*, 87.

31. Ronni Lundy, *Victuals: An Appalachian Journey, with Recipes* (New York: Clarkson Potter, 2016), 50; Quatrano, *Summerland*, 59.

32. Acheson, *New Turn in the South*, 33; Donald Link and Paula Disbrowe, *Down South: Bourbon, Pork, Gulf Shrimp & Second Helpings of Everything* (New York: Clarkson Potter, 2014), 31; Brock, *Heritage*, 265.

33. The statistics in this section were arrived at by cataloging all variations of *South*, excluding *south* as a direction (as in "south of New Orleans"), *South* as part of a proper name (as in "South Carolina"), *South* pertaining to a microregion (as in "Southern Georgia"), and *South* pertaining to a region outside the United States (as in "the South of France").

34. Willis, *Basic to Brilliant, Y'all*, 5 and 28; 5; 25; 26; 37; 43; 147.

35. Reusing, *Cooking in the Moment*, 20.

36. Brock, *Heritage*, 326.

37. Ibid., 50, 258.

38. Ibid., 280.

39. Ibid., 282.

40. Ibid., 62.

41. Ibid., 280.

42. Willis, *Basic to Brilliant, Y'all*, cover, 3.

43. Ibid., 49, 54, 75, 115.

44. Acheson, *New Turn in the South*, 20.

45. Ibid., 22.

46. Ibid., 24.

47. Ibid., 26.

48. John Currence, *Pickles, Pigs, and Whiskey* (Kansas City, MO: Andrews McMeel), 43.

49. Acheson, *New Turn in the South*, 100, 164.

50. This page credits Laura Palese and Rinne Allen as designers, but also gives credit for illustrations to Acheson, Allen, Susan Hable, Carolyn Holmes, and Jordan Noel. Allen is cited in the acknowledgments as photographer and designer.

51. Janet Theophano, *Eat My Words: Reading Women's Lives through the Cookbooks They Wrote* (New York: Palgrave Macmillan, 2002).

52. Willis, *Bon Appetit, Y'all*, back cover.

53. Ibid., vii.

54. Hastings, Hastings, and Cobbs, *Hot and Hot Fish Club Cookbook*, back cover; Andrew Ticer and Michael Hudman, *Collards & Carbonara: Southern Cooking, Italian Roots* (San Francisco: Olive Press, 2013), back cover.

55. Willis, *Bon Appetit Y'all*, back cover; Jean Anderson, *A Love Affair with Southern Cooking: Recipes and Recollections* (New York: William Morrow Cookbooks, 2007).

56. Currence, foreword to *Pickles, Pigs and Whiskey*; Brock, *Heritage*, back cover; Lee, *Smoke and Pickles*, back cover.

57. Currence, *Pickles, Pigs, and Whiskey*, 45, 128, 150–51, 240; Lee, *Smoke and Pickles*, 60, 133, 236; Brock, *Heritage*, 327.

58. Hastings, Hastings, and Cobbs, *Hot and Hot Fish Club Cookbook*, back cover.

59. Ticer and Hudman, *Collards & Carbonara*, back cover.

60. John Egerton, *The Americanization of Dixie: The Southernization of America* (New York: Harper's Magazine Press, 1974), xxi.

61. Scott Romine, *The Real South: Southern Narrative in the Age of Reproduction* (Baton Rouge: Louisiana State University Press, 2008), 2–3.

62. Michael Kreyling, *The South That Wasn't There: Postsouthern Memory and History* (Baton Rouge: Louisiana State University Press, 2010), 8.

63. Jennifer Rae Greeson, *Our South: Geographic Fantasy and the Rise of National Literature* (Cambridge, MA: Harvard University Press, 2010).

64. Allison Glock, "Southern Women: A New Generation of Women Who Are Redefining the Southern Belle," *Garden & Gun*, Aug/Sep 2011.

65. Link and Disbrowe, *Down South*, 9.

66. Meredith Abarca, "Authentic or Not, It's Original," *Food and Foodways* 12, no. 1 (January 2004): 1–25, JSTOR, https://doi.org/10.1080/07409710490467589.

67. Zach Everson, "Edward Lee on Paula Deen's Racist Comments and Anti-South 'Provocations,'" *Eater*, June 24, 2013, http://bit.ly/2pgDY16.

68. Michael Twitty, "Dear Sean, We Need to Talk," *Afroculinaria* (blog), March 23, 2016, https://afroculinaria.com/2016/03/23/dear-sean-we-need-to-talk/.

69. Brock, *Heritage*, 66.

70. Ibid.

71. Terry, *Afro-Vegan*, 101.

72. Barbara Smith, *B. Smith Cooks Southern-Style* (New York: Scribner, 2009), 2.

73. Timothy Tyson, *Blood Done Sign My Name* (New York: Broadway Books, 2005), 10.

74. Carolyn Eriksen Hill, "Changing Times in Composition Classes: *Kairos, Resonance, and the Pythagorean Connection,*" in *Rhetoric and Kairos: Essays in History, Theory, and Praxis,* ed. Philip Sipiora and James S. Baumlin (Albany: State University of New York Press, 2002), 217.

75. Brock, *Heritage*, 66.

76. Wendy Atkins-Sayre and Ashli Quesinberry Stokes, "Crafting the Cornbread Nation: The Southern Foodways Alliance and Southern Identity," *Southern Communication Journal* 79, no. 2 (April–June 2014): 79, https://doi.org/10.1080/10417 94X.2013.861010.

77. "About Us," *Southern Foodways Alliance,* https://www.southernfoodways.org /about-us/.

78. Atkins-Sayer and Stokes, "Crafting the Cornbread Nation," 89.

79. Abarca, "Authentic or Not, It's Original."

BIBLIOGRAPHY

Abarca, Meredith. "Authentic or Not, It's Original." *Food and Foodways* 12, no. 1 (January 2004): 1–25. JSTOR. https://doi.org/10.1080/07409710490467589.

"About Us." *Southern Foodways Alliance.* https://www.southernfoodways.org /about-us/.

Acheson, Hugh. *A New Turn in the South.* New York: Clarkson Potter, 2011.

Alexander, Kelly. *No Taste Like Home: A Celebration of Regional Southern Cooking and Hometown Flavor.* Birmingham, AL: Oxmoor House, 2013.

Aller, Joan E. *Cider Beans, Wild Greens, and Dandelion Jelly: Recipes from Southern Appalachia.* Kansas City, MO: Andrews McMeel, 2010.

Anderson, Jean. *A Love Affair with Southern Cooking: Recipes and Recollections.* New York: William Morrow Cookbooks, 2007.

Angelou, Maya. *Hallelujah! The Welcome Table.* New York: Random House, 2004.

Appadurai, Arjun. "How to Make a National Cuisine: Cookbooks in Contemporary India." *Comparative Studies in Society and History* 30, no. 1 (Jan 1988): 3–24. JSTOR.

Arnold, Sarah Camp. "Editor's Note." *Gravy* 46 (Dec 2012): 1.

Atkins-Sayre, Wendy, and Ashli Quesinberry Stokes. "Crafting the Cornbread Nation: The Southern Foodways Alliance and Southern Identity." *Southern Communication Journal* 79, no. 2 (April–June 2014): 77–93. https://doi.org/10.1080 /1041794X.2013.861010.

Atwood, Margaret. *The CanLit Foodbook: From Pen to Palate, a Collection of Tasty Literary Fare.* Toronto, Ontario: Totem Books, 1987.

Besh, John. *Besh's Big Easy: 101 Home Cooked New Orleans Recipes.* Kansas City, MO: Andrews McMeel, 2015.

Best, Stephen, and Sharon Marcus. "Surface Reading: An Introduction." *Representations* 108, no. 1 (Fall 2009): 1–21. JSTOR.

Biagioli, Mario, Peter Jaszi, and Martha Woodmansee, eds. *Making and Unmaking Intellectual Property: Creative Production in Legal and Cultural Perspective.* Chicago: University of Chicago Press, 2011.

Bitzer, Lloyd. "The Rhetorical Situation." *Rhetoric and Philosophy* 1, no. 1 (1968): 1–14. http://www.jstor.org/stable/40236733.

Bourdieu, Pierre. *Distinction: A Social Critique of the Judgement of Taste.* Translated by Richard Nice. Cambridge: Harvard University Press, 1984.

———. *The Field of Cultural Production.* Edited by Randal Johnson. New York: Columbia University Press, 1993.

Bower, Anne, ed. *Recipes for Reading: Community Cookbooks, Stories, Histories.* Amherst: University of Massachusetts Press, 1997.

Brock, Sean. *Heritage.* New York: Artisan, 2015.

"Brunswick County, Virginia–'The Original Home of Brunswick Stew' Marker, U-91."
    Marker History, accessed November 2014. http://bit.ly/2p3kklL.
Burke, Kenneth. *A Rhetoric of Motives*. Berkley: University of California Press, 1969.
——. "Terministic Screens." In *Language as Symbolic Action: Essays on Life, Literature,
    and Method*. Berkeley: University of California Press, 1966.
Caldwell, Patsy, and Amy Lyles Wilson. *Bless Your Heart: Saving the World One Covered
    Dish at a Time*. Nashville, TN: Thomas Nelson, 2010.
——. *Y'all Come Over: A Celebration of Southern Hospitality, Food, and Memories*.
    Nashville, TN: Thomas Nelson, 2013.
——. *You Be Sweet: Sharing Your Heart One Down-Home Dessert at a Time*. Nashville,
    TN: Thomas Nelson, 2012.
Carruth, Allison. *Global Appetites: American Power and the Literature of Food*. New York:
    Cambridge University Press, 2013.
Castle, Sheri. *The Southern Living Community Cookbook*. Birmingham, AL: Oxmoor
    House, 2014.
Charles, Dora, with Fran McCullough. *A Real Southern Cook: In Her Savannah Kitchen*.
    New York: Houghton Mifflin Harcourt, 2015.
Christensen, Ashley, and Kaitlyn Goalen. *Poole's: Recipes and Stories from a Modern Diner*.
    Berkeley, CA: Ten Speed Press, 2016.
Christensen, Emma. "Recipe Headnotes: Do We Really Need Them?" *Kitchn,* September 19,
    2011. http://bit.ly/2pyJPeZ.
Cobb, James C. *Away Down South: A History of Southern Identity*. New York: Oxford
    University Press, 2007.
Cognard-Black, Jennifer, and Melissa Goldthwaite. "Books That Cook: Teaching Food
    and Food Literature in the English Classroom." *College English* 70, no. 4 (March 2008):
    421–36. JSTOR.
Conroy, Pat, and Suzanne Williamson Pollack. *The Pat Conroy Cookbook: Recipes and
    Stories of My Life*. New York: Nan A. Talese, 2009.
Cooley, Angela Jill. "The Customer Is Always White: Food, Race and Contested Eating
    Space in the South." In Edge, Engelhardt, and Ownby, *Larder*, 240–72.
——. *To Live and Dine in Dixie: The Evolution of Urban Food Culture in the Jim Crow
    South*. Athens: University of Georgia Press, 2015.
Cotter, Collen. "Claiming a Piece of the Pie: How the Language of Recipes Defines
    Community." In Bower, *Recipes for Reading*, 51–71.
Crump, Nancy Carter. *Hearthside Cooking: Early American Southern Cuisine Updated for
    Today's Hearth and Cookstove*. 2nd ed. Chapel Hill: University of North Carolina Press,
    2008.
Currence, John. Pickles, Pigs, and Whiskey. Kansas City, MO: Andrews McMeel, 2013.
Danchev, Alex. "Provenance." Journal for Cultural Research 10, no.1 (2006): 23–33.
    Academic Search Complete.
Davis, Patricia G. Laying Claim: African American Cultural Memory and Southern
    Identity. Tuscaloosa: University of Alabama Press, 2016.
de Cereau, Michel, Luce Giard, and Pierre Mayol. *The Practice of Everyday Life, Vol 2:
    Living and Cooking*. Translated by Timothy J. Tomasik. Minneapolis: University of
    Minnesota Press, 1998.
Deen, Paula, and Melissa Clark. *Paula Deen's Southern Cooking Bible*. New York: Simon
    and Schuster, 2011.
DiBenedetto, David. "Editor's Letter." *Garden & Gun*, Oct/Nov 2011.

Dixler, Hillary. "How Gullah Cuisine Has Transformed Charleston Dining." *Eater,*
    March 22, 2016. http://www.eater.com/2016/3/22/11264104/gullah-food-charleston.
Dupree, Nathalie. *New Southern Cooking.* New York: Knopf, 1990.
Dupree, Nathalie, and Cynthia Graubart. *Mastering the Art of Southern Cooking.* Salt Lake
    City, UT: Gibbs Smith, 2012.
Edge, John T., ed. *A Gracious Plenty: Recipes and Recollections from the American South.*
    New York: G. P. Putnam's Sons, 1999.
———. *The Potlikker Papers: A Food History of the Modern South.* New York: Penguin
    Press, 2017.
Edge, John T., Elizabeth S. D. Engelhardt, and Ted Ownby, eds. *The Larder: Food Studies
    Methods from the American South.* Athens: University of Georgia Press, 2013.
Edge, John T., and Tunde Wey. "Who Owns Southern Food?" *Oxford American,* June 3,
    2016. http://www.oxfordamerican.org/magazine/item/870–who-owns-southern-food.
Editors of *Southern Living. The Southern Baker Book.* Birmingham, AL: Oxmoor House,
    2015.
———. *The Southern Cookie Book.* Birmingham, AL: Oxmoor House, 2016.
Egerton, John. *The Americanization of Dixie: The Southernization of America.* New York:
    Harper's Magazine Press, 1974.
———. *Southern Food: At Home, on the Road, and in History.* New York: Knopf, 1987.
Engelhardt, Elizabeth S. D. *A Mess of Greens: Southern Gender & Southern Food.* Athens:
    University of Georgia Press, 2011.
Estes, Rufus. *Rufus Estes's Good Things to Eat: The First Cookbook by an African American
    Chef.* Mineola, NY: Dover Publications, 2004.
Evans-Hylton, Patrick. *Dishing Up Virginia: 145 Recipes That Celebrate Colonial Traditions
    and Contemporary Flavors.* North Adams, MA: Storey Publishing, 2013.
Everson, Zach. "Edward Lee on Paula Deen's Racist Comments and Anti-South
    'Provocations.'" *Eater,* June 24, 2013. http://bit.ly/2pgDY16.
Fabe, Marilyn. *Closely Watched Films: An Introduction to the Art of Narrative Film
    Technique.* Oakland: University of California Press, 2014.
Faulkner, William. *Requiem for a Nun.* New York: Vintage, 1994.
Ferris, Marcie Cohen. *The Edible South: The Power of Food and the Making of an American
    Region.* Chapel Hill: University of North Carolina Press, 2014.
"First Pot of Brunswick Stew made on St Simon's Isle." *Way Marking,* last modified July 11,
    2009. http://bit.ly/2p3kN7B.
Fisher, Abby. *What Mrs. Fisher Knows about Old Southern Cooking.* Edited by Karen Hess.
    Bedford, MA: Applewood Books, 1995.
Foose, Martha Hall. *A Southerly Course: Recipes and Stories from Close to Home.* New
    York: Clarkson Potter, 2011.
Foster, Sara, and Carolyn Carreno. *Fresh Every Day: More Great Recipes from Foster's
    Market.* New York: Clarkson Potter, 2005.
———. *Sara Foster's Casual Cooking: More Fresh Simple Recipes from Foster's Market.*
    New York: Clarkson Potter, 2007.
Foster, Sara, and Sarah Belk King. *The Foster's Market Cookbook: Favorite Recipes for
    Morning, Noon, and Night.* New York: Random House. 2002.
Foster, Sara, and Tema Larter. *Sara Foster's Southern Kitchen.* New York: Random House,
    2011.
Foster, Sara, and Emily Wallace. *Foster's Market Favorites: 25th Anniversary Collection.*
    Dallas, TX: Brown Books, 2015.

Foucault, Michel. "Nietzsche, Genealogy, and History." In *The Foucault Reader,* edited by Paul Rabinow, 76–120. New York: Pantheon Books, 1984.

Fowler, Damon Lee. *Classical Southern Cooking.* Rev. ed. Salt Lake City, UT: Gibbs Smith, 2008.

———. *Essentials of Southern Cooking: Techniques and Flavors of a Classic American Cuisine.* Guilford, CT: Lyons Press, 2013.

"G&G and Le Creuset's Chefs' Roundtable." *Garden & Gun,* May 2, 2011. http://bit.ly/2omzItN.

Gabaccia, Donna. *We Are What We Eat: Ethnic Food and the Making of Americans.* Cambridge, MA: Harvard University Press, 1998.

Gillespie, Kevin, and David Joachim. *Fire in My Belly: Real Cooking.* Kansas City, MO: Andrews McMeel, 2012.

Glock, Allison. "Southern Women: A New Generation of Women Who Are Redefining the Southern Belle." *Garden & Gun,* August/September 2011.

Gomez, Asha, with Martha Hall Foose. *My Two Souths: Blending the Flavors of India into a Southern Kitchen.* Philadelphia: Running Press, 2016.

Goucher, Candice. *Congotay! Congotay! A Global History of Caribbean Food.* New York: Routledge, 2013.

Greeson, Jennifer Rae. *Our South: Geographic Fantasy and the Rise of National Literature.* Cambridge, MA: Harvard University Press, 2010.

Guillory, John. *Cultural Capital: The Problem of Literary Canon Formation.* Chicago: University of Chicago Press, 1995.

Gutierrez, Sandra. *The New Southern-Latino Table.* Chapel Hill: University of North Carolina Press, 2011.

Hanchett, Tom. "A Salad Bowl City: The Food Geography of Charlotte, North Carolina." In Edge, Engelhardt, and Ownby, *Larder,* 166–83.

Harris, Jessica. *High on the Hog: A Culinary Journey from Africa to America.* New York: Bloomsbury, 2011.

Hastings, Chris, Idie Hastings, and Katherine Cobbs. *Hot and Hot Fish Club Cookbook: A Celebration of Food, Family, and Traditions.* Philadelphia: Running Press, 2009.

Heldke, Lisa. *Exotic Appetites: Ruminations of a Food Adventurer.* New York: Routledge, 2003.

Hess, Karen. "Recipe for a Cookbook: Scissors and Paste." *Harper's Magazine* 269, no. 10 (October 1975): 85–90. Academic Search Complete.

Hill, Carolyn Eriksen. "Changing Times in Composition Classes: *Kairos,* Resonance, and the Pythagorean Connection." In *Rhetoric and Kairos: Essays in History, Theory, and Praxis,* edited by Philip Sipiora and James S. Baumlin, 211–25. Albany: State University of New York Press, 2002.

Hoffman, Gretchen. "What's the Difference between Soul Food and Southern Cooking? The Classification of Cookbooks in American Libraries." In Wallach, *Dethroning the Deceitful Pork Chop,* 61–76.

Holloway, Pippa. Introduction to *Other Souths: Diversity and Difference in the U.S. South, Reconstruction to Present.* Edited by Pippa Holloway. Athens: University of Georgia Press, 2008.

Jacob, Dianne. "What Makes a Recipe Headnote So Good You Want to Rush into the Kitchen?" *Will Write for Food* (blog). November 29, 2010. http://bit.ly/2oJwhiZ.

——. *Will Write for Food: The Complete Guide to Writing Cookbooks, Blogs, Reviews, Memoirs, and More*. 2nd ed. Cambridge, MA: Lifelong Books, 2010.

Jacobitti, Edmund E., ed. *Composing Useful Pasts*. Albany, NY: State University of New York Press, 2000.

Jaszi, Peter. "On the Author Effect: Contemporary Copyright and Collective Creativity." In Woodmansee and Jaszi, *Construction of Authorship*, 29–56.

Johnston, Josee, and Shyon Baumann. *Foodies: Democracy and Distinction in the Gourmet Foodscape*. New York: Routledge, 2010.

Jordan, Christy. *Come Home to Supper: Over 200 Casseroles, Skillets, and Sides (Desserts, Too) to Feed Your Family with Love*. New York: Workman Publishing, 2013.

Joshi, Khyati, and Jigna Desai. Introduction to *Asian Americans in Dixie: Race and Migration in the South*, edited by Khyati Joshi and Jigna Desai. Chicago: University of Illinois Press, 2013.

Keith, Don Lee. "Eudora Welty: 'I Worry Over My Stories.'" In *Conversations with Eudora Welty*, edited by Peggy Whitman Prenshaw, 141–53. Jackson: University Press of Mississippi, 1998.

Kelting, Lily. "The Entanglement of Nostalgia and Utopia in Contemporary Southern Food Cookbooks." *Food, Culture and Society* 19, no. 2 (2016): 361–87. https://doi.org/10.1080/15528014.2016.1178549.

Kirshenblatt-Gimblett, Barbara. "Playing to the Senses: Food as Performance Medium." *Performance Research* 4, no. 1 (1999): 1–30. JSTOR.

Kreyling, Michael. *The South That Wasn't There: Postsouthern Memory and History*. Baton Rouge: Louisiana State University Press, 2010.

Lam, Francis. "Edna Lewis and the Black Roots of Southern Cooking." *New York Times Magazine,* October 28, 2015. http://nyti.ms/2wC3bn8.

Lang, Rebecca. *Quick-Fix Southern: Homemade Hospitality in 30 Minutes or Less*. Kansas City, MO: Andrews McMeel, 2011.

Lee, Edward. *Smoke and Pickles: Recipes and Stories from a New Southern Kitchen*. New York: Artisan, 2013.

Lee, Matt, and Ted Lee. *The Lee Bros. Southern Cookbook: Stories and Recipes for Southerners and Would-Be Southerners*. New York: W. W. Norton, 2006.

Leonardi, Susan J. "Recipes for Reading: Pasta Salad, Lobster a la Riseholme, and Key Lime Pie." *PMLA* 104, no. 1 (1989): 340–47. JSTOR.

Lewis, Edna, and Scott Peacock, with David Nussbaum. *The Gift of Southern Cooking: Recipes and Revelations from Two Great Southern Cooks*. New York: Alfred A. Knopf, 2003.

Link, Donald, and Paula Disbrowe. *Down South: Bourbon, Pork, Gulf Shrimp & Second Helpings of Everything*. New York: Clarkson Potter, 2014.

Little, Stacey. "About Stacey." *The Southern Bite* (blog). http://southernbite.com/about/.

——. *The Southern Bite Cookbook*. Nashville, TN: Thomas Nelson, 2014.

Lundy, Ronni. *Victuals: An Appalachian Journey, with Recipes*. New York: Clarkson Potter, 2016.

Malakasis, Tasia. *Southern Made Fresh*. Birmingham, AL: Oxmoor House, 2015.

Martinelli, Katherine. "What It's Like to Be a Cookbook Ghostwriter." *Bon Appetit*, January 10, 2017. http://www.bonappetit.com/story/cookbook-ghostwriters.

Mazzone, Jason. *Copyfraud and Other Abuses of Intellectual Property Law*. Stanford, CA: Stanford Law Books, 2011.

Miller, Adrian. *Soul Food: The Surprising Story of an American Cuisine, One Plate at a Time*. Chapel Hill: University of North Carolina Press, 2013.

Mintz, Sidney. "Cuisine: High, Low, and Not at All." In *Tasting Food, Tasting Freedom: Excursions into Eating, Culture, and the Past*. Boston, MA: Beacon Press, 1996.

Montgomery, Robbie, with Ramin Ganeshram. *Sweetie Pie's Cookbook: Soulful Southern Recipes from My Family to Yours*. New York: Amistad, 2015.

Moore, Marilyn. *The Wooden Spoon Book of Home-Style Soups, Stews, Chowders, Chilis and Gumbos: Favorite Recipes from The Wooden Spoon Kitchen*. New York: Atlantic Monthly Press, 1994.

Moore, Matt. *A Southern Gentleman's Kitchen: Adventures in Cooking, Eating, and Living in the New South*. Birmingham, AL: Oxmoor House, 2015.

Moskin, Julia. "A Culinary Birthright in Dispute." *New York Times*, June 25, 2013, http://www.nytimes.com/2013/06/26/dining/paula-deens-words-ripple-among-southern-chefs.html.

———. "I Was a Cookbook Ghostwriter." *New York Times*, March 13, 2012. http://nyti.ms/20eXkjZ.

Moss, Robert F. *The Fried Green Tomato Swindle and Other Southern Culinary Adventures*. Mt. Pleasant, SC: Palmetto New Media, 2011.

Murphy, Morgan. *Bourbon and Bacon*. Birmingham, AL: Oxmoor House, 2014.

"Nathalie Dupree." Interview by April Grayson. *Southern Foodways Alliance*, October 7, 2004. http://bit.ly/2ppYkRq.

Neal, Bill. *Bill Neal's Southern Cooking*. Chapel Hill: University of North Carolina Press, 1989.

Nystrom, Justin A. "Italian New Orleans and the Business of Food in the Crescent City: There's More to the Muffuletta than Meets the Eye." In Edge, Engelhardt, and Ownby, *Larder*, 128–54.

Opie, Frederick Douglass. *Hog and Hominy: Soul Food from Africa to America*. New York: Columbia University Press, 2010.

———. *Southern Food and Civil Rights: Feeding the Revolution*. Charleston, SC: American Palate, 2017.

Ostmann, Barbara Gibbs, and Jane L. Baker. *The Recipe Writer's Handbook: Revised and Expanded*. Hoboken, NJ: John Wiley & Sons, 2001.

Pinner, Patty. *Sweets: Soul Food Desserts and Memories*. Berkeley, CA: Ten Speed Press, 2006.

Pollan, Michael. "Six Rules for Eating Wisely." *Time*, June 11, 2006. http://ti.me/2nPoaSL.

Porter, Faye. *At My Grandmother's Knee: Recipes & Memories Handed Down by Women of the South*. Nashville, TN: Thomas Nelson, 2011.

Powell, Tara, and David Davis. *Writing in the Kitchen: Essays on Southern Literature and Foodways*. Oxford: University Press of Mississippi, 2014.

Prewitt, Wiley. "Game Cookery." In *Foodways*, edited by John T. Edge, 55–57. Vol. 7 of *The New Encyclopedia of Southern Culture*. Chapel Hill: University of North Carolina Press, 2007.

Quatrano, Anne Stiles. *Summerland: Recipes for Celebrating with Southern Hospitality*. New York: Rizzoli, 2013.

Randall, Alice, and Caroline Randall Williams. *Soul Food Love: Healthy Recipes Inspired by 100 Years of Cooking in a Black Family*. New York: Clarkson Potter, 2015.

Randolph, Mary. *The Virginia Housewife*. Edited by Karen Hess. Columbia: University of South Carolina Press, 1996.

Reusing, Andrea. *Cooking in the Moment: A Year of Seasonal Recipes*. New York: Clarkson Potter, 2011.

Roahen, Sarah, and John T. Edge, eds. *The Southern Foodways Alliance Community Cookbook.* Athens: University of Georgia Press, 2010.

Romine, Scott. *The Real South: Southern Narrative in the Age of Reproduction*. Baton Rouge: Louisiana State University Press, 2008.

Samuels, Edward. *The Illustrated Story of Copyright*. New York: Thomas Dunne Books; St. Martin's Press, 2002.

Scafidi, Susan. *Who Owns Culture? Appropriation and Authenticity in American Law*. New Brunswick, NJ: Rutgers University Press, 2005.

Sharpless, Rebecca. *Cooking in Other Women's Kitchens: Domestic Workers in the South, 1865–1960*. Chapel Hill: University of North Carolina Press, 2010.

Smith, Andrew F. "False Memories: The Invention of Culinary Fakelore and Food Fallacies." In *Food and the Memory: Proceedings of the Oxford Colloquium on Food and Cookery 2000*, edited by Harlan Walker, 254–60. London: Prospect Books, 2001.

Smith, Art. *Back to the Table: The Reunion of Food and Family*. New York: Hyperion, 2001.

Smith, Barbara. *B. Smith Cooks Southern-Style*. New York: Scribner, 2009.

Sokolov, Raymond. *Fading Feast: A Compendium of Disappearing American Regional Foods*. New York: Farrar Strause Giroux, 1979.

Stanonis, Anthony. "Just Like Mammy Used to Make: Foodways in the Jim Crow South." In *Dixie Emporium: Tourism, Foodways, and Consumer Culture in the American South*, edited by Anthony Stanonis, 208–33. Athens: University of Georgia Press, 2008.

Stitt, Frank. *Frank Stitt's Southern Table: Recipes and Gracious Traditions from Highlands Bar and Grill*. New York: Artisan, 2004.

Stokes, Ashli Quesinberry, and Wendy Atkins-Sayre. *Consuming Identity: The Role of Food in Redefining the South*. Jackson: University Press of Mississippi, 2016.

Taylor, Diana. *The Archive and the Repertoire: Performing Cultural Memory in the Americas*. Durham, NC: Duke University Press, 2003.

Taylor, Joe Gray. *Eating, Drinking, and Visiting in the South*. Baton Rouge: Louisiana State University Press, 1982.

Taylor, Nicole A. *The Up South Cookbook: Chasing Dixie in a Brooklyn Kitchen*. New York: Countryman Press, 2015.

Taylor, Saddler. "Brunswick Stew." In *Foodways*, edited by John T. Edge, 131–33. Vol. 7 of *The New Encyclopedia of Southern Culture*. Chapel Hill: University of North Carolina Press, 2007.

Terry, Bryant. *Afro-Vegan: Farm-Fresh African, Caribbean, and Southern Flavors Remixed*. Berkeley, CA: Ten Speed Press, 2014.

———. *Vegan Soul Kitchen: Fresh, Healthy, and Creative African American Cuisine*. Cambridge, MA: De Capo Press, 2009.

Theophano, Janet. *Eat My Words: Reading Women's Lives through the Cookbooks They Wrote*. New York: Palgrave Macmillan, 2002.

Thompson, Ashley B., and Melissa M. Sloan. "Race as Region, Region as Race: How Black and White Southerners Understand Their Regional Identities." *Southern Cultures* 18, no. 4 (Winter 2012): 73. http://bit.ly/2fz2DdF.

Thompson, Tracy. *The New Mind of the South*. New York: Simon and Schuster, 2013.

Ticer, Andrew, and Michael Hudman. *Collards & Carbonara: Southern Cooking, Italian Roots*. San Francisco: Olive Press, 2013.

Tippen, Carrie Helms. "'Acting It Out Like a Play:' Flipping the Script of Kitchen Spaces in Faulkner's *Light in August*." *Southern Quarterly* 53, no. 2 (Winter 2017): 58–73. https://doi.org/10.1353/soq.2016.0017.

———. "Squirrel, if You're So Inclined: Recipes, Narrative, and the Rhetoric of Southern Identity." *Food, Culture, and Society* 17, no. 4 (Dec 2014): 555–70.

Tipton-Martin, Toni. *The Jemima Code*. Austin: University of Texas Press, 2015.

Twitty, Michael. "Dear Sean, We Need to Talk." *Afroculinaria* (blog). March 23, 2016. https://afroculinaria.com/2016/03/23/dear-sean-we-need-to-talk/.

———. "Saveur Blog Awards Was a Blast!" *Afroculinaria* (blog). September 30, 2016. https://afroculinaria.com/2016/09/30/saveur-blog-awards-was-a-blast/.

Tyson, Timothy. *Blood Done Sign My Name*. New York: Broadway Books, 2005.

Villas, James. *The Glory of Southern Cooking*. New York: John Wiley & Sons, 2007.

———. *Pig: King of the Southern Table*. New York, NY: John Wiley & Sons, 2010.

———. *Southern Fried: More Than 150 Recipes for Crab Cakes, Fried Chicken, Hush Puppies, and More*. New York: Houghton Mifflin Harcourt, 2013.

Wallach, Jennifer Jensen, ed. *Dethroning the Deceitful Pork Chop: Rethinking African American Foodways from Slavery to Obama*. Fayetteville: University of Arkansas Press, 2015.

Warnes, Andrew. "Edgeland *Terroir:* Authenticity and Invention in New Southern Foodways Strategy." In Edge, Engelhardt, and Ownby, *Larder*, 345–62.

———. *Hunger Overcome? Food and Resistance in Twentieth-Century African American Literature*. Athens: University of Georgia Press, 2004.

Washington, Martha. *Martha Washington's Booke of Cookery and Booke of Sweetmeats*. Edited by Karen Hess. New York: Columbia University Press, 1996.

"Welcome to the 2014 Brunswick Rockin' Stewbilee." Brunswick Rockin' Stewbilee. Last modified 2014. http://www.stewbilee.com/.

Welty, Eudora. "From Where I Live." In *Ocassions: Selected Writings,* edited by Pearl Amelia McHaney, [page range]. Jackson: University of Mississippi Press, 2009.

———. *One Writer's Beginnings*. Cambridge, MA: Harvard University Press, 2003.

White, Hayden. *Metahistory: The Historical Imagination in Nineteenth-Century Europe*. Baltimore, MD: Johns Hopkins University Press, 1973.

Whiting, John. "Authentic? Or Just Expensive?" In *Authenticity in the Kitchen: Proceedings of the Oxford Symposium on Food and Cookery 2005*, edited by Richard Hosking, 427–40. London: Prospect Books, 2006.

Whitman, Joan, and Dolores Simon. *Recipes into Type: A Handbook for Cookbook Writers and Editors*. New York: HarperCollins Publishers, 1993.

Wilcox, Estelle Woods. *Buckeye Cookery*. Minneapolis, MN, Buckeye Publishing, 1877. PDF. *Feeding America: The Historic American Cookbook Project*, Michigan State University. http://bit.ly/2wUWwUm.

———. *Dixie Cook-Book*. Atlanta, GA: L. A. Clarkson, 1883. PDF. http://bit.ly/2u AFDSe.

Williams-Forson, Psyche A. *Building Houses out of Chicken Legs: Black Women, Food & Power*. Chapel Hill: University of North Carolina Press, 2006.

Willis, Virginia. *Basic to Brilliant, Y'all: 150 Refined Southern Recipes and Ways to Dress Them Up for Company*. Berkeley, CA: Ten Speed Press, 2011.

———. *Bon Appetit, Y'all: Recipes and Stories from Three Generations of Southern Cooking*. Berkeley, CA: Ten Speed Press, 2008.

Winder, Delilah. *Delilah's Everyday Soul: Southern Cooking with Style*. Philadelphia: Running Press, 2006.

Witt, Doris. *Black Hunger: Food and the Politics of U.S. Identity*. New York: Oxford University Press, 1999.

Woodmansee, Martha. "On the Author Effect: Recovering Collectivity." In Woodmansee and Jaszi, *Construction of Authorship*, 15–28.

Woodmansee, Martha, and Peter Jaszi, eds. *The Construction of Authorship: Textual Appropriation in Law and Literature*. Durham, NC: Duke University Press, 1994.

INDEX